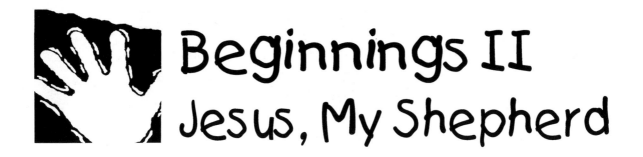

Beginnings II
Jesus, My Shepherd

NEW TESTAMENT LESSONS FOR YOUNG READERS

EXPLORER'S BIBLE STUDY

FOR

THE YOUNG BIBLE SCHOLAR

Remember now your Creator in the days of your youth....
Ecclesiastes 12:1

With my whole heart I have sought You;
Oh, let me not wander from Your commandments!
Your word I have hidden in my heart, that I might not sin against You.
Psalms 119:10-11

Published By

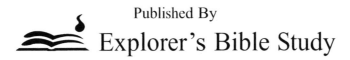 Explorer's Bible Study

Dickson, Tennessee

Curriculum Development/Author	Editor
Patricia Constance Russell	Dee M. Murtha
Cover Art	Project Editor
Troy D. Russell	Tom M. Constance, Jr.

*We believe the Bible is God's Word, a divine revelation, in the original language
verbally inspired in its entirety, and that it is the supreme infallible authority
in all matters of faith and conduct.*

(2 Peter 1:21; 2 Timothy 3:16)

Printed in the United States of America

Published by

Explorer's Bible Study
2652 Highway 46 South
Post Office Box 425
Dickson, Tennessee 37056-0425
615-446-7316
www.explorerbiblestudy.org

Contents

About the Author

Pat Russell has been a Christian educator for over 25 years. She began her teaching career by forming a preschool in her home. Later she accepted a position as a teacher in a private Christian School and also served as a curriculum coordinator and consultant. Most recently, she helped to co-found Park City Academy. Through years of writing and development, she has crafted a curriculum that comes from practical "hands on" experience. This curriculum has been "classroom tested" in Christian schools, in homeschool settings, as well as having been used in Explorer's Bible Study classes throughout the U.S.

Pat's goal in developing this curriculum is to provide the young Bible scholar with a chronological and historical method of Bible study. It is through this means that the Bible is seen in its entirety, not in broken pieces. The importance of understanding the true meaning of God's Word and His plan for each of us comes through careful study. Interpretation follows a knowledge of what God says, what God means, and finally how each individual applies this knowledge to his or her personal life experience.

How to Use This Book

The daily lessons in this book will help you as you teach your child about God. The goal is to give you a useful tool to give your child a better understanding of who God is and what His Word, the Bible says.

The core of each day's lesson is a Bible story and questions for your student to answer:

Bible Story is presented in an easy to understand language.

Questions: Thinking & Remembering will help your child recall and relate the story concepts in the lesson. Many of the questions are multiple choice, and in many instances, there is more than one correct choice. Sometimes all may be correct—this is deliberate. Typically, multiple choice answers are a matter of elimination. The purpose is to have the student read each answer and consider carefully what is included in the lesson. There are some answers that are obviously not to be considered and occasionally, there is an "all of the above." This is to prevent everything becoming so routine that the students stop thinking. The goal is to think!

In addition to the story and questions, the day's lesson may include one or more of the following elements:

Bible Words to Remember are provided to encourage and develop memorization skills. You may notice that some of the verses are abbreviated or paraphrased to make it easier for a young child to understand and remember. We have chosen the New King James version for this book.

Words to Know gives brief definitions to help explain difficult words or concepts.

Prayer Thought presents a short prayer as a model for learning to talk with God.

Think About is designed to help your child apply God's Word to his/her life.

Curriculum Implementation

These lessons may be used for students in 1st through 3rd grade. They are designed to be used by your child when he/she is old enough to read and write on their own. Early first grade students may have difficulty working the lessons without help at first, but as their reading and writing skills improve, they should be able to complete the lessons on their own.

Beginnings II is, as the name implies, the companion volume for our Beginnings I preschool curriculum. If you have younger children, the lessons are designed so that everyone is learning the same story and focusing on the same concepts—but in an age appropriate way. One of the goals of Explorer's Bible Study ministry has been to develop curriculum that allows families to study God's Word together. We hope that this book is an important and productive tool towards that end.

A Note to Parents and Teachers

If you have said "yes" to the call of God to teach, you have accepted one of the most important challenges in building the future kingdom. In James 3:1 we read not many should become teachers, knowing that there will be a stricter judgment. It takes a great commitment to put ourselves in a place of responsibility in which children and young students will make life-changing decisions based on the life and teaching we put before them. But knowing the high expectations God has for those who commit to this calling should not deter one from this wonderful and powerful opportunity to serve in this way. As you see the loving response to God from a child or student, it is difficult—if not impossible—to imagine NOT teaching! It becomes a compelling urgency that God rewards in so many ways that you'll wonder why there was ever a question mark after the words, "Should I consider teaching?"

Whether you are a home schooling parent, a Sunday School teacher, or a Christian educator, God has chosen you to teach! As a teacher, you will have a great influence in the lives of your children or students. You have been given the responsibility by God to mentor these lives spiritually. It is an awesome responsibility, but you don't have to do it alone! God is with you every step of the way.

Teach each child faithfully, prayerfully, and consistently in His Word . . . Knowing it, Believing it, Living it, and then Teaching it. Teaching is impossible without the first three. We hope this Bible curriculum will help guide you through this process.

During the writing of this curriculum, I have been constantly reminded of the awesome task that is set before us as teachers of God's Word. As with no other written word, we stand as facilitators in the greatest and most solemn responsibility. In the search for meaningful and thoughtful questions that would plant God's Words firmly in the hearts and minds of these precious ones who are so tender and receptive, it seemed that there was a need for much greater depth for our youngest of students than is often assumed.

The Bible stories do not just cover the familiar "wrapped in cotton" lessons. Rather, there has been a desire to tell the whole story within the child's frame of reference. It has been my prayerful desire to remain true to the biblical text. Some events may seem limited and you may consider expanding on the text. Let God be your ultimate guide in what you present.

The purpose is not only to show God's love for the people He created, but to also reveal God's great truth in His plan and purpose for each of us. The lessons deliberately do not seek to hide or cover the consequences of sin and wrongdoing, because omitting this leaves a child to wonder why there is a need for forgiveness. Sin is dealt with as the Bible deals with it, without a pretense that there is no judgment. But the compassion of God is evident. The child is never left with hopeless despair or the impression of an angry or distant God.

The lessons endeavor to teach the following:
>God's Care: His love is infinite.
>God's Concern: His ways of guiding and directing people and events show His love.
>God's Communication: He instructs and expresses His love in many ways.
>God's Consequences: There are results from our choices.
>God's Compassion: He does not stop loving us. God forgives and continues to
>help us grow and change.

It is my prayerful anticipation as you use this Bible curriculum that you will find and be delighted to observe, as I have, a response from those little ones that you teach. As they respond to God's love, may you be given the guidance that we all need as we seek HIM—the perfect one! These are exciting days with the most wondrous opportunities we can imagine.

Pray, seek, and study diligently; then teach with your heart.

Prayerfully,

Patricia Russell

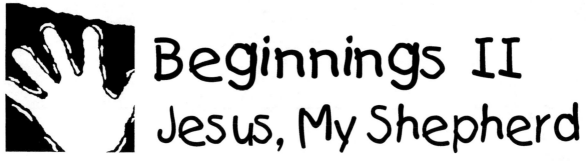

Beginnings II
Jesus, My Shepherd
New Testament Overview

STUDENT WORKBOOK

EXPLORER'S BIBLE STUDY

FOR

THE YOUNG BIBLE SCHOLAR

If you receive my words, and treasure my commands,
If you incline your ear to wisdom, and apply your heart to understanding,
If you seek her as silver, and search for hidden treasures,
Then you will understand and trust the Lord.

(from Proverbs 2:1-5)

Beginnings II

God: In the Beginning - Genesis

BIBLE WORDS TO REMEMBER

Jesus was in the beginning with God.
All things were made through Him. (from John 1:2-3)

Bible Story: A GREAT AND POWERFUL GOD

Before God **created** the world, there was complete darkness. How did everything get put into place? Why doesn't the sun fall down from the sky? What keeps the stars in the night sky? When you look at their **arrangement**, you might think that tomorrow or next year they will have changed. But the next time you look, they are there in the very same **pattern** as before—in perfect order. That's amazing!

God's power is stronger than any **force** that we can understand. There was a plan and **purpose** for everything. The **universe** did not just spin around and land somewhere to create the life and beauty we can see.

God was there in the beginning—and Jesus was with Him even before the world was created! God is now controlling the whole universe. And He will be there through **eternity**—forever! God always was and always will be.

How wonderful to know that God IS! We cannot see Him or touch Him because He is a spirit, but we can know that He is everywhere, in every place—anytime. His love can reach to everyone in the whole world.

WORDS TO KNOW

create:	to make out of nothing
arrangement:	a plan and a system for a design
pattern:	a design with order
force:	to make happen with energy and power
purpose:	the reason for something
universe:	the heavens and all of space everywhere
eternity:	forever, where there is no time; endless

Questions:
THINKING & REMEMBERING

Fill in the blanks or circle the letters of all that are right.

1. What is amazing about the world?
    a. It is always changing.
    b. It is in perfect order.
    c. It is old and falling apart.

2. What can you see about the stars over a period of time?
    a. They remain in the same pattern.
    b. They are never the same.
    c. After a few years they change.

3. What would it take to put everything in this perfect order?
    a. thousands of years
    b. a power stronger than any force we can understand
    c. millions of years of natural occurrence (happenings)

4. Who was in the beginning with God before the world was created?
    a. Adam and Eve
    b. just a few people and animals
    c. Jesus

5. What is God doing right now?
    a. making a new plan
    b. controlling the universe
    c. keeping a list of the wrong things we do

6. Why can't we see God or touch Him?
    a. because God is a spirit (John 4:24)
    b. because He stays in heaven
    c. because He is holy

7. God can be _____. His love can reach _____.

3

BIBLE WORDS TO REMEMBER

Jesus was in the beginning with God.
All things were made through Him. (from John 1:2-3)

Bible Story: LISTENING TO GOD

God speaks to us through His book, the Bible. The words that are in this wonderful book are the words that God gave to men to write down. Each one, whom God chose, carefully wrote **exactly** what God told him. He wanted all people always to be able to know how to live God's way. There are many words in God's book. You are beginning to learn what these words mean and what God is saying to you.

We may not hear God's voice with our ears, but when we listen to His word being read or we read it ourselves, we can know Him in our hearts. God is with you to help you **understand** His words. God's **Spirit** will help you know what is right and what is wrong.

God can put thoughts in your mind anytime, but especially when you are thinking about Him and praying. God will never tell you to do anything that will hurt you or hurt someone else. God will always help you love and be kind—those thoughts are from God. You can always trust Him. **Listen** carefully!

WORDS TO KNOW

exactly:	correctly; in the right way
understand:	to accept and believe
Spirit:	the Holy Spirit, the part of God that helps people understand God's words
listen:	to put your mind on what is being said

PRAYER THOUGHT

Dear God, Thank You for the ways in which You speak to me through Your words in the Bible. Help me trust You and listen carefully. When You are in my thoughts, I know that you will help me understand how You want me to live. In Jesus Name, Amen.

Questions:
THINKING & REMEMBERING

Fill in the blanks or circle the letters of all that are right.

1. How does God speak to us?
    a. through the words in His book, the Bible
    b. through angels, most of the time
    c. sometimes through our friends

2. Why did God choose certain people to write His words?
    a. so we could know which friends we will be nice to
    b. so people would know how to live God's way
    c. so the animals would have names

3. For whom did God want these words written?
    a. just for the people in the Bible times
    b. just for the people now in Israel, the land of the Bible
    c. for people thousands of years ago and for people today

4. How can we know what God is saying?
    a. by listening to His words and reading them
    b. by listening to the radio or watching TV
    c. by asking other people what He said

5. How will God help us when we listen?
    God is with us to help us _____ His words.

6. What will the Spirit of God help you know?
    God's Spirit will help me know what is _____ and what is
    _____.

7. When does God put thoughts in your mind?
    a. when you are praying
    b. when you are thinking about Him
    c. anytime

8. Whom can you ALWAYS trust? _____

5

BIBLE WORDS TO REMEMBER

Jesus was in the beginning with God.
All things were made through Him. (from John 1:2-3)

Bible Story: GOD'S GREAT LOVE

The Bible tells about **God's love**. The word LOVE is in the Bible many times. God shows His love in so many ways; we cannot even begin to count them. One of the very first ways He shows His love is through the **creation** of the world. He made everything **perfect** for us in the beginning.

We know that we cannot measure God's love. But we can know and see the many ways in which He loves us.

In our Bible lessons, we are going to learn more about what God did to show us His love. We are going to read about how God loved people even when they sinned and disobeyed Him. We are going to learn that God gave His very own Son, Jesus, to die for us so that we could live in heaven forever with Him.

We know that the **reason** God sent Jesus is that He loves us! That is the most wonderful part of all. We will also find out how to love God and others. God is giving YOU a gift. He will not make you take it. You will need to choose to **accept** His gift of love.

WORDS TO KNOW

God's love: the expression of all that is perfect
creation: everything that God made
perfect: just right
reason: why something is
accept: to take or receive

PRAYER THOUGHT

Dear God, Your love is all around me and does not change. Thank You for loving me so much! Help me to love others like You love me. Thank You for sending Jesus, Your gift of love to me! In Jesus Name, Amen.

Questions:
THINKING & REMEMBERING

Fill in the blanks or circle the letters of all that are right.

1. Where do we find out about God's love?
   a. in just the things God made
   b. in a certain place someone will tell us about
   c. in the Bible

2. How many ways does God show His love?
   a. there are too many to count
   b. about 100
   c. in the thousands

3. What are you going to learn in the Bible?
   a. about God's love
   b. about how God sent Jesus to show His love
   c. how to love God and others
   d. how we can live in heaven forever with Him

4. When does God love people?
   a. only when they do the right thing
   b. always—even when they sin and disobey Him
   c. sometimes, when He has time to remember the people He made

5. What plan did God have to show His love when people sinned?
   He sent His Son, _____.

6. Why did God send Jesus to earth?
   a. so we could live in heaven forever with Him
   b. so we can know how long the earth has been here
   c. so we can know how people are different from God

7. What do we need to do to be ready to live in heaven?
   a. accept God's gift
   b. believe in Jesus
   c. try to be good all by ourselves

8. God sent _____ to earth to show us His _____.

   If we believe in Him, we can live _____ in heaven with God.

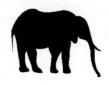

BIBLE WORDS TO REMEMBER

Jesus was in the beginning with God.
All things were made through Him. (from John 1:2-3)

Bible Story: GOD CARES ABOUT YOU

God's book, the Bible, tells us how He took care of those whom He loved. No matter what happens, God does not stop loving the people He made. He is watching over them all the time. God does not need to sleep. He is a spirit. He does not have a body that gets tired.

Every day when you wake up you can look at the sky and know that God is giving you a new day! He watches through the night and cares for you while you are asleep. The new day brings many **possibilities**. Every day you will learn many things to help you grow to be the person God wants you to be. He created you and knows that you can make others happy by being kind and loving them.

Whatever you do, God says to do the best work you can. Never think that something is not important enough to do well. God cares for you, and He cares that you do the right things. God has a **plan** for you for your whole life. He will always care what you think about, what you do every day, and what you will do each tomorrow!

WORDS TO KNOW

possibilities: all the things you can think about to do
plan: something that is thought about and decided how and
   what to do

PRAYER THOUGHT

Dear God, Help me to always do the best work every day for You. Help me to know what is really important to do well. Thank You for being with me and taking care of me. Thank You for showing me Your love in so many ways! In Jesus Name, Amen.

Questions:
THINKING & REMEMBERING

Fill in the blanks or circle the letters of all that are right.

1. What can you know for sure?
    a. It will not rain tomorrow.
    b. My friends will always be nice to me.
    c. God loves me very much.

2. What else can you know?
    a. that God will always be with me
    b. what will happen at 3 p.m. tomorrow
    c. that it will be sunny next week

3. How can God be watching all the time?
    God is a _____.

4. What is special about every morning when you awake?
    God is giving us a new day with many _____.

5. Put a check by the things you can do every day.
    _____ a. learn to be the person God wants me to be
    _____ b. listen to God's words and pray
    _____ c. make others happy by being kind and loving them
    _____ d. do my "best work" in all I am given to do

6. What has God already thought about for you?
    Find the words in the lesson to fill in the spaces.
    God has a _____ for my whole_____.

7. In what ways does God care about you?
    a. what I think
    b. what clothes I choose to wear (the green or the blue)
    c. what I do
    d. what I will do tomorrow

BIBLE WORDS TO REMEMBER
Jesus was in the beginning with God.
All things were made through Him. (from John 1:2-3)

Bible Story: GOD DOES NOT CHANGE

The Bible says, "For I am the LORD, I do not **change**." It's wonderful to know that God never changes. He will always be the same. He will always do what He says He will do. He promised to love you, and He does—God loved you even before you were born!

God's love and His words are something you can always **trust** and believe. God also wants you to believe His words in the Bible. He does not change His mind about love. He does not decide to do or say something different later today, tomorrow or next year.

It is **confusing** when people cannot always keep the promises they make. People often change their mind about what they think is right and wrong. In the Bible you will discover what is right and good. You will know what God hates and what will make you sad. Even though you will make mistakes and will not always keep your promises, God will forgive you when you ask Him. You will learn how to live in God's way and bring happiness to others. It is exciting to find out what God says and what He has planned!

WORDS TO KNOW

change: to turn away from doing one thing and do something different
trust: knowing that God loves you and will take care of you
confusing: puzzling, mixed up—when you can't know for sure

PRAYER THOUGHT

Dear God, Thank You for never changing. Help me remember that You love me and want what is best for me. I want to love you more and live in ways that will serve You and bring happiness to others. Amen.

Questions:
THINKING & REMEMBERING

Fill in the blanks or circle the letters of all that are right.

1. Who will never change? _____

2. How do you know that God will love you?

    a. from the words in the Bible

    b. because of His promises

    c. He doesn't have a choice—He has to love me because He made me.

3. Whom does God love? _____

4. What does God want you to believe?

    God wants me to believe His words in the _____.

5. Does God ever change what is written in His word?

    yes_____ no_____

6. What is sometimes confusing?

    a. God sometimes gets mad and doesn't love us.

    b. when people change their mind about what they think

    c. when people do not keep their promises

    d. when people say that something is right and then do wrong

7. What exciting things can you find out by reading God's word?

    a. that He loved me—even before I was born!

    b. what God has planned for the people He made

    c. how to live in the right way

    d. how to love God and others

8. Fill in the missing words from John 1:2-3.

    Jesus was in the beginning with _____.

    All things were _____ through Him.

God: His Promises

BIBLE WORDS TO REMEMBER

In Him was life ... the light of men.
And the light shines in the darkness. (John 1:4-5)

Bible Story: GOD'S PROMISE TO ADAM AND EVE
from Genesis 1-3; John 1

In coming to the wonderful stories of Jesus we have to go back to the very beginning. Remember that there was only darkness before God created the heavens and the earth. And then when God spoke the words, "Let there be light," the world started happening! God is the beginning and ending of all things.

The Bible tells us that Jesus was in the beginning with God. "All things were made through Him, and without Him nothing was made." These are wonderful words to begin knowing about Jesus, God's only Son!

God's perfect plan was that His children, starting with Adam and Eve, would live in beautiful **peace** and **harmony** in the wonderful world He created. But the first people **chose** to go their own way and not listen to God. That was a sad day. God promised Adam and Eve that He would send a Savior to free people from sin and Satan.

The happy part is that God does not stop loving people when they **disobey**. God planned a way for everyone to come back to Him. **The Way** is through Jesus. Jesus is God's very special gift to the world.

WORDS TO KNOW

peace: calm and quiet

harmony: to be in agreement with each other

chose: decided between more than one thing

disobey: to choose to do wrong

The Way: In the Bible it says that JESUS is "The Way" for people to come to God.

Questions:
THINKING & REMEMBERING

Fill in the blanks or circle the letters of all that are right.

1. What do you need to remember before you hear the stories of Jesus?
    a. God is the beginning and ending of all things.
    b. There was only darkness before God created the world.
    c. Jesus was with God in the beginning.

2. What was God's perfect plan?
    a. People would never have work to do.
    b. People would live in peace and harmony.
    c. People would be able to do whatever they wanted.

3. Who were the first people who disobeyed God and sinned?
    a. Noah and his wife
    b. Abraham and Sarah
    c. Adam and Eve

4. Did God stop loving people because they disobeyed?
    yes_____ no_____

5. What way did God plan for people to come back to Him?
    a. Jesus is the Way. He came to earth and died for our sins.
    b. God told people to try harder to be good.
    c. God said He would give them one more chance.

6. Fill in the Bible words from John 1:4-5.
    In Him (Jesus) was _____ ...the light of men.
    And the _____ shines in the darkness.

PRAYER THOUGHT

Thank You God, for caring about me and making a perfect plan for me to live with You in heaven forever. Help me to listen to Your words and obey. In Jesus Name, Amen.

BIBLE WORDS TO REMEMBER

In Him was life … the light of men.
And the light shines in the darkness. (John 1:4-5)

Bible Story: GOD'S PROMISE TO NOAH
from Genesis 6-9

There were many people on the earth. They forgot their loving God—except for one man named Noah who obeyed God. God was very sad when He saw the people doing bad things. God told Noah that He would send rain for many days until the earth was destroyed by the waters. Because Noah loved God, he and his family would be safe.

God told Noah to build an **ark**. He gave him directions and Noah followed God's instructions. Noah told the people what God was going to do because they didn't love Him, but they just laughed at Him!

God told Noah to **gather** two of every kind of animal to put in the ark. When Noah and his family and the animals were safely inside, God closed the door.

It rained for forty days and nights. When the rain stopped, they waited until the land was dry. They came out of the ark and thanked God for taking care of them. God made a promise that He would never send another flood to destroy the earth again. As a sign of His promise, God put the very first rainbow in the sky!

WORDS TO KNOW

ark: a huge wooden boat   **gather:** collect

PRAYER THOUGHT

Dear God, Thank You for the wonderful rainbow to help me remember Your promise. I want to learn more about You and love You more! In Jesus Name, Amen.

 # Questions:
THINKING & REMEMBERING

Fill in the blanks or circle the letters of all that are right.

1. What had happened on the earth?

   The people forgot _____.

2. What was the name of the one man who loved and obeyed God?

   _____

3. What did God tell Noah would happen?

   He would send _____ and _____ the _____.

4. Who would be saved from the flood of waters?
   a. Noah and his family
   b. two of every kind of animal
   c. just Noah

5. What did God tell Noah to build? _____

6. How did Noah know how to build it?

   God gave him _____.

7. What did the people do when Noah told them what was going to happen?

   _____

8. How many of each kind of animal was taken on the ark? _____

9. Who closed the door of the ark? _____

10. How long did it rain? _____

11. What did the family do when they came out of the ark?

    They thanked _____ for taking care of them.

12. What did God show as a sign of His promise to never send another flood to

    destroy the earth again? _____

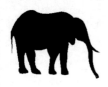

BIBLE WORDS TO REMEMBER

In Him was life … the light of men.
And the light shines in the darkness. (John 1:4-5)

Bible Story: GOD'S PROMISE TO ABRAHAM
from Genesis 12, 15, 18, 21

A man named Abraham loved God and **worshiped** Him, even when all the people around him were worshiping other gods. God told Abraham to move to a new land that He would show him. God promised Abraham that his family would grow to be a very great **nation**. God said that there would be as many people in his family as there were stars in the sky and sand on the seashore! That is more than anyone can count!

Abraham and Sarah waited and many years passed. They still did not have children. They wondered how God would keep His **promise**. They thought that they were too old to have children. But God always keeps His promises. God said, "Is anything too hard for the Lord?"

A son was finally born! His name was Isaac. When Isaac grew up, he married Rebekah. The family was starting to grow bigger! This was all part of God's plan to send a **Savior** to save people from their **sin** and make them free. Jesus came from Abraham's family many years later and God's promise came true!

WORDS TO KNOW

worship: showing respect in honoring and praising God
nation: a group of people living together in the same land
promise: to say that for sure something will be done or given
Savior: One who saves others and makes them free
sin: thinking and doing wrong—not obeying and loving God

PRAYER THOUGHT

Thank You God, for Your wonderful promises. I know that You will always keep Your promises. Help me to keep the promises I make to show others that I love You. In Jesus Name, Amen.

Questions:
Thinking & Remembering

Fill in the blanks or circle the letters of all that are right.

1. What was the name of the man in the lesson who loved and worshiped God?
   a. Samuel
   b. Abraham
   c. Moses

2. What were the people around him doing?
   a. worshiping God
   b. worshiping other gods
   c. loving the God of Abraham

3. What did God tell Abraham to do?
   a. talk to the other people about God
   b. move into his father's house
   c. move to a new land

4. How would Abraham know where to go?
   a. God would give him a map.
   b. God would show him the way.
   c. He would have to ask people along the way.

5. What did God promise Abraham?
   a. His family would be a great nation.
   b. There would be as many people as sand on the seashore.
   c. There would be as many people as stars in the sky.

6. How long did Abraham and Sarah wait for the promise to come true?
   a. five years
   b. two years
   c. many years

7. What was the name of the son that was born? _____

8. What was God's plan?
   a. to send a Savior (Jesus)
   b. to give Abraham and Sarah a new place to live

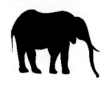

BIBLE WORDS TO REMEMBER

In Him was life ... the light of men.
And the light shines in the darkness. (John 1:4-5)

Bible Story: JACOB REMEMBERS GOD'S PROMISE
from Genesis 25, 28

Two baby boys (**twins**) were born to Isaac and Rebekah. While the boys were growing up, Jacob and his brother Esau were told about God's wonderful promise. They told them how **important** the promise was to God's people. Someday, the Savior of all people was going to be part of the family that God promised to Abraham.

Esau and Jacob were very different from each other. Jacob was gentle and liked to help at home with the gardens and listen to his mother talk about God's promise. Esau was a hunter and did not want to listen to stories about God. God's promise to **save** people from their sins was not important to Esau. He only thought about himself and what he wanted—just like we do many times!

Jacob thought about God's promise to his family and he was excited! He remembered what God told his grandfather Abraham. He knew that God promised that his family would be a great nation with many people. God talked to Jacob and said, "Do not be afraid. I will always be with you. I will keep My promise."

WORDS TO KNOW

twins: two babies born one after the other at the same time
important: something that you should think about seriously and know that it has great value
save: to make a way to live in God's perfect heaven someday

PRAYER THOUGHT

Dear God, Thank You for Your love and care. Help me to trust you and not be afraid. In Jesus Name, Amen.

Questions:
THINKING & REMEMBERING

Fill in the blanks or circle the letters of all that are right.

1. How did Jacob and Esau know about God's promise?
   a. They read about it.
   b. Their parents, Isaac and Rebekah, told them.
   c. Their friends knew about it.

2. For whom was this promise important?
   a. for Abraham, Isaac and Jacob
   b. for all of God's people
   c. just for people in Bible times

3. Who was born from this family who is the Savior? _____

4. Which brother liked to hear about God? _____

5. Which brother did not think God was important? _____

6. What did Jacob think about and remember?

   a. God's promise to Abraham
   b. that God was sad that people were sinning
   c. that his parents would take care of him

7. What did God tell Jacob? (Find the words in your lesson.)
   "Do not be _____. I will always be with you.
   I will keep my _____."

THINK ABOUT

God shows you His love in many different ways. God will always be
with you and help you. If you are ever afraid, remember to ask God
to help you feel His love. God keeps His promises!

Say the words that God said and tell them to someone else.
God said, "Do not be afraid. I will always be with you. I will keep
My promises."

BIBLE WORDS TO REMEMBER

In Him was life … the light of men.
And the light shines in the darkness. (John 1:4-5)

Bible Story: DAVID LOVES GOD

from 1 Samuel-2 Samuel; 1 Kings 1-2

When David was a young boy, he took care of his father's sheep. He took his sheep to **pastures** where there was lots of green grass to eat. He took them to clear streams so they could have good water to drink. He didn't want them to get hurt so he watched to keep them safe from wild animals. One time he used a **sling** and killed a bear that was attacking his sheep!

David thought a lot about God. He prayed and asked God to help him take good care of the sheep. He played a harp and sang songs about God's love. He wrote words that said we are like God's sheep—He loves us and takes care of us.

David was not afraid. When a giant laughed at God and God's people, David said, "God is on our side. I will kill the giant." He used his sling again and God's enemies ran away.

When David grew up, God chose him to be the king of Israel. David was from the family of Abraham and Jesus was born from this family to live on the earth to be ***"God with us"***!

WORDS TO KNOW

pastures:　　　meadows of green grass

sling:　　　a leather strap in which a stone can be thrown

"God with us": Jesus was God born on earth as a human baby to show us how much He loves us!

PRAYER THOUGHT

Dear God, Thank You for the Bible with Your wonderful words. Help me to remember Your promises. Help me to listen to Your words to learn how You want me to live. In Jesus Name, Amen.

Questions:
THINKING & REMEMBERING

Fill in the blanks or circle the letters of all that are right.

1. What did David do when he was a young boy?

   He took care of his father's _____.

2. How did David accept his responsibility to care for them?

   a. He loved them.

   b. He kept them safe from wild animals.

   c. He made sure they had good food and water.

3. Whom did David think about while he was taking care of the sheep?

   _____

4. What did David ask God to help him do?

   He asked His help to take good _____ of the _____.

5. How did David express his love to God?

   He played a _____ and _____ about God's love.

6. How do we know that David was not afraid?

   a. He protected his sheep by killing a bear.

   b. He believed that God loved and cared about him.

   c. He fought the giant.

7. What did the enemies of God do?

   a. They killed God's people.

   b. They ran away.

   c. They wanted to become friends with David.

8. What did David do when he grew up?

   He was the _____ of Israel.

9. Who was born from the family of Abraham and David?

   _____

Beginnings II

The Promise: Watching and Waiting

BIBLE WORDS TO REMEMBER

The people who walked in darkness have
seen a great light. (Isaiah 9:2)

Bible Story: REMEMBERING THE PROMISE
from Isaiah 7

Many times the people of God were reminded by His special messengers that
God loved them and wanted them to come back to Him. The people would not
listen. They thought about earthly kings and kingdoms—they wanted to have
power and be important—without God telling them what to do. They thought
that the **commandments** which God had given them were too **difficult**.

Sometimes the grandmothers and grandfathers remembered the time when the
Israelites saw the miracles God did. They knew that God had opened up the Red
Sea and let the people walk across on dry land. God had fed them in the desert
with bread from heaven. He had helped them win wars against their enemies and
kept them safe. But soon, the stories seemed far away and long ago. Other things
became more important than God.

The **prophet** Isaiah told the king of Israel, "If you will not believe, God will not
protect you." The king had to **choose**. God did not want to give up on His
people, but He would let them choose—just as He always had and always will.

WORDS TO KNOW

commandments:	rules to follow
difficult:	something hard to do
prophet:	someone whom God has told what will happen before it happens
protect:	to take care of and keep safe
choose:	to decide between more than one thing

THINK ABOUT

The Bible tells us that God loves the people He made. God is very sad
when people choose to sin (disobey Him) and choose not to love Him.
God will always help you do the right thing when you ask Him!

Questions:
THINKING & REMEMBERING

Fill in the blanks or circle the letters of all that are right.

1. Whom did God send to the people to tell them to come back to God?
   a. prophets
   b. special messengers

2. What did they remind the people of?
   God _____ them and wanted them to come back to _____.

3. What did God want the people to remember?
   He wanted them to remember that they were His _____.

4. What did the people think about most?
   a. being rich
   b. being powerful
   c. themselves

5. How did they feel about God's commandments?
   a. They were too difficult.
   b. They forgot what the commandments were.
   c. They wanted other people to follow the rules.

6. What were some of the miracles God had showed them?
   a. He opened up the Red Sea.
   b. He fed them in the desert with bread from heaven.
   c. He helped them win wars against their enemies.

7. What did the prophet Isaiah tell the King of Israel?
   a. If you will not believe, God will not protect you.
   b. to choose whether or not he would follow God
   c. God did not want to give up on His people, but He would let them choose to follow Him.

Remember: God will always let you choose to love Him.

PRAYER THOUGHT

Dear God, You ask me to believe. You ask me to obey. You ask me to wait for Your promises. Help me to choose to follow You. In Jesus Name, Amen.

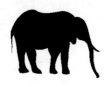

BIBLE WORDS TO REMEMBER

The people who walked in darkness have
seen a great light. (Isaiah 9:2)

Bible Story: GOD WITH US!
from Isaiah 7, 9

God said that He would send a Savior who would make all people free from sin. He would die so that it would be **possible** for people to live in heaven forever. This promise was given in the very beginning to Adam and Eve who were the first people. He gave the promise to Abraham, Isaac and Jacob. God also told King David about this wonderful promise to keep the people He loved from being destroyed by Satan.

Isaiah was a prophet who told many things about the **Messiah** who would be called Jesus. He told about the special birth of Jesus. He would have an earthly mother (just like you have) but His heavenly Father was God. Isaiah said that the Messiah would also be called **Immanuel**, which means "God with us."

The promise came true! When the time was just right, Jesus was born. When the time was just right, Jesus died for the sins of the world. When the time was just right, Jesus was alive again and death was no longer a problem for those who believed in Him. The promise has been **fulfilled**!

WORDS TO KNOW

possible: what can happen if certain conditions are met
Messiah: the King promised by God
Immanuel: God with us
fulfilled: it happened already!

THINK ABOUT

God's love was very big and great to make a plan for us to live in heaven forever. God knew the plan from the beginning. Everything happened to make it come true!

Questions:
THINKING & REMEMBERING

Fill in the blanks or circle the letters of all that are right.

1. What did God promise to do?
    a. send a Savior
    b. make everyone love Him
    c. force people to choose to believe

2. Why did God send a Savior?
    a. to make people free from sin
    b. to make it possible for us to live in heaven forever
    c. so people could do what they felt like doing

3. When was the promise first given?
    a. to King David
    b. to Adam and Eve
    c. to Abraham

4. Who is God's enemy that tries to make people sin?_____

5. Which prophet told about the coming Messiah?_____

6. Was Jesus' birth very ordinary?   yes_____   no_____

7. What does the name of Jesus "Immanuel" mean?

    _____

8. What happened when the time was "just right"?
    a. Jesus was born.
    b. Jesus died for the sins of the world.
    c. Jesus was alive again.

9. What would no longer be a problem for those who believed?

    _____

BIBLE WORDS TO REMEMBER

The people who walked in darkness have
seen a great light. (Isaiah 9:2)

Bible Story: WHY JESUS CAME FROM HEAVEN

from Isaiah 11

The Bible tells us that Jesus was in the very beginning. Jesus was with God, and Jesus is God. That is a lot to think about! And we must think about it because it is important to understand why Jesus came to earth.

Being in **heaven** is living in the most wonderful place there is. We read in the Bible that in heaven there is no darkness, there are no tears, and there is no sickness. It is more beautiful than anything you can think or dream about on earth.

Jesus was in heaven with God when creation happened. Jesus left this most **perfect** place in heaven and came to earth where there is sin and sadness. All people have sinned since the first people, Adam and Eve, disobeyed God.

God loves us so much that He wanted us to be in heaven with Him forever. But God is perfect. And to live in a perfect heaven with a perfect God, we would have to be perfect. That is why Jesus came—to die for your sins and my sins. By **believing** in Him, we can be **accepted** by a perfect God.

WORDS TO KNOW

heaven: the place where there is perfect peace
perfect: without sin; there is nothing that is missing
believe: to know that something is true
accept: to agree with and believe
separate: to keep apart

THINK ABOUT

God is perfect and all people have sinned. Sin **separates** us from God.
Jesus is the way back to God. What a wonderful plan!

Questions:
THINKING & REMEMBERING

Fill in the blanks or circle the letters of all that are right.

1. Who was in the very beginning with God? _____

2. What things are not in heaven that happen on earth?
    a. There is no darkness.
    b. There are no tears.
    c. There is no sickness.

3. What kind of place did Jesus leave to come to a place of sin and sadness?

    _____

4. Why did God plan for Jesus to come to earth?
    a. He wanted Jesus to see the earth for Himself.
    b. He wanted Jesus to make the earth just like heaven.
    c. He wanted us to be in heaven with Him forever.

5. What would we need to be like to live in a perfect heaven with a perfect God?
    a. We would need to be perfect, also.
    b. We would need to be as good as we can be.
    c. We would need to work hard to get to heaven.

6. What have all people done since the first people, Adam and Eve, sinned and disobeyed God?
    a. loved God whenever we could
    b. continued to sin and disobey God
    c. thought about how we could get to heaven on our own

7. What must we do to live in heaven with God?
    a. know that we have sinned
    b. believe in Jesus
    c. ask Jesus to be our Savior and live in us

Remember: The Holy Spirit gives us power to live for God!

BIBLE WORDS TO REMEMBER

The people who walked in darkness have
seen a great light. (Isaiah 9:2)

Bible Story: WHEN WILL HE COME?
from Isaiah 40

God never wanted anyone to be hurt or sad. For more than two thousand years
since the beginning of the world, God told people that He loved them. God chose
them, but people did not always choose God.

When Jesus came to earth the first time, people were **suffering**. They had **rulers**
who did not love God. They were cruel and unfair. Everything seemed dark in the
world. There was **cheating**, **lying**, and killing. People did not love each other and
thought only of themselves. Mothers, fathers, and even children hated each other.
They were not kind and did not take care of sick people. God looked at all of this
sadness, and He knew that the time was right for His plan to send Jesus to earth.

When Jesus came He told people that were sad about God's love. He made the
sick well. He showed people how to be kind to each other. Then He showed God's
love in the only way that would make it **possible** for people to live in a perfect
heaven. He died for all people to free them from their sin and sadness. It is His
gift of life.

WORDS TO KNOW

suffering: knowing pain and difficulty
rulers: those who tell others what to do
cheating: tricking other people
lying: telling what is not true
possible: something that can happen to make things right
dismayed: discouraged
respond: to answer with words or actions

THINK ABOUT

God said: "Fear not, for I am with you. Do not be **dismayed**, for I am your
God. I will make you strong. Yes, I will help you." (Isaiah 41:10)

Questions:
THINKING & REMEMBERING

Fill in the blanks or circle the letters of all that are right.

1. What two things do we know that God said about His people?
   a. I love you.
   b. Because you have sinned, you are no longer my people.
   c. I have chosen you.

2. How did the people **respond** to God's love?
   They did not always_____ God.

3. What was happening on earth before Jesus came?
   a. People were _____.
   b. They had rulers who were _____ and _____.
   c. People did not _____ each other.

4. What did people think about most? _____

5. What did God decide to do when He saw all this sadness?
   a. He wanted the people to suffer longer.
   b. He wanted the people to work out things on their own.
   c. He sent Jesus to earth.

6. What things did Jesus do?
   a. He told people about God's love.
   b. He made the sick well.
   c. He showed people how to be kind to each other.

7. What great and wonderful gift did Jesus give when He died on the cross for our sins?
   He gave the gift of _____ so that we can live in heaven forever with Him. To receive this gift, we must accept it.

PRAYER THOUGHT

Dear God, Help me to understand and accept Your gift of love and life forever. I am sorry for all the wrong things I have done to hurt You and others. I choose to love You and want You to live in my heart. I believe that Jesus died for my sins. Help me to follow You every day in every way. In Jesus Name, Amen.

BIBLE WORDS TO REMEMBER

The people who walked in darkness have
seen a great light. (Isaiah 9:2)

Bible Story: PROMISES KEPT

from Luke 1

God is so wonderful and powerful; He can do anything! Even though we sometimes think about God being up above the clouds, God is a spirit and can be everywhere at the same time. We know from the Bible that God sends angels to give special **messages** to people and to **protect** those who love Him. He also sends angels on **extraordinary assignments**.

Before Jesus was born, an angel had an assignment to tell a man named Zacharias that he and his wife (who were very old) would have a son who would be named John. This was not very ordinary, either—but nothing is **impossible** for God to do!

John would help people get ready for Jesus and remember the promise God made to Abraham. Abraham believed God and His promise. There was a nation from this family called Israel. There were as many people from Abraham's family as there were stars in the sky and grains of sand on the shore. It was just as God promised. God's promises all come true. Even if there is a long waiting time, we can trust and believe God. What He says He will do—always!

WORDS TO KNOW

message: to tell something to someone
protect: to take care of and keep from danger
extraordinary: unusual and amazing
assignment: a job someone is given to do or to which someone is sent
impossible: hopeless; something you think cannot happen

PRAYER THOUGHT

Dear God, I can't understand everything about You, but I know that You love me and I can believe everything in Your Word. Help me to have faith and hear Your words so that I can love You more. In Jesus Name, Amen.

Questions:
THINKING & REMEMBERING

Fill in the blanks or circle the letters of all that are right.

1. How can God be everywhere? God is a _____.

2. Whom does God send to be special messengers?_____

3. What else do they do? _____

4. What was the name of the special child born to Zacharias?
   a. Abraham
   b. Isaac
   c. John

5. What special work did God have planned for him?
   a. to get people ready for Jesus
   b. to help build a church
   c. to help the people remember God's promise

6. What is the name of the nation that is from Abraham's family?
   a. Egypt
   b. Israel
   c. Syria

7. How many people did God say would be in this nation?
   There would be as many as there are _____ in the sky, and as
   many as there are grains of _____ on the shore.

8. What do we know about all of God's promises?
   They will all come _____.

9. Does God ever change His mind or forget what He promised?
   yes_____   no_____

10. Write your Bible words:

   _____

   _____

   _____

   _____

   _____

Beginnings II

God: His Messengers

BIBLE WORDS TO REMEMBER

And He will be called Wonderful, Counselor, Mighty God, Everlasting Father, Prince of Peace. (from Isaiah 9:6)

Bible Story: AN ANGEL VISIT

from Luke 1

God loved His people and He promised to send a Savior to save people from their sins. By believing this promise and loving Jesus we will live **forever** in heaven with God!

Many years had passed since God first gave this wonderful promise. Many people forgot about God—they chose not to remember. They started worshiping other gods and idols. The Romans took over the land that God had given to the Israelites. God's people were not free.

But not everyone forgot God. A **priest** named Zacharias remembered God's promise. He and his wife, Elizabeth, prayed every day that God's promise would come true. They followed God's commandments. They prayed that someday they could have a child who loved and served the Lord.

One day, while Zacharias was worshiping God at the **temple**, a voice spoke to him. It was an **angel** talking to him! The angel said, "Don't be afraid. God has heard your prayer. You will have a very special child. His name will be John. He will tell people what they must do to be ready for the Savior to come."

WORDS TO KNOW

forever: a time that never ends
priest: a special person in charge of worship
temple: a place where people worshiped God
angel: a heavenly being who worships and serves God

THINK ABOUT

Angels bring special messages from God to people. They take care of us and watch over us. They sometimes show us what to do or where to go. They sometimes even get us out of trouble. Isn't God wonderful to have such special messengers?

 # Questions:
THINKING & REMEMBERING

Fill in the blanks or circle the letters of all that are right.

1. What was God's promise to His people?
   a. He would get rid of the Romans.
   b. He would make their life easy.
   c. He would send a Savior.

2. What do people need to do so they can live forever in heaven?

   By _____ this _____ and loving

   _____ we can live forever in heaven.

3. What did some of the people do instead of following God?
   a. They worshiped other gods and idols.
   b. They celebrated and had parties.
   c. They wanted God to make the rules easier.

4. What happened when they forgot God?
   a. They had rulers who did not love God.
   b. They were not free—they became slaves.
   c. They didn't have to worry about pleasing God.

5. Who remembered God's promise?

   _____ Zacharias _____ Jezebel _____Elizabeth

6. What did Zacharias and his wife pray and ask God for?

   _____

7. What did the angel say to Zacharias when he was at the temple?

   "Don't be _____. God has heard your _____."

8. What did the angel say their son's name would be? _____

9. What would John do?

   He would tell people what they must do to get ready for the Savior to come.

   true _____   false_____

BIBLE WORDS TO REMEMBER

And He will be called Wonderful, Counselor, Mighty God, Everlasting Father, Prince of Peace. (from Isaiah 9:6)

Bible Story: THE SPECIAL NEWS
from Luke 1

Do you remember what the angel told Zacharias? Zacharias and his wife were going to have a baby boy! His name would be John and he would be the special one that would tell the people that the Savior was coming.

Zacharias listened to the angel tell him this news but couldn't believe it! They had prayed for a child, but now they were very old. Zacharias asked, "How can I know that what you are telling me is true? This cannot be possible!"

The angel spoke to Zacharias again. "I am Gabriel, who stands in the **presence** of God, and was sent to speak to you and bring you these glad **tidings**. Because you did not believe my words, you will not be able to speak until after the child is born."

When Zacharias came out of the temple, he could not speak—just as the angel had told him. All the people around him wondered what had happened. They thought that maybe he had seen a **vision**—but Zacharias knew why he was silent. He had not believed that God could do what was impossible for man. With God, all things are possible!

WORDS TO KNOW

presence: to be close to
tidings: news or message
vision: dream

PRAYER THOUGHT

Dear Heavenly Father, I know that you have planned everything and that you will always love me and be with me. Help me to trust you every day and show others that I have confidence in Your love and that nothing is impossible with You. Amen.

Questions:
THINKING & REMEMBERING

Fill in the blanks or circle the letters of all that are right.

1. Why didn't Zacharias believe what the angel told him?
   a. He was shocked.
   b. He and his wife were old.
   c. He thought that it would be hard to take care of a baby.

2. What question did Zacharias ask the angel?
   a. Did God really send you to give me a message?
   b. How am I to tell my wife Elizabeth?
   c. How can I know that what you are telling me is true?

3. What else did Zacharias say to the angel?
   This cannot be _____.

4. What happened when Zacharias did not believe the angel's message?
   a. The angel repeated the message so he would understand.
   b. He could not speak.
   c. He sat down to rest.

5. How long would Zacharias have this condition?
   a. until the baby was born
   b. until he told his wife
   c. until he told the people

6. What did the people think had happened to Zacharias?
   They thought he had seen a _____.

7. Did Zacharias know and understand why he was silent? _____

8. Finish this verse from the Bible:
   With God all things are _____ . (Matthew 19:26)

THINK ABOUT

When God is part of your thoughts and plans, you can know that He will make your dreams for good things that please Him happen. Begin your day by thinking of wonderful possibilities—think of ways to be helpful and to show God's love to others.

BIBLE WORDS TO REMEMBER

And He will be called Wonderful, Counselor, Mighty God, Everlasting Father, Prince of Peace. (from Isaiah 9:6)

Bible Story: A MESSENGER IS BORN
from Luke 1

What the angel said came true. That is because the words the angel spoke were from God. God only says what is true. He always keeps His promises. A son was born to Zacharias and Elizabeth. They were very happy that God had given them this special son. All of their friends and family **celebrated** with them on the birthday of their son.

It was time to choose a name for the new baby. Everyone thought that the baby would have the same name as his father. They thought that "Zacharias" was the perfect name for the special baby that was born to old parents. This baby was not just an **ordinary** baby!

Zacharias had not spoken one word for many months, since the visit of the angel in the temple. Zacharias wrote the name that the angel had told him for the baby boy. His name is JOHN.

Everyone was surprised. And they were even more surprised when Zacharias started speaking aloud. He was praising God for remembering His people. As the people listened, they started to wonder what kind of a child JOHN would be. They would find out very soon.

WORDS TO KNOW

celebrated: to have a happy party when something special has happened
ordinary: just like everyone else

PRAYER THOUGHT

Dear God, Your plan is so perfect and wonderful! The promises You make are never forgotten! Help me to remember that whatever You say, You will do. In Jesus Name, Amen.

Questions:
THINKING & REMEMBERING

Fill in the blanks or circle the letters of all that are right.

1. What can we always know about God?
   a. His words are true.
   b. He keeps His promises.
   c. He changes His mind.

2. What name did the family and friends of Zacharias think the baby should have? his _____ name, Zacharias

3. Why was this baby not an ordinary baby?
   a. His parents were too old to have children.
   b. God planned for this baby to be born for a special purpose.
   c. He had a different name than his father had.

4. How did Zacharias let everyone know what the baby's name should be?
   a. He could suddenly talk and he shouted the name.
   b. He told his wife in another room.
   c. He wrote it—JOHN.

5. What happened next for Zacharias?
   a. He ate his dinner.
   b. He could speak.
   c. He held the baby.

6. What did Zacharias do?
   a. He praised God for remembering His people.
   b. He said how cute the baby was.
   c. He asked what they were going to eat.

THINK ABOUT

God is awesome! He is always ready to show His love to you whenever you need Him—and whenever you ask Him. He is like a warm blanket wrapped around you to keep you safe and secure. Remember to pray. God hears the words you say to Him—even if you whisper!

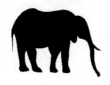

BIBLE WORDS TO REMEMBER

And He will be called Wonderful, Counselor, Mighty God, Everlasting Father, Prince of Peace. (from Isaiah 9:6)

Bible Story: ZACHARIAS SEES THE FUTURE
from Luke 1

Zacharias knew what kind of a child John would be. God told him that the Savior was coming, and how John, his son, would get people ready for Him. Zacharias said, "God will send a Savior who will come from the family of David. God loves us and will forgive us for turning away from Him. He will not forget what He promised to Abraham."

Zacharias said that John would be called the prophet of God. John would **prepare** the people who remembered God's promise and were waiting for it to happen. He was going to tell people that the light (Jesus) would shine in the darkness. He was going to tell them to ask God's forgiveness for the wrong things they had done. He would tell them that God would **guide** their feet into the way of peace.

The Bible says that before John gave the people this message, he grew and became strong in spirit. John learned from his parents and from the written words of God what the prophets had told about the Savior, God's Son, who was coming to save people from their sins.

WORDS TO KNOW

prepare: to get ready   **guide:** to show how

THINK ABOUT

While you are waiting, stop and think about what is really important. God waits, too. He waits for you to believe in Him—He loves you so much!

 # Questions:
THINKING & REMEMBERING

Fill in the blanks or circle the letters of all that are right.

1. How did Zacharias know what John would do?
   a. Elizabeth told him.
   b. God told him.
   c. Another priest told him.

2. Which family would the Savior come from who was a king?
   a. Isaac
   b. Noah
   c. David

3. To whom had God made the promise?
   a. Abraham
   b. Elizabeth
   c. Isaiah

4. What did Zacharias remind the people that God would do?
   a. love them
   b. forgive them
   c. not forget what He promised

5. What would John be called?
   a. a king
   b. a carpenter
   c. the prophet of God

6. What was John going to do before Jesus came?
   a. tell the people to get ready
   b. tell the people to listen to the king
   c. tell the people not to eat certain foods

7. What was John going to tell them?
   a. that the light (Jesus) would shine in the darkness
   b. to tell God they were sorry they had sinned
   c. to prepare for the Savior to come

8. What would God do if they listened?
   He would guide their feet into the way of _____.

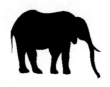

BIBLE WORDS TO REMEMBER

And He will be called Wonderful, Counselor, Mighty God, Everlasting Father, Prince of Peace. (from Isaiah 9:6)

Bible Story: BELIEVING THE IMPOSSIBLE
from Luke 1

God likes to **surprise** and **delight** His people. In the Bible, we read that God's people should not have been so surprised when He did what He had promised to do. It is easy for us to think that they should have said, "Yes! We are ready and waiting!"

But they didn't believe what God said. Even when an angel gave the message, there were questions like, "How is God going to do that?" "Why now?" God can do what is impossible for people to do because He is God. Nothing is impossible for God!

Many times people act like there are things that God cannot do, even though we can know that all of God's promises came true. There are more promises and God will keep every promise He made.

Zacharias learned very quickly that God means what He says. He was unable to speak when he didn't believe that God could do what He said He would do. God did not **expect** Zacharias to make it happen. That was for God to do—the impossible. God expected Zacharias to say "yes" to a wonderful plan that would get people ready for Jesus.

WORDS TO KNOW

surprise: what you did not know was going to happen

delight: something that gives joy

expect: to believe that something will happen

PRAYER THOUGHT

Dear God, Help me to believe all of Your words and know that whatever is impossible for me to do is possible for You to do when it is part of Your plan. Help me to understand how much You love me. Please forgive me when I do not remember Your promises and try to do things "all by myself." In Jesus Name, Amen.

Questions:
THINKING & REMEMBERING

Fill in the blanks or circle the letters of all that are right.

1. Should the people in the Bible have been surprised when God kept His
   promises?   yes_____   no_____
   God _____keeps His _____.

2. What do you think you would have said?
   a. "I am ready."
   b. "Wait awhile until I'm older."

3. Check true or false:
   a. People sometimes don't believe what God says.
      true_____   false_____
   b. Some things are impossible for God to do.
      true_____   false_____
   c. Everything God promised in the Bible He will do.
      true_____   false_____

4. What did Zacharias learn about God?
   a. Everything He says is true.
   b. He means what He says.
   c. He will keep His promises, even if we don't believe.

5. How did God give a message to Zacharias?
   a. He used a helper at the temple.
   b. He sent Moses to tell him.
   c. An angel brought the message.

6. What did Zacharias need to do to make the impossible happen?
   a. believe God
   b. go to a doctor
   c. ask someone else what to do

7. From the Bible Words to Remember, what names did the prophet Isaiah call
   Jesus the Savior?
   a. Prince of Peace   b. Mighty God   c. Counselor
   d. Everlasting Father   e. Kingdom Maker   f. Wonderful

Beginnings II

Jesus: Getting Ready

BIBLE WORDS TO REMEMBER

You shall call His name Jesus,
for He will save people from their sins. (from Matthew 1:21)

Bible Story: JOHN LISTENS TO GOD
from Matthew 3; Mark 1

God had a very special and important work for John to do. He was going to tell the people that Jesus was coming. The people were not ready for Him! They had forgotten all about God's promise to send a Savior.

But first, John had to prepare. He stayed in the desert listening to God and praying. He needed to know God in a very special way that would make him a brave and strong messenger. God wanted John to tell people that they had sinned.

While he was alone in the **wilderness**, meeting with God, he lived a very simple life so that he could think about God and his work. He made clothes of camel's hair and wore a leather belt around his waist. He ate **locusts** and wild honey. At night he would look up at the stars and remember God's promise to send a Savior that would be born on the earth to show people how great God's love is.

John planned what he would say to the people who would listen to him. He would tell them, "Be sorry for your sins, the kingdom of heaven is coming soon! Get ready!"

WORDS TO KNOW

wilderness: desert; a place where people are not living

locusts: an insect that is like a grasshopper

PRAYER THOUGHT

Dear loving God, You have special work for me when I believe in You. Help me to listen to You and pray for You to show me how important it is to know what You want me to do. In Jesus Name, Amen.

Questions:
THINKING & REMEMBERING

Fill in the blanks or circle the letters of all that are right.

1. What special plan did God have for John?
   a. to live in the desert and eat different food
   b. to tell the people that Jesus was coming
   c. to get the people ready for Jesus

2. Were the people excited and ready for Jesus to come?
   a. No. They had forgotten God's promise.
   b. No. They were not ready.
   c. They thought that it would never happen.

3. Where did John prepare for his work?
   a. in the wilderness (desert)
   b. in the temple
   c. at home with his mother

4. How did John prepare for his work?
   a. He sang songs in the desert.
   b. He hunted for bears.
   c. He listened to God and prayed.

5. What happened during that time?
   a. He became a brave and strong messenger.
   b. He was scared of the wild animals.
   c. He learned to know God in a very special way.

6. Why was John's assignment so difficult?
   a. The people had stopped believing in God's promise of a Savior.
   b. He needed to tell people that they had been doing wrong things.
   c. He had to tell them they should be sorry for what they were doing.

7. What kind of a life did John have in the desert?
   a. He lived a simple life.
   b. He wore clothes made of camel's hair and a leather belt.
   c. He ate locusts and honey.

8. What did he think about and remember at night?
   He remembered God's _____ to send a Savior to show
   God's great _____ for all people.

BIBLE WORDS TO REMEMBER

You shall call His name Jesus,
for He will save people from their sins. (from Matthew 1:21)

Bible Story: JOHN'S MESSAGE

from Luke 3

John did not try to make his words **pleasing** to the people. John told the people to **repent**. He told them that if they expected God to help them and save them, they would have to love and obey Him. They thought that no matter what they did, God would always get them out of their troubles.

The people did not like to hear what John told them, but they knew that he was right. John knew that he had to tell them the truth. He knew that they weren't happy because there was sin in their hearts. They had forgotten God and lived only for themselves. They did not want to change their ways, they just wanted God to make life easy for them—to fix their problems and hurt their enemies.

John told the people what God wanted him to say. God is a **righteous** judge. Everyone who believes and obeys God will live forever in heaven. Those who refuse God's love are choosing to go to a place where they are **separated** from God. That makes God very sad.

WORDS TO KNOW

pleasing: what makes one feel good
repent: to be sorry for doing wrong
righteous: pure and perfect
separated: be apart from

THINK ABOUT

Talking is easy when we are saying what someone wants to hear. God wants us to show kindness and love. When we know from God's Word that what people are doing is wrong and makes God sad, we can say in a loving way, "Whatever hurts God; hurts me, too."

 # Questions:
THINKING & REMEMBERING

Fill in the blanks or circle the letters of all that are right.

1. John just told the people what would make them feel good.
   true_____false _____

2. What did he say that they were expecting God to do?
   a. get them out of trouble
   b. save them from their enemies
   c. accept whatever they did

3. What did he say they should do if they expected God to do this?
   a. try to be good on their own
   b. love and obey Him
   c. go to the temple every day

4. How did John know what and how to speak to the people?
   a. He got instructions from his father.
   b. His friends told him.
   c. God told him.

5. What kind of a judge did John say God was?
   a. a kind judge
   b. a righteous judge
   c. a judge who would try to be fair

6. Who will be rewarded and go to heaven?
   Those who _____ and _____ God will go to heaven.

7. What will happen to those who choose not to believe?
   a. They will be choosing to go to a place where they are separated from God.
   b. God won't punish them if they are just doing the best they can.
   c. If they work hard and go to church they can go to heaven.

8. Will God choose for anyone to be separated from Him?
   a. Yes. He only loves certain people.
   b. No! He loves everyone and wants all people to choose to believe and be in heaven. He is very sad when someone chooses not to be with Him.

BIBLE WORDS TO REMEMBER

You shall call His name Jesus,
for He will save people from their sins. (from Matthew 1:21)

Bible Story: THE PEOPLE ARE SORRY

from Luke 3

The people who listened to John tell them God's words said, "What should we do? We know that what you have told us is true. We believe that God sent you to tell us His words. We are sorry for disobeying God and doing wrong things."

John told the people that they must repent—that means telling God they were sorry for their sins. The Bible says that sin is not believing God. It is not believing that His promises are true. It is not obeying what His word tells us to do. It is not only doing wrong things, but it is thinking wrong things. It is having hate instead of love in our hearts. It is to keep doing **evil** when we know it is hurting God, others and ourselves.

When someone understands that they have done wrong against God—and everyone has done wrong, they will do more than just say the words, "I'm sorry." If they mean those words and are **sincere**, they will stop doing wrong things. It is impossible to think and do right things all by ourselves. We need God's help every minute. That is why God sent Jesus to be with us and love us enough to die for our sins.

WORDS TO KNOW

evil: to keep doing wrong things (sinning) on purpose

sincere: truthful and honest about what you say

PRAYER THOUGHT

Dear God, Help me to listen and obey Your word. I know that I cannot believe and do the right things without Your help. In Jesus Name, Amen.

Questions:
THINKING & REMEMBERING

Fill in the blanks or circle the letters of all that are right.

1. What question did the people ask?
   a. "What should we do? "
   b. "Why don't you tell God we're following some of the commandments?"
   c. "Who gave you the right to tell us what to do?"

2. How did the people show that they had understood what John said?
   a. They said, "We know that what you say is true."
   b. They said, "We know that God sent you."
   c. They said, "We are sorry; we didn't obey and listen to God."

3. What did John tell them they must do?
   a. start to be nice to everyone
   b. repent—tell God they were sorry
   c. tell God they would try harder to be good

4. What does the Bible say that sin is?
   a. not believing God
   b. doing wrong things
   c. thinking wrong things

5. What does sin do in our hearts? It makes us _____ instead of _____.

6. Whom does evil hurt?
   a. God
   b. others
   c. ourselves

7. In the Bible, we are told that everyone has sinned. true_____ false_____

8. It is possible to "be good" and do right by ourselves. true_____ false_____

9. Who will help us do the right things and love God and others? _____

10. Why did God send Jesus?
    He sent Jesus to _____ for our _____.

BIBLE WORDS TO REMEMBER

You shall call His name Jesus,
for He will save people from their sins. (from Matthew 1:21)

Bible Story: LIVING FOR GOD
from Luke 3

The people listening to John's message knew that they must change. They were sorry for the wrong things they had been doing. They had told God they were sorry. They wanted John to tell them more about what God wanted them to do. They wanted to know how they could be different and show that they wanted to live God's way.

John said that to love God you must also love others. "If you have two coats, give one to someone who doesn't have any. If you have extra food, give some to those who are hungry. Be honest. Don't take more money from people than what they are supposed to pay. Don't **accuse** anyone of doing what they have not done. And be **content** with what you get paid."

Those who were sorry for their sins were **baptized**. This was a way of telling everyone that they had turned away from their sins and had asked God to forgive them.

Each one who had decided to follow God followed John to the Jordan River. Grownups and children went into the water and John baptized them so that others would know that they had decided to follow God from now on and that they believed in God's promise to send a Savior.

WORDS TO KNOW

accuse: to blame someone for something

content: to be satisfied (not complaining)

baptized: to use water to show that you have been washed inside and outside. It means that you have asked God to forgive you for your sins and want to follow Him.

THINK ABOUT

What are some easy choices you have to make? What is the most important decision you will ever make? Why is this decision so important? Will God ever force you to love Him?

Questions:
THINKING & REMEMBERING

Fill in the blanks or circle the letters of all that are right.

1. What did the people know they must do?
   a. They must change.
   b. They must make John to stop speaking and go away.
   c. They must tell the priests that John was making them feel bad.

2. What were they sorry for doing?
   _____

3. What did they want John to tell them?
   a. more about what God wanted them to do
   b. how they could be different
   c. how to show others that they wanted to live for God

4. What did John say they should do?
   a. love others
   b. share extra things you have
   c. give others the things you don't want anymore

5. What did John say about telling what is true?
   John said to be _____.

6. What things did he tell them they should not do?
   a. Do not take more than what someone is supposed to pay.
   b. Do not accuse someone for something they didn't do.
   c. Do not talk to others.

7. What does being baptized mean?
   It shows that you have been washed free from your _____ and that
   you _____ in God's _____ to send a Savior.

PRAYER THOUGHT
(Here are some words you can tell God if you are ready to decide.)

*Dear God, Help me know and understand what is most important—
loving YOU. I am sorry for all the wrong things I have done to hurt You and
hurt others. I choose to love You and want You to live in my heart. I believe that
Jesus died for my sins. Help me to follow You every day in every way.
In Jesus Name, Amen.*

BIBLE WORDS TO REMEMBER

You shall call His name Jesus,
for He will save people from their sins. (from Matthew 1:21)

Bible Story: THINKING ABOUT GOD'S PLAN
from Luke 3

The Bible is like a giant puzzle! Each time we put in a new piece, the picture of God's love gets better and clearer. God created a perfect world. People made the picture ugly because of sin. But God made a plan that would make things beautiful again.

Some people heard John's words, but didn't believe. Others listened and believed. They repented and were baptized. They started doing what God wanted instead of thinking only of themselves. It was very important for the people to be ready for Jesus. He was on earth to do many wonderful things—but most of all, He came to show the greatest love that can ever be given to the people God made. He died on the cross for everyone.

It is important for us to be ready for Jesus in our hearts. He will come again to earth to take us to be with Him in heaven if we love Him and believe in Him. We have been given more pieces to the puzzle than the people who listened to John the Baptist. We have more of the story of Jesus than they knew because we can read the words in the Bible. Be ready!

PRAYER THOUGHT

Dear God, You must love me a lot to care enough to send Jesus. Help me to be ready for Jesus and to show Your love to others. I know that when I love others it is one way of showing You that I love You. In Jesus Name, Amen.

Questions:
THINKING & REMEMBERING

Fill in the blanks or circle the letters of all that are right.

1. What can we think of the Bible being like?
   a. a giant puzzle
   b. a confusing book
   c. a book of poems

2. What happens when we put a new piece into the puzzle?
   The picture of God's _____ gets better and _____.

3. What kind of a world did God create?
   God created a _____ world.

4. What happened that spoiled what God had created?
   a. The people listened to Satan and sinned.
   b. Adam and Eve wanted to live somewhere else.
   c. The animals God made were mean to each other.

5. What did God decide to do?
   a. He would not speak to Adam anymore.
   b. He decided that people could live in an ugly world.
   c. He made a plan so that it would be beautiful again.

6. Who was sent with a message to the people about what God was going to do?
   a. Adam
   b. John the Baptist
   c. Elizabeth

7. What did John tell the people to do?
   He told the people to get ready for _____.

8. How did God want to show His greatest love?
   He showed His great _____ by sending _____.

9. What was Jesus coming to do?
   a. die on the cross for our sins
   b. kill all the bad people
   c. make people love God

Beginnings II

Jesus: From Darkness to Light

BIBLE WORDS TO REMEMBER

His name will be "Immanuel,"
which means "God with us." (from Matthew 1:23)

Bible Story: THE ANGEL TELLS MARY THE NEWS
from Luke 1:26-38

One day, an angel named Gabriel was sent by God to a young girl whose name was Mary. Mary was so surprised! She didn't expect an angel to come to her! The angel said to her, "Don't be afraid, Mary. God loves you very much. You are going to be the mother of a special baby boy. He will be God's own Son. His name will be Jesus. He will be great, and His kingdom will last forever. You are chosen because you have obeyed God."

Mary smiled. This was **certainly** the most wonderful and exciting news! But then she looked puzzled. Mary had planned to be married to Joseph, a carpenter from Nazareth. She asked the angel, "How can I have a baby? I don't have a husband."

The angel was very kind to Mary and said, "You will have a baby by the power of God. Mary, with God, nothing is impossible."

Mary said, with joy in her heart, "I am the **servant** of the Lord and I am **willing** to do whatever He tells me to do."

When the angel was gone, Mary thought and thought about this wonderful promise. Mary was so happy she sang praises to God. She said, "I am rejoicing in God my Savior! **Holy** is His name!"

WORDS TO KNOW

certainly: something positive; absolutely for sure
servant: to do what someone else wishes or requests
willing: something one chooses to do
Holy: pure and perfect
miracle: something only God can do

Questions:
THINKING & REMEMBERING

Fill in the blanks or circle the letters of all that are right.

1. Whom did God send to give Mary a special message?
   a. Joseph
   b. an angel
   c. her mother

2. What were the first words that the visitor said?
   "Don't be _____."

3. Why was Mary so surprised?
   a. She was not given any warning.
   b. She had not invited this special visitor.
   c. She did not expect an angel to visit her!

4. What was the message from the angel?
   a. God loved her.
   b. She was chosen to be the mother of a special baby boy.
   c. Maybe God would choose her to bring Jesus to the earth.

5. Who was this special baby?
   This special baby was God's own_____.

6. What did the angel say that the baby's name would be? _____

7. What words did the angel say to tell Mary that this was a **miracle** birth?
   a. "Nothing is impossible with God."
   b. "God can do things in a different way."
   c. "You will find out later."

8. How did Mary respond?
   a. "Ask God to choose some other girl. I can't be the right one."
   b. "I am willing to do whatever He tells me to do."
   c. "I don't think I am good enough to be the mother of God's own Son."

9. What did Mary do after the angel left?
   a. She thought about this wonderful promise.
   b. She went to tell her parents.
   c. She sang praises to God.

BIBLE WORDS TO REMEMBER

His name will be "Immanuel,"
which means "God with us." (from Matthew 1:23)

Bible Story: AN ANGEL GIVES JOSEPH A SPECIAL MESSAGE
from Matthew 1:18-25

Joseph was thinking about Mary. He loved Mary so much! Soon, he and Mary would have a **wedding** and they could be together all the time.

Then Mary came to tell Joseph that she was going to be the mother of the Savior. Joseph loved God and knew that God would keep His promise to send a Savior to the world. But Joseph was worried, too. Would the other people in Nazareth understand and believe?

That night, while Joseph was sleeping, the angel Gabriel came to Joseph in a dream. The angel gave him a special message from God. "Do not be afraid to make Mary your wife, Joseph. She will be the mother of God's Son from the power of God, the **Holy Spirit**." Joseph thought, this was the Savior they had been waiting for! He would save people from their sins!

Joseph remembered that the prophets had said that God would come in this way. He was very happy! Just as Mary had been chosen to be the mother of God's Son, Joseph knew that he was chosen for an important part. God wanted him to be Jesus' father on earth to protect and care for Jesus while He was growing up.

WORDS TO KNOW

wedding: a ceremony where two people get married

Holy Spirit: the part of God that is present in the world to help us see Jesus and live in us

PRAYER THOUGHT

Dear God, Help me to listen to You and know the words in Your wonderful book, the Bible, so that I can make the right choices and the right decisions to live in the right way. In Jesus Name, Amen.

Questions:
THINKING & REMEMBERING

Fill in the blanks or circle the letters of all that are right.

1. What did Mary tell Joseph after the angel visited her?
   a. She was going to be the mother of the Savior.
   b. She couldn't marry him.
   c. She was more special to God than he was.

2. Joseph loved God and believed in God's promise to send a Savior.
   true_____ false_____

3. What worried Joseph?
   a. God would change His mind.
   b. Other people in Nazareth wouldn't understand and believe.
   c. Mary would be afraid to do what God told her.

4. How/When/Where (underline the right word) did the angel come to Joseph?
   a. in a dream
   b. in the carpenter shop
   c. in the morning

5. What message did the angel give to Joseph?
   The angel told Joseph that Mary would be the _____ of
   _____ Son.

6. What did the angel tell Joseph to do?
   a. to get married to Mary after the baby was born
   b. not to take Mary as his wife
   c. to make Mary his wife

7. How was this going to be a miracle birth?
   The birth of Jesus was by the _____ of the Holy Spirit.

8. How was Joseph an important part of God's plan?
   Joseph was Jesus' father on earth to _____and _____
   for Him while he was growing up.

55

BIBLE WORDS TO REMEMBER

His name will be "Immanuel,"
which means "God with us." (from Matthew 1:23)

Bible Story: AN IMPORTANT VISIT
from Luke 1

Zacharias, Mary and Joseph heard the news from God's angel. Mary and Elizabeth were both chosen by God for something very wonderful and special. Elizabeth was going to have a son who would prepare the people for the Savior to come. His name was John. Mary was going to be the mother of Jesus, Whom God was sending as a Savior to the world. God's promise and plan was coming true—and Mary and Elizabeth were part of God's plan to complete God's purpose.

Mary was so excited, she decided to visit Elizabeth who lived in a small town close to Nazareth. She had just come into the house when something happened to Elizabeth. The baby inside her moved around like it was **leaping** for joy! Elizabeth said to Mary, "You are **blessed**! You are to be the mother of my Lord."

Mary and Elizabeth spent happy days together **rejoicing** and talking about God's promise. They knew the time was just right for the Savior to come. Soon they would be able to tell everyone about the wonderful plan God had. He was sending Jesus, His precious and Holy Son to bring **glorious** light to the whole world.

WORDS TO KNOW

leaping: jumping and moving
blessed: favored by God with special joy and happiness
rejoicing: to feel or show much happiness
glorious: heavenly light
unique: the only one

THINK ABOUT

It is hard to wait for one special day to give a gift to someone you love. Gifts of love are like that. God promised the most wonderful gift many years before it happened. God's gift of love waited until just the right time.

Questions:
Thinking & Remembering

Fill in the blanks or circle the letters of all that are right.

1. Which of the following people heard the wonderful news from an angel?
   a. Elizabeth
   b. Mary
   c. Zacharias
   d. Joseph

2. Which two women in the lesson are special and important?
   a. Mary
   b. Elizabeth
   c. Sarah

3. What was special about Elizabeth's son?
   a. He was going to be born before Jesus.
   b. He liked to wear strange clothes.
   c. He was going to prepare the people for Jesus.

4. What was **unique** about Jesus?
   a. He was going to be a good son and never do wrong.
   b. He was coming as God's Son to be the Savior of the world.
   c. He was going to help Joseph in a carpenter shop.

5. Why did Mary visit Elizabeth?
   a. She wanted to get away from Nazareth.
   b. She was so excited. She wanted to tell her about the good news.
   c. She wanted to ask Elizabeth if God's promises were true.

6. What did Elizabeth's baby do when Mary came into the house?
   The baby was leaping for _____ inside his mother.

7. Did Elizabeth know that Mary was the mother of the Messiah?
   yes_____   no_____

8. Who was coming at just the right time?
   God's precious and Holy Son, _____ the Messiah, was coming
   at just the right time.

BIBLE WORDS TO REMEMBER

His name will be "Immanuel,"
which means "God with us." (from Matthew 1:23)

Bible Story: A LONG TRIP

from Luke 2:1-5

Soon the baby Jesus would be born. Mary thought about the special baby. She thought about being chosen to have this wonderful child who would change the whole world—nothing would ever be the same. People who were **suffering** and sad could believe in Jesus and everything would look new and bright. Jesus would be the light of the world to bring people out of darkness.

Then, just about the time that baby Jesus was to be born, the king in the land made an **order** that everyone must go back to the city where they had been born. It didn't matter where they lived or how far they had to travel, they must go. It didn't matter to the king that Mary was going to have a special baby. She and Joseph must obey the king and travel from Nazareth to a town far away. The town was called Bethlehem. Mary and Joseph had a donkey for the long trip. They walked and walked and walked.

"When will we get to Bethlehem?" Mary asked Joseph. "We will get there soon so you can rest, Mary," said Joseph. Joseph walked faster and the donkey walked faster, too. Something very important was going to happen very soon in Bethlehem!

WORDS TO KNOW

suffering: hurting   **order:** a command to obey

PRAYER THOUGHT

Dear God, It makes me so thankful to know that You are in charge of today and tomorrow and forever. Help me to always show others the confidence I have in You and trust You every day. In Jesus Name, Amen.

Questions:
THINKING & REMEMBERING

Fill in the blanks or circle the letters of all that are right.

1. What did Mary think about while she was waiting for Jesus to be born?
   a. She thought about God's Son changing the world.
   b. She thought about buying new clothes for herself.
   c. She thought about the new furniture she wanted Joseph to make.

2. What would Jesus make different?
   a. He would be the light that would bring people out of darkness.
   b. He would help people who were suffering and sad.
   c. Those who believed in Him would have a new life.

3. Why did Mary and Joseph go on a long trip when Mary was going to have a baby?
   a. They wanted to find a new place to live.
   b. The king made an order that everyone must go back to the city of their birth.
   c. There was a good doctor where they were going.

4. Was the king worried about people who had to travel a long way?
   yes_____ no_____

5. The king knew that a very special baby was about to be born.
   true_____ false_____

6. What was the name of the city where Mary and Joseph lived?
   a. Jerusalem
   b. Nazareth
   c. Bethlehem

7. To which town did they have to travel?
   a. Bethlehem
   b. Jerusalem
   c. Jericho

8. With what animal did they use to travel?
   a. horse
   b. camel
   c. donkey

BIBLE WORDS TO REMEMBER

His name will be "Immanuel,"
which means "God with us." (from Matthew 1:23)

Bible Story: JESUS IS BORN
from Luke 2; Matthew 1

This was going to be a very special night. Mary and Joseph came into Bethlehem after their long trip from the city of Nazareth. There were many other people in Bethlehem, too. They looked for a place to sleep. There was no room anywhere. All the **inns** were full of people already. Finally one man said, "Wait, I do have room for you in the **stable**."

Well, we might think that a stable was not the place for the mother of baby Jesus to stay. How could the king of the world be born in such a place? Mary and Joseph were very tired. Joseph looked at Mary and Mary said, "Thank you. You are very kind." And that very night in the stable God's promise came true—baby Jesus was born.

There wasn't a fine baby bed for baby Jesus, but Mary took a clean cloth and wrapped it around Jesus and laid Him very carefully on clean straw in a **manger**. Did it seem that everything went wrong for the coming of baby Jesus that night? We may have planned everything differently. But it all happened just as God had planned for it to happen. God took care of Mary and baby Jesus.

WORDS TO KNOW

inn: a hotel

stable: a place where the animals slept

manger: a box for the animals' food

PRAYER THOUGHT

Dear God, I am so thankful that You loved me so much! When You sent Jesus to the earth from heaven, it was the most wonderful gift I could ever receive. Help me to understand that it cost You a lot to send Your Son. I want to accept Your gift of love. In Jesus Name, Amen.

Questions:
THINKING & REMEMBERING

Fill in the blanks or circle the letters of all that are right.

1. What important thing was about to happen in Bethlehem?
   a. People were going to pay their taxes.
   b. There was a special celebration for the king.
   c. Baby Jesus was going to be born.

2. Why didn't Mary and Joseph stay at the inn for the baby's birth?
   a. There was no room at the inn.
   b. Mary and Joseph wanted Jesus to be born in a palace.
   c. The inn didn't have a baby bed.

3. Where did Mary and Joseph stay?
   a. in a tent
   b. in the stable
   c. out in the field

4. If you were choosing a place for Jesus to be born, where would you choose?
   a. a hospital
   b. a palace
   c. a house

5. Why was the birth of Jesus so important?
   _____ was God's _____ coming true.

6. How did Mary take care of baby Jesus?
   a. She took a clean cloth and wrapped it around Jesus.
   b. She laid Him carefully on clean straw in a manger.
   c. She took him outside the stable.

7. How did Joseph do his part in caring for Mary and Jesus?
   a. He found the best place there was, even though it was a stable.
   b. He took good care of Mary.
   c. He cared for baby Jesus so that He was safe.

8. Who planned everything that happened? _____

Jesus: A New Beginning

BIBLE WORDS TO REMEMBER

For unto us a Child is born,
Unto us a Son is given. (Isaiah 9:6)

Bible Story: THE SHEPHERDS HEAR THE GOOD NEWS
from Luke 2

No one knew except Mary and Joseph that Jesus, God's Son had been born. Baby Jesus slept on the straw. Mary had him wrapped warmly in a blanket. Even though He looked like any other new baby, this baby was different. Many things had happened to show that Jesus was God's own special Son.

The night that Jesus was born there were shepherds in a field nearby who were taking care of their sheep. Everything was so quiet. And then suddenly there was a beautiful light shining in the sky above them. An angel was in the sky!

The shepherds could not believe what they were seeing. Why would an angel come to them, they wondered! They were very surprised and afraid! But the angel said, "Don't be afraid. I have good news! A Savior has been born. He is in Bethlehem right now, lying in a manger." The shepherds were so happy to hear the glad news! The Savior they had waited for had come! God had kept His promise!

THINK ABOUT

Jesus has given us hope for what we can anticipate for every day and for the future. Because Jesus came to show us God's love and the way to eternal life, we can be confident that God is in control of everything that happens now and everything that will happen. For those who know Jesus, being hopeful is not just wishful thinking!

PRAYER THOUGHT

I thank You God, for caring about me and making a perfect plan for me to live with You in heaven forever. Help me to listen to Your words and obey. In Jesus Name, Amen.

Questions:
THINKING & REMEMBERING

Fill in the blanks or circle the letters of all that are right.

1. Who knew that Jesus, God's Son, had been born?
   a. the king
   b. Mary
   c. Joseph

2. How was baby Jesus different from all other babies?
   a. He was God's Son.
   b. He cried a lot.
   c. He was very tiny.

3. Who was near Bethlehem taking care of sheep?
   a. wise men
   b. shepherds
   c. farmers

4. What happened that changed the quiet and darkness of the night?
   a. There was a noisy celebration at the inn.
   b. People were trying to find a place to stay.
   c. A beautiful light; an angel appeared in the sky.

5. What words tell that the shepherds knew that this was unusual?
   They were _____.

6. What words did the angel say to help them not to fear?
   a. "Do not be afraid."
   b. "I have good news."
   c. "I will not hurt you."

7. What was the angel's message?
   A Savior has been _____.

8. The angel told the shepherds where Jesus was.
   true_____   false_____

9. Why were the shepherds so happy?
   God had kept His _____. A Savior had been born.

63

Bible Story: THE ANGELS SING
from Luke 2

The shepherds were **bowing** their heads to the ground after they heard the good news that the angel had brought to them. They had never seen an angel before! They had never heard such a wonderful message! A Savior has been born! They must have thought of all the years people had been waiting for this special One who would come to take away sin and sadness.

The sky was bright and there were many angels in the heavens singing and praising God. "Glory to God in the highest, and on earth peace and **goodwill!**" What a **glorious** and fantastic sight this was! The shepherds must have wondered and been **amazed** that this **announcement** was made to them. They were just **ordinary** people, they thought. But God had chosen to tell them.

Suddenly, the angels were gone. The singing was gone. The brightness in the sky had faded. The fields were quiet, but just for a moment. The shepherds looked at each other. They knew that what they had seen and heard was not a dream. They knew what they would do. They said to each other, "Let's go to Bethlehem and see the Baby the angel told us about!"

WORDS TO KNOW

bowing:	to kneel down on knees
goodwill:	a wish for all that is right and fair
glorious:	bright and brilliant
amazed:	to look at with wonder and surprise
announcement:	to tell that something has happened
ordinary:	plain and simple; not very special

THINK ABOUT

When you are happy and delighted with what you see and do, you are looking on the bright side of life instead of the dark side of life. Living on the bright side is what we should do naturally if we love Jesus. Jesus has given us hope for every day and for the future. Jesus is the light of the world. We can be confident that God is in control of everything that happens now and everything that will happen. For those who know God's love, being hopeful is not just wishful thinking!

Questions:
THINKING & REMEMBERING

Fill in the blanks or circle the letters of all that are right.

1. What did the shepherds do after they heard the good news?
   a. They woke up the sheep.
   b. They bowed their heads to the ground.
   c. They ran to tell their friends.

2. What had never happened before?
   a. The shepherds had never seen an angel before.
   b. They had never heard such a wonderful message.
   c. The Savior had never come into the world before.

3. What was the Savior sent to do?
   a. He was sent to take away sin and sadness.
   b. He was sent to show God's love to the world.
   c. He was sent to tell people that they were bad.

4. What happened in the sky?
   a. It was bright.
   b. Many angels were singing.
   c. The angels were praising God.

5. What were the words the angels were singing?
   "Glory to _____ in the highest, and on earth _____ and goodwill!"

6. Why were the shepherds so amazed that God had chosen to tell them?
   They were just _____ people.
   Choose the word given in the story: ordinary   common   average

7. The shepherds thought they had just been dreaming. true_____ false_____
   They were certain of what they had _____ and _____.

8. What did the shepherds say they would do?
   a. They would go and find the Baby in Bethlehem.
   b. They would go back to sleep.
   c. They would go to Bethlehem in the morning.

Bible Story: HE HAS COME!
from Luke 2

The shepherds were standing in **amazement** after the coming of the angel—after the bright sky and the angels singing. They couldn't wait to get to the place where the angel told them that Jesus was. They hurried across the fields and up the hills. They were very quiet as they walked through the streets because the people in the city were still asleep. They had not seen the angel. They did not know about the exciting news!

Finally they came to the stable where Jesus was. They looked inside and saw Mary. They saw Joseph. There were sheep in the stable—and goats and cows. They saw a manger with **hay** in it. And there, all **snuggled** in the hay was Baby Jesus!

Quietly the shepherds knelt down and thanked God for sending Jesus. But the shepherds were not quiet for very long. They wanted to tell everyone about the wonderful thing that had happened. They didn't stop to think that maybe people would not listen and believe what just ordinary shepherds were telling them. They were so excited that the people who heard their story knew that it could not be a **make-believe** story. It was true what the angel had told them!

WORDS TO KNOW

amazement:	awe and wonder
hay:	food for the animals
snuggled:	curled up and nestled inside something
make-believe:	pretend; something not true

PRAYER THOUGHT

Dear God, I can know for sure that the message is true. Jesus came and He is Your very own Son. I can believe Your words and know that You will keep Your promises until the end of the story when Jesus comes back to earth—and then it will be another beginning for those who ask Jesus to live in their hearts. Heaven will be forever! In Jesus Name, Amen.

Questions:
THINKING & REMEMBERING

Fill in the blanks or circle the letters of all that are right.

1. How did the shepherds react after they saw the angel and heard the angels singing?
   a. They stood in amazement.
   b. They thought they were dreaming.
   c. They thought that the angels made a mistake to come to shepherds.

2. What words tell that they went quickly?
   a. rushed
   b. slowly
   c. hurried

3. The people in Bethlehem saw the angel.
   true_____ false _____

4. What did the shepherds see inside the stable?
   a. Mary
   b. Joseph
   c. animals
   d. Baby Jesus

5. What did the shepherds do when they saw Jesus?
   a. They said he was a nice baby.
   b. They knelt down and thanked God.
   c. They kissed the baby.

6. What did the shepherds want to do?
   a. They wanted to tell everyone what had happened.
   b. They wanted to go back to the fields.
   c. They wanted to find a place to sleep.

7. Why did the people who heard the shepherds believe what they said?
   a. They were so excited.
   b. They were so sure of what they had seen and heard.
   c. They could not have made up a story so wonderful.

BIBLE WORDS TO REMEMBER

For unto us a Child is born,
Unto us a Son is given. (Isaiah 9:6)

Bible Story: A CHANGED WORLD
from Luke 2

On the night that Jesus was born, the town of Bethlehem was crowded with people. Some were there to pay their taxes to the king. They were tired from traveling. Some were looking for an inn to stay in for the night, as Mary and Joseph had tried to do. Others were hungry and looking for a place to eat and rest.

The people who had found an inn, were already sleeping. The young who were not tired might have been having a party and talking and laughing with their friends. They did not know that something was happening in a quiet stable that was going to change the whole world.

Jesus was being born. It was quiet and still in the stable. The angels were ready to give the message to the shepherds who were quiet and still out in the fields outside of Bethlehem watching their sheep. They were the ones who heard the angels singing, "Peace on earth"—not the people in Bethlehem.

"Peace on earth" is the peace that comes to you when you think of God's love for you—and for the whole world. Jesus came in peace to bring peace. He will help us show His peace to others!

PRAYER THOUGHT

Dear God, You sent Jesus to bring peace. Sometimes I say wrong things that hurt others and I am angry and feel like fighting. That is not peaceful. I know that You will help me when I ask You. Help me to have peace and show others Your peace. In Jesus Name, Amen.

Questions:
THINKING & REMEMBERING

Fill in the blanks or circle the letters of all that are right.

1. What was Bethlehem like on the night Jesus was born?
   a. It was an ordinary night in a little town.
   b. There were many people in Bethlehem.
   c. The people were probably busy, tired and hungry.

2. The people in Bethlehem knew that something important was happening that night.   true_____ false_____

3. What happened that changed the whole world?
   _____ was born. God's _____ came to earth.

4. It was busy and noisy in Bethlehem. Where was it quiet?
   It was quiet in the _____.

5. To whom did the angels give the special message that Jesus had been born?
   a. the shepherds
   b. the priests
   c. the tax collectors

6. Where were these special ones who heard the news first?
   a. in Bethlehem
   b. in their houses
   c. in the fields outside of Bethlehem

7. What were they doing when they saw and heard the angels?
   a. sleeping in the field
   b. watching their sheep
   c. eating their dinner

8. What wonderful words did the shepherds hear the angels say?
   "_____"

9. When can you know peace?
   Peace comes to you when you think of God's _____ for you.
   Jesus came in _____ to bring _____ for the world.

BIBLE WORDS TO REMEMBER

For unto us a Child is born,
Unto us a Son is given. (Isaiah 9:6)

Bible Story: JESUS, THE TRUE LIGHT
from John 1:1-9; John 8:12

The shepherds saw a wonderful light in the sky the night that Jesus was born. It was an angel telling them the joyful news. The real light was Jesus Himself, coming into the world.

There are many different kinds of light but there is only one true light. The true light is Jesus. The Bible tells us that Jesus is the light that will never go out.

When we think of the light that Jesus is, it is even more than being able to see with our eyes. He helps us see with our hearts. Sadness is like darkness. Jesus will make that sadness turn to joy and happiness when we know and love Him.

Jesus will always give you His light when you ask Him to help you. Sometimes it is when your pet dies and you feel so sad you can't even see the sunshine at all. Ask Jesus and He will open up your heart to see His light. Jesus said these words for us to remember: "I am the light of the world. He who follows Me shall not walk in darkness, but have the light of life."

THINK ABOUT

The message that changed the world! Jesus is the light that helps us see with our hearts. We have heard the whole wonderful story in the Bible. God wants us to know and believe. What are you going to decide to do about what you know?

PRAYER THOUGHT

Dear God, Thank You for sending me the light of Jesus. Help me to let the light of Jesus shine in my heart so others can see Him and find His light. In Jesus Name, Amen.

 # Questions:
THINKING & REMEMBERING

Fill in the blanks or circle the letters of all that are right.

1. Who is the only One who is the true light of the world?_____

2. What does the Bible tell us about the light that Jesus gives?
   a. It will be there only when we are good.
   b. It will always be there for us.
   c. It will never go away.

3. How is Jesus different from all other light?
   a. He helps us see with our hearts.
   b. He knows when we feel sad.
   c. He knows when we are in darkness.

4. What does Jesus turn sadness into when we know and love Him?
   a. joy
   b. peace
   c. happiness

5. When will Jesus give you His light?
   a. whenever you ask Him to help you
   b. only when we are doing the right thing
   c. just when we are helping others

6. What happens when we think of the light of Jesus?
   a. He helps us see with our hearts.
   b. He makes life easy all the time.
   c. He helps us see when others do wrong things.

7. What did Jesus say to do so that you won't be walking in the dark?
   "I am the _____ of the world. He who _____ Me
   shall not walk in _____, but have the _____
   of _____." (John 8:12)

Beginnings II

Jesus: God with Us!

BIBLE WORDS TO REMEMBER

Jesus is the true light. He gives light to
everyone coming into the world. (from John 1:9)

Bible Story: A FIRST VISIT
from Luke 2

When Jesus was still a tiny baby, Mary and Joseph took Him to the temple in Jerusalem. Mary and Joseph were very happy that God had sent Jesus to live in their home. They wanted to say a special thank you to God for baby Jesus. This was Jesus' first visit to God's house.

Most people traveled by donkey, so we can think that this is how Mary and Joseph went to the temple. They took two pigeons as an offering as God said they should. They took little baby Jesus into the temple where they prayed and presented their offering. They thanked God for sending Jesus to them and asked God to bless Him and take care of Him always.

This was such an important and special time for the family of Jesus. Mary and Joseph knew that Jesus was God's own Son and that He was born on earth to save people from their sins and be the promised Messiah.

Mary and Joseph made a promise at the temple, too. They would take good care of Jesus and they would teach Him to love and obey God.

PRAYER THOUGHT

Dear God, I want to love You and worship You in the right way. Help me to worship You in many ways, every day—not just when I go to church. In Jesus Name, Amen.

Questions:
Thinking & Remembering

Fill in the blanks or circle the letters of all that are right.

1. Where did Mary and Joseph take Jesus when He was still a tiny baby?
   a. to see his grandparents in Nazareth
   b. to the temple in Jerusalem
   c. to visit friends in another town

2. What was important for Mary and Joseph to do?
   a. to thank God for sending Jesus
   b. to show everyone how proud they were of baby Jesus
   c. to compare Jesus with other babies

3. How do we think Mary and Joseph traveled to the temple?
   a. They rode on a donkey.
   b. They walked.
   c. They rode in a small carriage.

4. What did they take as an offering?
   a. They took as many coins as they could afford.
   b. They took two pigeons.
   c. They took one goat.

5. What did they do at the temple?
   a. They prayed and thanked God.
   b. They presented their offering.
   c. They worshiped God and praised Him.

6. What did they ask God to do?
   a. They asked God to help them have more money.
   b. They asked God to bless Jesus.
   c. They asked God to help them be good parents.

7. Mary and Joseph knew why Jesus had come to earth as God's Son.
   true_____ false_____

8. What promise did Mary and Joseph make to God?
   a. They would take good care of Jesus.
   b. They would teach Him to love and obey God.
   c. They would teach him God's commandments.

BIBLE WORDS TO REMEMBER

Jesus is the true light. He gives light to
everyone coming into the world. (from John 1:9)

Bible Story: A PRAYER IS ANSWERED
from Luke 2

Simeon loved God and prayed that God's promise would come true while he was alive. God gave Simeon a **certain** hope that he would not die until he had seen the Savior.

One day the Spirit told Simeon to go to the temple. It was on this day that Mary and Joseph brought Jesus to the temple. Simeon knew **immediately** that this was the Savior that God had promised. He took Jesus in his arms and blessed God. He said, "Now I am ready to die in peace. Your Word has been kept, Lord. I have seen Your salvation which You have shown to everyone. This child is a light that will tell everyone that God loves them."

Simeon blessed Mary and Joseph and Jesus. He told Mary that there would be sadness for her someday because of what Jesus had come to do—to die for the sins of the world.

But the wonderful news is that because Jesus came to die, many can live! Jesus paid the price for sin so that we can live forever in heaven with Him.

WORDS TO KNOW

certain: for sure   **immediately:** right away

PRAYER THOUGHT

Dear God, I am so glad that You can be everywhere—there are so many places where people gather together to worship You. Help me remember why I come together with others at church and think about You and thank You for Your love. In Jesus Name, Amen.

Questions:
THINKING & REMEMBERING

Fill in the blanks or circle the letters of all that are right.

1. What did Simeon pray that God would let him do before he died?
   a. see the Savior
   b. go to the temple
   c. meet John the Baptist

2. God gave Simeon a certain hope that he would not die until he had seen the Savior.   true_____ false_____

3. The word *certain* means:
   a. doubtful
   b. for sure
   c. undecided

4. Whom did God send to help Simeon know that his prayer would be answered and that he should go to the temple?
   a. Mary and Joseph
   b. the Holy Spirit
   c. the temple priest

5. When did Simeon know that Jesus was the Savior?
   a. when he held Jesus in his arms
   b. immediately after he saw him with his own eyes
   c. when he asked Mary and Joseph some questions

6. What did Simeon say he was ready to do after seeing God's salvation?
   a. go tell others about Jesus
   b. get people prepared to accept Jesus, the Messiah
   c. die in peace

7. Simeon said that Jesus would be a _____ to everyone.

8. The wonderful news is that because Jesus came to die, many can _____!
   Jesus paid the price for _____ so that we can live forever in
   _____ with Him.

BIBLE WORDS TO REMEMBER

Jesus is the true light. He gives light to
everyone coming into the world. (from John 1:9)

Bible Story: NO LONGER WAITING

from Luke 2

A woman named Anna had also been waiting for God's promise to come true. For many years she stayed at the temple, serving God.

Anna knew all about the promises God had made to Israel. She knew that Abraham had been faithful in believing God's promise to make Israel a great nation. From the nation Israel the Savior of the world would come. Anna knew that the **prophets** had told God's people to get ready and watch for the coming of the Savior.

Anna served God by **fasting** and praying night and day. Then one day, she saw Jesus right there in the temple. Can you imagine how wonderful it was for Anna to finally be able to look at the face of the Son of God? She did not wonder at all if the Savior *would* come. She only knew that when the time was exactly right, God would send the Savior Jesus.

Anna gave thanks to the Lord and ran to tell everyone that Jesus, the Savior had come to Jerusalem. The waiting was over—the Savior had come!

WORDS TO KNOW

prophets: those who listened to God and told what would happen before it happened

fasting: to stop eating food for a time

PRAYER THOUGHT

Dear God, You will bring me joy when I ask You. Help me to remember that the clouds of sadness will go away when I believe in You to be the light of my life. In Jesus Name, Amen

Questions:
Thinking & Remembering

Fill in the blanks or circle the letters of all that are right.

1. What was the name of the woman who was waiting to see Jesus?
   a. Anna
   b. Mary
   c. Elizabeth

2. What did she believe that God would do someday?
   a. He would keep His promises.
   b. He would send the Messiah (Jesus).
   c. He would help Israel have a new ruler.

3. Where did she stay?
   a. She stayed at her house.
   b. She stayed with her friends.
   c. She stayed at the temple.

4. What did she do every day and every night?
   a. She fasted and prayed.
   b. She cooked meals at the temple.
   c. She talked to people about God's promise.

5. She sometimes thought that God had forgotten Israel.
   true_____ false_____

6. What had the prophets told God's people?
   a. They should get ready for the Savior.
   b. They could believe what they wanted.
   c. They should watch for the coming of the Savior.

7. Anna knew that the baby she was seeing was the Messiah.
   true_____ false_____

8. What two things did Anna do after she saw Jesus?
   a. She thanked God.
   b. She went to tell everyone that the Savior had come.
   c. She fasted and prayed.

Bible Story: THE PROMISE CAME TRUE
from Luke 2; Isaiah 49

Simeon had waited a very long time for something wonderful to happen. Anna also was praying and waiting. They weren't waiting for something they had just dreamed about or **imagined**. Simeon and Anna loved God and God's people. They believed that God would keep His promise. They read what the prophets had said about Jesus coming and why He would come.

The prophet Isaiah told what the Lord God said: "I will make Israel a light for other nations. Then it will be possible for the whole world to be **saved**."

So those who read these words waited, hoping to see God's special King, the Christ. Simeon saw all the people in darkness. He saw that they were sad. But he knew that when Jesus came, He would bring light to their hearts.

Anna was a **prophetess**—someone who told others the Word of God. She knew that the coming of Jesus would bring freedom for all people who believed in Him.

Many people were waiting, but when Jesus came, *they kept on waiting*! They didn't know that the waiting was over. The Light had come. Simeon and Anna were two that knew.

WORDS TO KNOW

imagine: to think about in your mind

saved: to make free; to rescue (from sin)

prophetess: a woman who tells others the Word of God

THINK ABOUT

God always answers your prayers. But since God knows exactly what is best for you, He may not answer them in the way you want. Sometimes God will just ask you to wait because the time is not right. Anna prayed and waited. She knew that God would send Jesus at the right time.

Questions:
THINKING & REMEMBERING

Circle the letters of all that are right.

1. Which two people in the Bible story waited for Jesus to come?
   a. Simeon
   b. Isaiah
   c. Anna

2. How did they know for sure that God was sending a Savior?
   a. They had a dream one night and an angel told them.
   b. They read what God had told the prophets.
   c. They imagined that this was true.

3. Who were God's special people in the Bible?
   a. the Israelites
   b. the Romans
   c. the Gentiles

4. What did God say about Israel?
   a. He would make Israel a light.
   b. Through Jesus, who was an Israelite, the world would be saved.
   c. Because they sinned, he would choose another people.

5. What did Simeon observe about God's people?
   a. They were sad.
   b. They were in darkness—not knowing what to do.
   c. They were happy the way they were.

6. What would happen when Jesus came?
   a. He would bring freedom for all people who believed in Him.
   b. He would punish people.
   c. He would bring light to people's hearts.

7. Did everyone see the Light when Jesus was born?
   a. Some thought that the Savior would be more powerful.
   b. Some didn't know yet that Jesus was the Light.
   c. Some kept on waiting.

BIBLE WORDS TO REMEMBER

Jesus is the true light. He gives light to
everyone coming into the world. (from John 1:9)

Bible Story: SEEING AND BELIEVING
from Luke 2; Matthew 2

Jesus was still a tiny baby when Mary and Joseph traveled to Jerusalem for His
first visit to the temple. Others traveling on the same road must have seen this
mother and father with a baby. They did not know that this was a special baby.
They didn't notice anything different about Jesus. He was just like all other babies,
they thought.

Mary and Joseph did what other parents did when they brought their baby for
the first time to thank God for their child. They gave an offering of two pigeons
just like many others coming to worship in the temple.

But there were those who saw Jesus and knew who He was.

First, Mary and Joseph, of course knew that Jesus was very special—that He was
the Son of God. The angel had told them this wonderful news. The shepherds also
knew and ran to worship the Savior that God had sent. At the temple, Simeon and
Anna knew who Jesus was. God had kept His promise. They did not need to wait
any longer.

At this very time, the wise men were on their journey—following a great star to
find Jesus. They, too, knew that a king had been born! Do you know the King
Jesus?

PRAYER THOUGHT

*Dear God, I know that You sent Jesus to be my light. I don't
need to be in darkness and be sad, because Jesus brings love
and joy to all who will believe. Thank You, God! In Jesus Name,
Amen.*

Questions:
THINKING & REMEMBERING

Fill in the blanks or circle the letters of all that are right.

1. The people traveling to Jerusalem knew that Jesus was special.
   true_____ false_____

2. There were some people who saw Jesus and knew who He was.
   true_____ false_____

3. Which people saw and knew that Jesus was the Son of God on earth?
   a. Mary   d. the shepherds
   b. Simeon   e. Anna
   c. Abraham   f. Joseph

4. Match the people below with something about them:

   a. Simeon   (1) _____fasted and prayed at the temple
   b. Mary   (2) _____the husband of Mary
   c. Shepherds   (3) _____did not want to die before seeing the
                              Savior
   d. Joseph   (4) _____mother of Jesus
   e. Anna   (5) _____heard the angel's singing

5. Who else was coming to find Jesus?
   a. the king of Egypt
   b. the wise men
   c. people from Bethlehem

6. How were they going to find Jesus?
   a. A wonderful star was guiding them.
   b. They had a map that showed where He was.
   c. They were going to ask people along the way.

7. How can you know that Jesus is the King sent from God?
   a. Someone will tell me.
   b. The signs in the sky show me.
   c. God's Word and the Holy Spirit guide me.

Beginnings II

Jesus: A King on Earth

BIBLE WORDS TO REMEMBER
Jesus said, "I am the light of the world."
(from John 8:12)

Bible Story: A WONDERFUL STAR
from Matthew 2

In a country far away from Bethlehem where Jesus was born, some very wise men looked up into the sky and saw a brilliant star. The star was brighter than all the other stars in the sky, and it was a star they had never seen before.

The wise men, who had studied the stars and learned many things from books, knew the new star meant that a king had been born.

They wanted to go and find the new king to worship Him. They hurried and prepared for their journey. It would be a long trip and would take many days and months. They thought the star would lead them to the city of Jerusalem. The new king would certainly be born in a wonderful and beautiful palace! Surely, this new king would be the ruler of the greatest nation in the world—and armies would obey his every command!

In their bags they took some very special gifts to give to the new king. "We must give him the very best gifts we have because this king is sent from God." The wise men started on their long journey.

PRAYER THOUGHT
Dear God, You have shown Your love in the greatest way possible—by sending Your Son to give us Your love. Help me to know ways to show You that I love You and to tell others about Your love. In Jesus Name, Amen.

Questions:
THINKING & REMEMBERING

Circle the letters of all that are right.

1. Why were these men called "wise" men?
    a. They talked to the king.
    b. They went to school.
    c. They studied the stars and read many books.

2. What was special about the star they saw in the sky?
    a. A new star meant that a king had been born.
    b. The star was brighter than all the other stars in the sky.
    c. They had never seen this star before.

3. What did the wise men want to do?
    a. They wanted to ask someone what the star meant.
    b. They wanted to wait awhile and see if it went away.
    c. They wanted to follow the star to find the new king.

4. What would they do when they found the king?
    a. They would ask him questions.
    b. They would worship Him.
    c. They would tell the old king that there was a new king.

5. About how long did they have to travel?
    a. a few days
    b. many days and months
    c. two weeks

6. Where did they think the new king would be born?
    a. in a palace
    b. in a stable
    c. in Jerusalem

7. What did they take to give to the new king?
    a. new clothes
    b. their very best gifts
    c. a book about kings

8. Whom did they think had sent this king?
    a. God
    b. another ruler
    c. an angel

Bible Story: THE WISE MEN BRING GIFTS TO JESUS
from Matthew 2

The wise men followed the star and traveled for many days and months. When they arrived in Jerusalem, they asked where they could find the new king. When King Herod heard about this, he was very upset and **troubled**. He did not want a new king to take his place! He thought he was the greatest king!

King Herod pretended that he wanted to know where the new king was so that he could worship Him, too. However, he really wanted to find Him so that he could stop another king from taking his place. He called the men to the **palace** who had studied the **Scriptures**. They knew that the king, who was **Christ**, would be born in the city of Bethlehem.

The wise men continued their journey. They followed the star until they came to Bethlehem. When they came to the house where Jesus was, they were very tired, but they were too excited to think about that. They were going to see a very special king!

They went into the house and there were Mary and Joseph—and Jesus! The wise men said, "This is the King we have waited to see!" They fell down and worshiped Him. Then they opened their treasures and presented their finest gifts: gold, **frankincense**, and **myrrh**.

WORDS TO KNOW

troubled:	worried
palace:	large mansion where kings and queens live
Scriptures:	God's words written for people to read and study
Christ:	God's chosen One
frankincense and **myrrh:**	precious spices and perfume

THINK ABOUT

Sometimes when we think of gifts—especially at Christmas—we think mostly of what we will get, not what we can give. The wise men took gifts to honor Jesus. They brought the very best gifts they had to give. The gift they received was being able to see God's love come to earth. God gave the best He could give—His very own Son.

Questions:
THINKING & REMEMBERING

Fill in the blanks or circle the letters of all that are right.

1. How did the wise men know which direction to travel?
   a. They had a map.
   b. They asked directions.
   c. They followed the star.

2. King Herod was happy about a new king being born.
   true_____   false_____

3. Why was king Herod so troubled?
   a. He didn't want a new king to take his place.
   b. He wanted to pick a new king himself.
   c. He thought he was the greatest king.

4. Herod really wanted to worship Jesus when the wise men found Him.
   true_____   false_____

5. How was it known that the new king was Christ and was born in Bethlehem?
   a. They had a dream about it.
   b. The king remembered.
   c. The men who studied the Scriptures, God's Word, told them.

6. When they continued their journey, what did they follow?
   a. the main road
   b. the star
   c. a person who said they would guide them

7. What did they do when they saw Jesus?
   a. They bowed down and worshiped Him.
   b. They went to tell the king.
   c. They wanted to hold him.

8. What gifts did the wise men bring to Jesus?
   a. gold
   b. frankincense
   c. myrrh

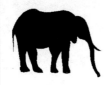

BIBLE WORDS TO REMEMBER
Jesus said, "I am the light of the world."
(from John 8:12)

Bible Story: A CRUEL KING
from Matthew 2

The wise men found the king they were looking for! The many days of traveling over the desert following the star had been worth it. Nothing would ever be the same for them again. They had seen and worshiped the Savior that God sent to save the world from sin. They **rejoiced** with **exceedingly** great joy!

Then the wise men remembered their visit to King Herod in Jerusalem. Herod told them to find Jesus and come back and tell him so that he could also "worship Him." As they were thinking about going back to Jerusalem to report to the king, God told them in a dream that Herod was going to do evil and try to harm Jesus. God told them not to return to Herod, but to go back to their country another way.

King Herod found out that the wise men returned home without telling him about Jesus. He was very **angry**! He ordered his soldiers to go to Bethlehem and kill all the baby boys. Herod thought that killing them would take care of his problem of a new king! But God was taking care of Jesus. He would not be hurt by the **cruel** king.

WORDS TO KNOW

rejoiced:	celebrate with great happiness
exceedingly:	extraordinary; immense
angry:	very mad
cruel:	vicious and violent

PRAYER THOUGHT

Dear God, I know that I have two choices—just like Adam and Eve had in the garden—just like Herod had. I can choose to follow You or I can choose to follow Satan. I want to choose to obey and follow You. Help me say "no" to Satan. In Jesus Name, Amen.

Questions:
Thinking & Remembering

Fill in the blanks or circle the letters of all that are right.

1. Whom did the wise men find by following the star?
   a. King Herod
   b. shepherds
   c. the Savior

2. Why did God send His Son to earth?
   a. to save the world from sin
   b. to tell people to be kind to each other
   c. to get a report about the earth to take to heaven

3. What words describe how the wise men felt about finding Jesus?
   a. They thought He would be a good shepherd.
   b. They were excited they had been right about the special star.
   c. They rejoiced with exceedingly great joy!

4. What did King Herod want the wise men to do when they found Jesus?
   a. make him the new king
   b. come and tell him where Jesus was
   c. return to their homes

5. Herod was going to worship Jesus.
   true_____   false_____

6. How did the wise men know that they should not go back to report to Herod?
   a. Mary and Joseph told them not to go.
   b. They were in a hurry to get back home.
   c. God told them in a dream.

7. What evil did Herod order his soldiers to do?
   a. hurt Mary
   b. kill the baby boys in Bethlehem
   c. punish the wise men for not reporting where Jesus was

8. God was taking care of _____. He would not be _____.

9. Fill in the missing words from John 8:12.
   Jesus said, "I am the _____ of the _____."

BIBLE WORDS TO REMEMBER
Jesus said, "I am the light of the world."
(from John 8:12)

Bible Story: ESCAPE INTO EGYPT
from Matthew 2

The wise men had worshiped Jesus and left to go to their own country. Mary and Joseph did not know that king Herod was planning to kill Jesus. But very soon they knew!

The angel of the Lord **appeared** to Joseph in a dream. The angel said, "Get up and take Jesus and Mary and **escape** to the country of Egypt. Stay there until I come to tell you that it will be safe to leave. Herod is coming to find Jesus and destroy Him."

Joseph didn't wait until morning to do what the angel said! He quickly got out of bed and woke up Mary. He told her they must hurry and leave Bethlehem. Gently, Mary held Jesus tightly in her arms. Nothing must happen to harm Jesus! Joseph prepared the donkey and quietly the family escaped in the night into Egypt. Joseph took good care of Jesus and Mary. He knew that God would help him protect God's precious and only Son.

The family stayed in Egypt until the wicked King Herod was dead. The prophet Isaiah had written these words from God many years before: "Out of Egypt I called My Son." These words came true!

WORDS TO KNOW
appeared: to come into view; to be seen
escape: to get away from danger

PRAYER THOUGHT

Dear God, I want You to live in my heart. Help me listen and follow Your directions. Your Word tells me how we can live for You. Choosing to love You is the most important thing I will ever do. Keep me on the path You have for me. In Jesus Name, Amen.

Questions:
THINKING & REMEMBERING

Fill in the blanks or circle the letters of all that are right.

1. Mary and Joseph knew that King Herod was trying to find Jesus.
   true_____   false_____

2. Who appeared to Joseph in a dream?
   a. an angel of the Lord
   b. God
   c. many angels

3. What was Joseph told to do?
   a. to go back to Nazareth
   b. to take Mary and Jesus to Egypt
   c. to stay in Bethlehem for awhile

4. How long were they told to stay in another country?
   a. four years
   b. two years
   c. until the angel told them it was safe to leave

5. Why did they leave Bethlehem in such a hurry?
   a. Herod wanted to destroy Jesus.
   b. It would be best to travel at night.
   c. They wouldn't have to explain to others why they were leaving.

6. Complete the sentences from your story:
   Joseph took good care of _____ and Mary. He knew that
   _____ would help him protect His precious and only _____.

7. When was the family able to leave Egypt?
   a. when the weather was good to travel
   b. after Herod was dead
   c. after six years

8. What words were written by Isaiah the prophet many years before?
   a. "Herod will try to destroy Jesus"
   b. "Out of Egypt I called My Son."
   c. "The Savior will do God's work in the land of Egypt."

89

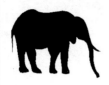

BIBLE WORDS TO REMEMBER
Jesus said, "I am the light of the world."
(from John 8:12)

Bible Story: GOD'S PLAN KEEPS MAKING HISTORY
from Matthew 2

King Herod thought that he was the greatest king and wanted his **kingdom** to last **forever**. He built large palaces and had large armies to **defend** the **fortresses** and strong walls around his houses and beautiful gardens. But this king could not win against the plan of God. The walls of the wonderful palaces **crumbled** and what was left was only part of a memory of his greatness.

People today **design** and build great buildings. They think that they are strong enough to last a very long time, too—just like King Herod. But many things happen to change what people build. God helps people do pretty amazing things but in the end, it is not what we do, but who we are inside that really matters. Nothing we can do or make **compares** to God's wonderful creation.

We are part of God's plan in belonging to His kingdom—not on earth, but in heaven. Each person is more important to God than the strongest building ever built on earth. But God is looking at the inside and asking us to be made clean from sin. The only way we can be clean on the inside is to ask Jesus to be in our hearts and make Him our King.

WORDS TO KNOW
kingdom: a nation or land which is ruled by a king
forever: always
defend: protect, guard
fortresses: walls and buildings that are extra strong
crumbled: broken up in small pieces
design: to draw plans for something
compares: shows a difference between more than one thing

 **Questions:**
THINKING & REMEMBERING

Circle the letters of all that are right.

1. King Herod thought his kingdom would last:
   a. a short time
   b. for a long time
   c. forever

2. What did Herod build to show his greatness?
   a. large palaces
   b. strong walls
   c. beautiful gardens

3. What did Herod have to protect all that he had?
   a. large armies
   b. slaves
   c. common people

4. What happened to the walls and palaces Herod built?
   a. They are still standing like they were when he built them.
   b. Some of them have been torn down.
   c. They all crumbled and there are just parts left.

5. What do people still try to do today?
   a. They try to make strong buildings.
   b. They try to build great buildings.
   c. They try to build things that will last thousands of years.

6. What is really the most important thing?
   a. how strong you are
   b. how you look and how you dress
   c. how many friends you have
   d. how much money you have
   e. who you are inside

7. How can you be a part of God's plan?
   a. ask Jesus to be in my heart and make Him my King
   b. be as good as I can
   c. do a lot of nice things

Beginnings II

Jesus: His Beginnings on Earth

BIBLE WORDS TO REMEMBER

"He who follows Me shall not walk in darkness,
but have the light of life." (from John 8:12)

Bible Story: GOING BACK TO NAZARETH

from Matthew 2

Jesus was safe in Egypt. Then an angel appeared to Joseph in a dream and said, "**Arise**, take the young Child and His mother and go to the land of Israel, because those who wanted to **harm** Him are dead." The Israelites did not need to be afraid of king Herod any longer. He had made the people sad with his **anger** and **jealousy**. But earthly kings do not live forever. Jesus is a heavenly king and His kingdom will have no end.

Jesus was sent to earth by God to save people from their sin and sadness. He came from heaven to be on earth until His work was done. He came to show God's perfect love by dying on a cross for our sins so that by believing in Him, we could live in heaven forever. That would not be possible unless Jesus came. This was all part of God's plan.

Joseph followed God's directions. He knew that while Jesus, God's own Son was on earth, that he was part of God's plan to keep Jesus safe and to help Him grow in the right way. Mary and Joseph were happy that they could finally go back to their home in Nazareth.

WORDS TO KNOW

arise:	get up and go
harm:	to hurt
anger:	to be very upset and mad at someone or about something
jealousy:	to hate someone for thinking they have something you want

PRAYER THOUGHT

Dear God, You are a loving Heavenly Father and You care about me in a perfect way! Thank You for sending Jesus. I want to show love to You in special ways, too. Help me to listen to Your directions. In Jesus Name, Amen.

Questions:
THINKING & REMEMBERING

Fill in the blanks or circle the letters of all that are right.

1. What was the name of the king who wanted to kill Jesus?
   a. Pharaoh
   b. David
   c. Herod

2. What kind of a king is Jesus?
   a. an earthly king
   b. a heavenly king

3. How long will Jesus' kingdom last?
   a. a thousand years
   b. two thousand years
   c. forever

4. What did Jesus come to earth to do?
   a. He came to be a good person.
   b. He came to take power away from the Romans.
   c. He came to the show God's perfect love.

5. How would Jesus prove to us how much we matter to God?
   a. die for our sins
   b. make it possible for us to live in heaven
   c. give us eternal life if we believe on Him

6. What did the angel tell Joseph to do?
   a. go back to the land of Israel
   b. stay in Egypt until Jesus was older
   c. live in Bethlehem

7. Joseph followed God's instructions and listened to God so that he could keep Jesus safe.
   true_____   false_____

8. Where was the home that Mary and Joseph had lived before?
   a. Jerusalem
   b. Bethlehem
   c. Nazareth

BIBLE WORDS TO REMEMBER

"He who follows Me shall not walk in darkness,
but have the light of life." (from John 8:12)

Bible Story: JESUS GROWS UP

from Luke 2

Can you imagine what a day would be like for Jesus? Waking up to a new day and doing all the things that every child does every day? He was just your age at one time on earth!

Jesus would help Mary and do what she asked when it was time to eat their meals. When the food was ready, they would thank God for their food. Jesus helped Joseph in his carpenter shop, too. He obeyed Mary and Joseph in everything they asked Him to do. He knew that obeying His earthly parents was what God wanted Him to do.

All around Jesus' house there were green grassy hills where He could run and play. Jesus loved the hills and all of the beautiful things God had made.

At nighttime, Jesus' family would talk about God. They would tell God's stories over and over until Jesus knew them all by heart. Then Jesus would say His prayers before bedtime...and the stars would come out...and all the little town of Nazareth would go to sleep.

He knew that someday He would leave His home and friends to finish the work God sent Him to do, but He understood that there was a right time for everything.

PRAYER THOUGHT

Dear God, I know that Jesus grew just like I do. Sometimes He must have been hurt, too. I know that You took care of Jesus and that You will take care of me, too. In Jesus Name, Amen.

Questions:
THINKING & REMEMBERING

Answer the questions below.

1. What important things can you think about when you consider Jesus' time on earth? _____

   _____

2. What other things can you remember about Jesus? _____

   _____

3. What did Jesus do while He was growing up that you can also do?

   _____

4. Do you need to wait until you are grown up to do something for God?

   _____

5. Tell some ways that you can do God's work right now.

   _____

   _____

   _____

THINK ABOUT

Sometimes we forget that Jesus grew up just like you are growing up right now. We think of Jesus being born in Bethlehem at Christmas. We think of Jesus and the wonderful things He showed about God's love. We think of why He came—to die for our sins so that we might live forever in heaven. We think about Him coming again and hope it will be soon.

All of these things are important. But it is also important to remember that: Jesus was a baby. Jesus was a little boy. Jesus was also a teenager. Jesus was a young man.

And all of this time, Jesus was doing good things. He didn't wait until He was all grown up to do God's work!

BIBLE WORDS TO REMEMBER

"He who follows Me shall not walk in darkness,
but have the light of life." (from John 8:12)

Bible Story: WHERE IS JESUS?
from Luke 2

When Jesus was twelve years old the family made their **journey** from Nazareth to Jerusalem so they could worship at the temple. Jesus was so excited! He couldn't wait to talk to the great teachers about God.

Too soon, it seemed, it was time to return to Nazareth. Jesus was not with Mary and Joseph as they started their trip home. But they were not worried at first. But then the whole day passed, and they still hadn't seen Jesus. Now they were upset!

Mary and Joseph hurried back to Jerusalem. They searched for three days! Finally, they came to the temple, and there they found Jesus. He was listening to the teachers and asking them questions. The teachers were **amazed**! How could this young boy know so many things about God? He understood many things that they could not ever understand.

Mary and Joseph were glad that Jesus was safe, but they had been so worried. His mother said to Him, "Son, why have You done this to us? We have been looking everywhere for You." Jesus was sorry they had been concerned. He said, "I must do the work that My Father sent Me to do." Then Mary remembered that Jesus was not only her boy, He was God's Son.

WORDS TO KNOW

journey: to travel somewhere and go on a trip
amazed: with great surprise

PRAYER THOUGHT

Dear Heavenly Father, I want to follow You—even though I am young. Help me to love others and be obedient to my parents like Jesus was. In Jesus Name, Amen.

Questions:
THINKING & REMEMBERING

Fill in the blanks or circle the letters of all that are right.

1. How old was Jesus when he went to the temple in Jerusalem?
   a. twelve
   b. eight
   c. fourteen

2. Jesus was excited about talking to the great teachers about God.
   true_____   false_____

3. When it was time to return to Nazareth, what happened?
   a. Jesus was not with Mary and Joseph.
   b. Jesus was with His friends.
   c. Jesus told His parents He would catch up later.

4. When did Mary and Joseph begin to worry?
   a. after two days
   b. after the day had passed
   c. in three hours

5. Where did Mary and Joseph go to look for Jesus?
   a. a town near Jerusalem
   b. near Nazareth
   c. in Jerusalem

6. How many days did Mary and Joseph search for Jesus?
   a. one day
   b. three days
   c. two days

7. What was Jesus doing when they found Him?
   a. He was playing with friends.
   b. He was listening to the teachers.
   c. He was asking questions.

8. Why were the teachers amazed?
   a. Jesus knew so much about God.
   b. Jesus understood things they could not understand.
   c. He was so young to have such knowledge.

BIBLE WORDS TO REMEMBER

"He who follows Me shall not walk in darkness,
but have the light of life." (from John 8:12)

Bible Story: JESUS IS BAPTIZED

from Matthew 3

One day Jesus knew it was the right time for Him to leave His home. He left His family and friends. Jesus, God's Son, was ready to go tell the people about God's great love for them and to save them from their sins.

John was a special messenger to tell the people about Jesus' coming and to get people ready for Jesus. One day as John was speaking to the people, he saw Jesus coming. He said, "Here comes the man I have been telling you about, God's own Son who will take away the sins of the world."

When Jesus asked John to baptize Him, John didn't think he should because Jesus had never sinned. But Jesus told him that it was part of God's plan. John baptized Jesus, and when He came up out of the water, a wonderful thing happened. The sky opened up and the Holy Spirit in the **form** of a dove rested on Jesus. Everyone heard God's voice saying, "This is my **beloved** Son and I am very **pleased** with Him." Then they knew that Jesus really was the Son of God—God had sent Him to show His love to everyone!

WORDS TO KNOW

form: appearance, to look like

beloved: loved very much in a special and honored way (Jesus lived a perfect and holy life)

pleased: satisfied

PRAYER THOUGHT

Dear God, Thank You for Your perfect love. Help me show others Your love, too. Help me to be like Jesus and obey my parents. In Jesus Name, Amen.

Questions:
THINKING & REMEMBERING

Circle the letters of all that are right.

1. Why did Jesus leave His home in Nazareth?
   a. He was going to work at a carpenter shop in Bethlehem.
   b. He wanted to preach with John the Baptist.
   c. It was time for Him to tell others about God's great love for them.

2. Whom did God choose to tell others that Jesus was coming?
   a. John
   b. Herod
   c. Zacharias

3. What was the important message He would tell?
   a. The king was a bad person.
   b. They should try to do good things so they could go to heaven.
   c. They should get ready for Jesus, the Savior of the world.

4. What did Jesus want John to do before He started His work?
   a. to tell Him how to live in the wilderness
   b. to baptize Him
   c. to stop making people feel sad for their sins

5. What did John tell the people when he saw Jesus coming?
   a. "Here comes the man I have been telling you about!"
   b. "This is the man you must listen to."
   c. "This is God's own Son who will take away the sins of the world."

6. Why did John say Jesus did not need to be baptized?
   a. because He was God's Son
   b. because Jesus had never sinned and was perfect
   c. because there were too many other people to baptize

7. What wonderful thing happened when Jesus came up out of the water
   a. The sky opened up.
   b. They heard God's voice saying, "This is my beloved Son and I am very pleased with Him."
   c. The Spirit of God came in the form of a dove and rested on Jesus.

Bible Story: JESUS IS TEMPTED BY SATAN
from Matthew 4

After Jesus was baptized, He went into the desert for forty days and forty nights to pray and listen to God. **Satan** knew Jesus was there and he wanted Jesus to sin.

When Satan saw that Jesus was hungry, he said, "If you are the Son of God, why don't you turn these stones into bread?" Jesus said, "God says that man should not live by bread alone, but by every word of God."

Then Satan took Jesus to the top of the temple and said, "If you really are the Son of God, throw yourself down to the ground. God will send His angels to take care of You." Jesus said, "God says not to **tempt** Him."

Next, Satan took Jesus to a high mountain, and showed Him all the beautiful kingdoms of the world. He said, "I will give you all of this if you will fall down and worship me." Jesus said, "God's Word says we must worship only God."

Satan knew that he could not make Jesus sin, so he went away. Then God sent His angels to be with Jesus in the desert. They took care of Jesus and gave Him what He needed.

WORDS TO KNOW

Satan: the devil; the enemy of God

tempt: to try to get someone to do something that is wrong by making it look right

---

PRAYER THOUGHT

Dear God, I know that You will always be near me. Even when Satan tries to get me to disobey You, I will choose to say "no" and choose to do the things that will please You. In Jesus Name, Amen.

 **Questions:**
THINKING & REMEMBERING

Fill in the blanks or circle the letters of all that are right.

1. Where did Jesus go after He was baptized?
   a. to visit His family in Nazareth
   b. to Jerusalem
   c. into the desert

2. How long was Jesus there?
   a. forty days and forty nights
   b. two weeks
   c. several days

3. What did Jesus do there?
   a. He prayed.
   b. He listened to God.
   c. He waited for John to come.

4. Who knew that Jesus was there?
   a. John the Baptist
   b. His mother
   c. Satan

5. What did he want Jesus to do?
   a. eat some food with him
   b. talk to him about His work
   c. sin

6. How many times did Satan tempt Jesus to sin?
   a. one time   b. seven times   c. three times

7. Complete the sentences with the right word: *worship   temple   bread*

   a. Satan tried to get Jesus to make stones into _____.
   b. Satan tried to get Jesus to throw Himself from the top of the

      _____.
   c. Satan tried to get Jesus to bow down and _____ him
      so Jesus could have all the kingdoms of the world.

8. Who came to take care of Jesus and give Him what He needed?

   a. John the Baptist   b. angels   c. friends

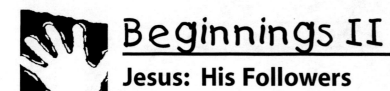

Beginnings II

Jesus: His Followers

BIBLE WORDS TO REMEMBER

Jesus said, "Follow Me, and I will make you fishers of men."
(from Matthew 4:19)

Bible Story: FROM FISHERMEN TO FOLLOWERS

from Matthew 4; Mark 1; Luke 5

One day Jesus was walking along the beautiful Sea of Galilee. He saw two men out in the lake fishing. It was Peter and Andrew. They had fished all night and had not caught even one fish. Then Jesus called to them and said, "Let down your nets." Peter said, "Master, we have worked all night, but we will do as You say." Immediately there were so many fish in the net that it was about to break!

Then Jesus said, "Come with Me, and I will make you fishers of men." They left their nets right away and followed Him. They had listened to John and they believed the message that he had given about Jesus being the Savior. They wanted to be with Jesus and be His **helpers**.

They walked along the sea and met two other **fishermen**. Their names were James and John. Jesus called to them too. They were so happy that Jesus invited them to come with Him! They left their boat and their nets and followed Jesus.

Now Jesus had four special helpers to go with Him to tell others about God. He was looking for even more followers who could be with Him to do God's important work.

WORDS TO KNOW

helpers: to work together so that something can get done

fishermen: those who catch fish and sell them

PRAYER THOUGHT

Dear God, I know that You need many followers to help tell others about Jesus and His love. Show me the ways in which I can help You best, even when I am young. In Jesus Name, Amen.

 # Questions:
THINKING & REMEMBERING

Circle the letters of all that are right.

1. Where was Jesus walking one day?
   a. along the Red Sea
   b. along the beautiful Sea of Galilee
   c. by the Jordan River

2. Whom did He see?
   a. John the Baptist
   b. people on the shore
   c. Peter and Andrew

3. What were they doing?
   a. having breakfast
   b. fishing
   c. cleaning the fish they had caught

4. How long had the men been fishing?
   a. a few hours
   b. all night
   c. for a day

5. What did Jesus tell them to do?
   a. "Let down your nets again."
   b. "Give up fishing!"
   c. "Go back home because you haven't caught any fish."

6. What happened next?
   a. They caught a few fish for their breakfast.
   b. Their nets were so full of fish they were ready to break.
   c. They still didn't catch any fish.

7. What did Jesus ask them to do after that?
   a. He said to follow Him and He would make them fishers of men.
   b. He said to go back to fishing.
   c. He said to tell others they were leaving to help Jesus.

8. What are the names of the other fishermen who followed Jesus?
   a. Mark   b. James   c. John

BIBLE WORDS TO REMEMBER

Jesus said, "Follow Me, and I will make you fishers of men."
(from Matthew 4:19)

Bible Story: MORE SPECIAL HELPERS
from Mark 1-3

Before Jesus chose more **disciples**, He went into the mountains to pray. He knew that it was important that His helpers were the right ones. Then He called the names of those who would be His disciples. There were twelve men. They were all different, but one thing was the same. They all loved Jesus. They knew He was the Son of God, the **Messiah**. They wanted to go everywhere with Him. They wanted to listen to Him teach, and they wanted to help people know who He was so they could believe in Him, too. They saw Jesus do miracles and they wanted to help others, too.

There were many people who were sick and needed to be healed. There were people who were sad and lonely. They needed to hear that God loved them. There were people who had done many wrong things and had sinned against God. Jesus told them that God would **forgive** them if they believed.

Everyone needs Jesus and His love! Are you one of Jesus' helpers? He wants you to be. You can find many ways to **serve** Him. There is still a lot of work to do!

WORDS TO KNOW

disciple:	someone who has a teacher and is learning
Messiah:	Christ, the One God sent to the world to show His love
forgive:	to make someone free from the wrong they have done
serve:	help

PRAYER THOUGHT

Dear God, Help me to think of ways to serve You. Put the thoughts in my mind that will keep me where You want me to be and doing what You want me to do. In Jesus Name, Amen.

Questions:
THINKING & REMEMBERING

Circle the letters of all that are right.

1. What did Jesus do before He chose each disciple?
    a. He asked them lots of questions.
    b. He prayed to God the Father.
    c. He talked to their families.

2. How many helpers were chosen?
    a. four   b. eight   c. twelve

3. What special name were these helpers called?
    a. friends   b. disciples   c. workers

4. What things were the same for each disciple? (There are six right choices.)
    a. They loved Jesus.
    b. They knew He was the Messiah.
    c. They wanted to go with Him and follow Him.
    d. They wanted to listen to Him teach.
    e. They all liked to travel.
    f. They wanted to help others.
    g. They wanted others to believe in Jesus.

5. Which people need Jesus and His love?
    a. the people who thought that they were good
    b. the sick people
    c. the sad and lonely people
    d. the people who sinned
    e. Everybody needs Jesus.

6. How did Jesus help people who sinned? (That is everybody!)
    a. He told them to go to the temple.
    b. He showed them the ten commandments.
    c. He forgave them.

7. Think of some ways that you can help and serve Jesus right now.

    _____

    _____

    _____

BIBLE WORDS TO REMEMBER

Jesus said, "Follow Me, and I will make you fishers of men."
(from Matthew 4:19)

Bible Story: THE QUEEN'S REVENGE

from Matthew 14

The new king Herod did not like the message of John the Baptist. When John said that Herod and the queen were not following God's commandments, the queen was angry! She wanted John to be killed. So the king put John in **prison**. But the queen would not be happy until John was dead.

The queen had a terrible and evil plan. On Herod's birthday, the queen's daughter danced at the party for the king. The king liked the dance so much that he said that she could have anything she wanted. The queen had already decided what it would be—the head of John the Baptist!

John was killed. But he had already done the work that God asked him to do. John had given God's message to the people about the Savior coming. He knew that he would live in heaven with God because He believed and obeyed God's Word.

Jesus was sorry when he heard what happened to John. Jesus was ready to show the people how much God loved them. He would finish His work by dying on a cross for the sins of the world. Everyone can choose to live in heaven forever by believing in Jesus.

WORDS TO KNOW

prison: a terrible place where someone is locked in and cannot leave

PRAYER THOUGHT

Dear God, Thank You for sending Jesus to bring Your love to me. Because of Jesus, I can be close to You again. Because of Jesus I have a Savior and Friend. In Jesus Name, Amen.

 # Questions:
THINKING & REMEMBERING

Circle the letters of all that are right.

1. Why did the queen hate John the Baptist?
   a. He said the king and queen were disobeying God's commandments.
   b. He said the queen was ugly.
   c. He said that Jesus was a king.

2. What did the queen want to happen to John?
   a. She wanted him to be put in prison.
   b. She wanted him killed.
   c. She wanted him to tell her she was doing the right thing.

3. What did the king promise the queen's daughter?
   a. anything she wanted
   b. just some new clothes
   c. some gold

4. What was the queen's plan?
   a. Her daughter would ask for some jewels.
   b. She would ask for her own party.
   c. She would ask for the head of John the Baptist.

5. What happened to John the Baptist?
   a. He was put in prison for life.
   b. He was killed.
   c. He was sent back to the desert.

6. Why was John not afraid?
   a. He knew he would be in heaven with God when he died.
   b. He knew he had done what God wanted him to do.
   c. He wanted to be away from people.

7. What was Jesus going to do because of the terrible sins of people?
   a. He was going to die on a cross.
   b. He was going to teach people for many years.
   c. He was going to finish His work on earth.

BIBLE WORDS TO REMEMBER

Jesus said, "Follow Me, and I will make you fishers of men."
(from Matthew 4:19)

Bible Story: JESUS CHOOSES ORDINARY PEOPLE
from Matthew 16; Mark 3, 8; Luke 6, 9

All of Jesus' special helpers were ordinary people who had ordinary jobs. Some were bold (like Peter); some were noisy and talked a lot. Some were quiet and thoughtful. All of them believed Jesus and His message. They wanted Jesus to be their king on earth. They did not yet understand that Jesus came to die on a cross for the sins of the world and go back to heaven.

One day, the disciples were talking about Jesus. They called Him "Rabbi," which means teacher. Andrew said, "We have found the Messiah," which means, the Christ. Phillip said, "We have found the one the prophets wrote about"—Jesus of Nazareth, the son of Joseph. When Jesus asked Peter, "Who do you say that I am?" Peter said, "Lord, to whom shall we go? You have the words of eternal life. Also we believe and know that You are the Christ, the Son of the living God."

Jesus knew His disciples were special because they believed His words. Sometimes we feel like we are ordinary. But Jesus looks at us through His eyes and sees what we can become. He thinks you are wonderful!

THINK ABOUT

Have you ever started a project and then decided it was too hard so you just wanted to give up? It happens to little children, big children, parents, teachers and grandmas and grandpas, too! Easy things are mostly fun to do. Difficult things make us work hard to figure out and finish. We should always try to finish what we start to do. God wants us to do well, whatever we do. We can always quit and say, "I can't do it," or "I won't do it," but God will be pleased if you do your work and do it to the finish line. You will feel better, too, when you work and get it done!

Questions:
THINKING & REMEMBERING

Fill in the blanks or circle the letters of all that are right.

1. What kind of helpers did Jesus choose?
   a. religious leaders
   b. ordinary people
   c. people who were teachers

2. Which words tell what the disciples were like?
   a. bold
   b. noisy
   c. quiet
   d. thoughtful
   e. selfish

3. From the list above, which kind of person do you think you are more like?

   _____

4. What did the disciple's believe?
   a. Jesus was from God.
   b. Jesus was the Christ.
   c. Jesus was the Messiah.

5. What didn't the disciple's understand?
   a. Jesus was not an earthly king.
   b. Jesus was not going to lead an army.
   c. Jesus was a heavenly king and was going to die and go back to heaven.

6. What did the disciples want Jesus to be?
   a. a king on earth
   b. someone that would have power over other rulers
   c. someone who would make things perfect on earth

7. How did Peter answer Jesus' question about who He was?
   "You are the _____, the Son of the living _____."

BIBLE WORDS TO REMEMBER

Jesus said, "Follow Me, and I will make you fishers of men."
(from Matthew 4:19)

Bible Story: WHO IS JESUS?
from Matthew 16

There were many people who saw Jesus when He was on earth. Some thought He was a wonderful teacher. They liked what He said about the kingdom of God. They thought Jesus was a great healer. He made sick people well.

There were some people who just wanted to see Jesus do miracles—they liked the excitement. Jesus knew that they really didn't believe in Him. He knew what they were thinking and the reason why.

Others thought that Jesus was doing things by **magic**, not by the power of God. There were some religious leaders who were very angry. They hated Jesus and wanted to kill Him because He said He was the Son of God. They liked being powerful and did not want Jesus to **disturb** their comfortable way of life.

Jesus asks you to decide who you think He is. If you love Jesus and know that He came to die for all the wrong things you have done and will do, you can say, "I am sorry for my sins, Jesus. I know that you will forgive me. I believe that You are God's Son." Jesus wants us to believe so that we can be in heaven forever with Him!

WORDS TO KNOW

magic: using tricks to make things happen

disturb: to bother or upset someone or something

PRAYER THOUGHT

Dear God, You sent Jesus to show Your love. Help me to know and believe and love You. I'm sorry for all the wrong things I have done. I want you to live in my heart. In Jesus Name, Amen.

Questions:
THINKING & REMEMBERING

Circle the letters of all that are right.

1. What did people think about Jesus when He was on earth?
   a. He was a great healer.
   b. He was friendly and happy.
   c. He was a wonderful teacher.

2. What did some people want Jesus to do for their own excitement?
   a. do magic tricks
   b. tell stories
   c. do miracles

3. What did some people say about the miracle's Jesus did?
   a. They were done by magic.
   b. Jesus did not have God's power.
   c. He was good at tricking them.

4. What did some of the religious leaders think about Jesus?
   a. He was a Savior sent from God.
   b. He should change the government.
   c. He was going to take away their power.

5. Why were they so angry that they wanted to kill Him?
   a. He said He was the Son of God.
   b. He wanted people to be happy.
   c. He talked about the kingdom of God.

6. What did Jesus come to earth to do?
   a. He came to die for all the wrong things we have done and will do.
   b. He came to make a happy life for everyone on earth.
   c. He came to tell delightful stories.

7. Why does Jesus want us to believe in Him?
   a. so we will be happy all the time
   b. so that we can do things for other people
   c. so that we can live in heaven forever with Him

Jesus: His Miracles

Bible Story: A MIRACLE AT A WEDDING
from John 2

Jesus did not stay in one place very long! He walked from one town to another and along the sea where many people worked and lived. Jesus cared about all of the people He saw and talked to them about God. He was interested in the things they did.

One day, Jesus went to a wedding in the village of Cana. Mary, Jesus' mother, was also there. Everyone watched the bride and groom make a special promise to each other. After the ceremony, the celebration began. It was a wonderful party with good food and wine.

As the people were enjoying the celebration, the servants discovered that the wine was almost gone. Mary looked at Jesus and knew that He could help. She told the servants, "Do whatever He tells you to do."

Jesus saw six large water jugs. He said, "Fill each with water, then pour some into a glass and take it to the host." They did as Jesus said. The host was amazed! He said, "Why did you save the best wine for now? You should have served this first." This was the first miracle that Jesus did to show that He had God's power.

PRAYER THOUGHT

Dear God, I know that You sent Jesus to show Your love. Miracles were one way that You showed Your love. Help me to see the miracles in my life every day. . .little things and big things. In Jesus Name, Amen.

Questions:
THINKING & REMEMBERING

Circle the letters of all that are right.

1. Which two sentences in the lesson tell that Jesus traveled.
   a. It was a wonderful party.
   b. Jesus didn't stay in one place very long!
   c. He walked from one town to another.

2. Which sentence tells that Jesus cared and was interested in people?
   a. Jesus saw six large water jugs.
   b. He went where people lived and worked to tell them about God.
   c. The host was amazed!

3. Where was the wedding celebration that Jesus went to one day?
   a. in Cana   b. in Nazareth   c. in Bethlehem

4. Who else was invited that was close to Jesus?
   a. his brother   b. one of the disciples   c. his mother

5. What did the bride and groom do at the ceremony?
   a. They made a special promise to each other.
   b. They danced.
   c. They ate food and drank wine.

6. What happened after the ceremony?
   a. Everyone went home.
   b. The celebration began with food and wine.
   c. They opened gifts.

7. What did the servants discover before the celebration was over?
   a. The food was gone.
   b. People were tired.
   c. The wine was almost gone.

8. What happened when the servants did what Jesus told them to do?
   a. They had water instead of wine to drink.
   b. The people went to another party.
   c. Jesus did a miracle and turned the water into wine.

9. This was the first miracle that Jesus did to show that He had God's power.
   true_____ false_____

BIBLE WORDS TO REMEMBER

He who hears My word and believes
in Him who sent Me has everlasting life. (from John 5:24)

Bible Story: JESUS MAKES A SICK BOY WELL
from John 4

More and more people started following Jesus when they saw and heard the wonderful things He was doing. Many people believed what Jesus told them about God. They wanted to be followers and live as God wanted them to live.

One day a very important man came to Jesus. His son was so sick he was afraid that he would die. Jesus saw that the man loved his son very much. He was a **rich** man, but having a lot of money could not help his son. The man said, "Please hurry and come to my house, Jesus!"

Jesus looked at the man who loved his son more than anything. He said, "You can go home now. Your son is already well." The man thanked Jesus and started home again. He knew that Jesus could make his son well even though he did not go to his house.

Before the man got to his home, his **servants** ran to meet him. "Your son is well again," they shouted. The father was so happy. He knew that Jesus had healed his boy just at the time that He had said the words. The man and his family believed that Jesus was the Son of God.

WORDS TO KNOW

rich: to have a lot of money
servant: someone who works for another person

PRAYER THOUGHT

Dear God, Help my words show love to others. Help me to speak softly and to be gentle in my words and actions. In Jesus Name, Amen.

Questions:
THINKING & REMEMBERING

Circle the letters of all that are right.

1. When people believed what Jesus told them about God, what did they want to do?
   a. They wanted to be Jesus' followers.
   b. They wanted to get money and be rich.
   c. They wanted to live like God wanted them to live.

2. What does the story tell about the man who came to see Jesus?
   a. He was important.
   b. He was a beggar.
   c. He was rich.

3. What was the most important thing to this man?
   a. his money
   b. being important
   c. his son

4. What happened to the man's son?
   a. He was very sick.
   b. He fell down and was hurt.
   c. He was going to die.

5. Why did the man come to find Jesus?
   a. He thought Jesus was kind.
   b. He knew Jesus could make his son well.
   c. He wanted to talk to Jesus.

6. What did the man ask Jesus to do?
   a. come to his house
   b. have dinner with him
   c. make his son well

7. What did Jesus tell the man?
   a. He said to go home because his son was already well.
   b. He said that he would come to his house later.
   c. He said to call a doctor.

Bible Story: MIRACLES OF HEALING
from Mark 1

Jesus was in Nazareth and people came to see what miracles He would do. Jesus knew that many were just **curious**. They didn't really want to believe that He was God's Son.

Jesus and His friends came to the house of Peter. They had planned to stop there and have **dinner**. But when they arrived, they found out that Peter's mother-in-law had a **fever**. She was lying down and was very sick.

Peter asked Jesus to come quickly to the room where she was. Jesus stood beside the woman's bed. He took her hand in His. The woman looked up at Jesus and the fever was gone. She did not want to stay in bed to rest! She quickly got up and went into the kitchen. She fixed a wonderful meal for Jesus and His friends to eat.

Soon, there were people all around the house where Jesus was. The healthy people were helping the sick people come to Jesus so that He could touch them and **heal** them. Jesus loved people! Even though He knew that they only wanted healing for their body, and not their **soul**, He put His hands on them and they were not sick anymore.

WORDS TO KNOW

curious: to wonder and want to know the how or why of something

dinner: a meal that is served in the evening

fever: being hot when your body is sick

heal: to make the body well from sickness

soul: spirit; the part inside a person that can feel and know and love

---

THINK ABOUT

Do you know any children that were born in a different country? Always remember that God loves each child from every country in the whole world. He does not look on the outside of a person but on the inside. He sees how precious they are, and they are His treasures.

Questions:
THINKING & REMEMBERING

Circle the letters of all that are right.

1. What did the people in Nazareth want to see Jesus do in their city?
   a. preach at the church
   b. teach about God
   c. do miracles and heal people

2. What did Jesus know about the people?
   a. They were just curious.
   b. They wanted to see Him do miracles.
   c. They really didn't want to believe that He was God's Son.

3. Where did Jesus and His friends plan to go for dinner?
   a. to Jesus' mother's house
   b. to the house of Peter
   c. to a friend's house

4. What did they find out when they arrived?
   a. Peter's mother-in-law had a fever and was sick.
   b. There was not any food in the house.
   c. It was too late for dinner.

5. What did Jesus do?
   a. He took the sick woman's hand and the fever was gone.
   b. He gave her some medicine.
   c. He healed her.

6. What did she do after Jesus was in the room?
   a. She wanted to rest awhile.
   b. She asked them to bring food to the room.
   c. She fixed the meal.

7. Why did other people come to the house?
   a. They came to be healed physically (for their body).
   b. They came to be healed spiritually (for their soul).
   c. They came to see what Jesus was doing at Peter's house.

117

BIBLE WORDS TO REMEMBER

He who hears My word and believes
in Him who sent Me has everlasting life. (from John 5:24)

Bible Story: FOUR FRIENDS WHO CARED
from Luke 5

Many people were **rushing** out into the streets of the town. They were all going in one **direction**. They came to a house and went in. Soon there were too many people to fit in the house. Jesus was the one they wanted to see!

There was a very sad man living in that town who was so sick he couldn't sit up or move his arms and legs. He could only lie there and think. Even his thoughts made him sad because he could only think of all the bad things he had done. He wished he could go see Jesus! Jesus could heal his body. Maybe Jesus would even forgive him for all the wrong things he had done because He was God's Son. But he thought that he would never be able to see Jesus.

Then four friends remembered the sick man. They were sorry he was so sad. One of the friends said, "Let's take him to Jesus! Jesus will help our friend." The men picked up their friend's mat and carried him to the house where Jesus was talking. They were hoping that people would let them get their friend close to Jesus.

WORDS TO KNOW

rushing: to hurry to a place

direction: to proceed (go) in a certain way

plan: to think of a way to make something happen

PRAYER THOUGHT

Dear God, You have sent Jesus to make sick people well and to make sad people happy. Show me how I can tell my friends this wonderful news! In Jesus Name, Amen.

Questions:
THINKING & REMEMBERING

Fill in the blanks or circle the letters of all that are right.

1. Where were the people in this town going?
   a. They were going to see Jesus.
   b. They were going to the church.
   c. They were going shopping.

2. Where was Jesus?
   a. Jesus was in a park.
   b. Jesus was in a house.
   c. Jesus was in a church.

3. What happened at this place?
   a. There were so many people some could not get close to Jesus.
   b. People were pushing each other.
   c. Everyone could see Jesus.

4. Why couldn't one man who was sick go to see Jesus?
   a. He couldn't sit up or move his arms or legs.
   b. He didn't want to see Jesus.
   c. He wanted Jesus to come to his house.

5. What did the man think about most?
   a. wanting someone to come and talk to him
   b. the wrong things he had done
   c. how badly he was feeling

6. What two things did he wish Jesus could do for him?
   a. heal his body
   b. give him some money
   c. forgive his sins

7. The sick man thought that he would never be able to see Jesus, whom he believed was God's Son.   true_____   false _____

8. What **plan** did the man's friends have?
   a. to take their friend to Jesus
   b. to tell him to get up and try to get to Jesus
   c. to pick up the mat so they could carry him and he wouldn't need to walk

BIBLE WORDS TO REMEMBER

He who hears My word and believes
in Him who sent Me has everlasting life. (from John 5:24)

Bible Story: A Great Plan
from Luke 5

The four friends tried to get close to Jesus with their sick friend on a mat. The people did not move away. The friends were sad and the sick man thought that he would never see Jesus.

Then his friends had a great plan. They carried their sick friend up the outside stairs to the roof of the house. They made a big hole in the roof and let their friend down with ropes tied on each corner of his mat right in front of Jesus!

The people inside were so surprised! They looked at Jesus to see if He would be angry. But He looked happy. Jesus wanted to help the sick man. Jesus knew the man had a sad heart, too, and that he was sorry for his sins. Jesus said, "Your sins are forgiven." Then the man wasn't sad anymore. Jesus had forgiven him! Then Jesus showed how strong and loving God is. He told the man to pick up his bed and walk.

Now he was the happiest man in the town. He rolled up his mat and thanked God, telling everyone he saw how wonderful God is!

Remember: Jesus is with you always! Ask Him to help you feel His love wherever you are.

PRAYER THOUGHT

Dear God, Thank You for the friends who care about me. Help me to care about others and tell them about what You can do—heal sickness and sadness! In Jesus Name, Amen.

 # Questions:
THINKING & REMEMBERING

Fill in the blanks or circle the letters of all that are right.

1. How did the friends take the man to Jesus?
   a. They walked beside him and helped him.
   b. They carried him on his mat.
   c. They put him in a cart with wheels.

2. What was their plan to get close to Jesus?
   a. to go up to the roof
   b. tie ropes to the four corners of the mat
   c. open up the roof
   d. let the man down carefully in front of where Jesus was

3. What was special about the friends the sick man had?
   a. They cared about him.
   b. They were kind to him.
   c. They wanted their friend to be well.
   d. They didn't give up easily.

4. The people in the house were surprised when the man came through the roof.   true _____   false _____

5. Jesus was angry at the friends for bringing their friend through the roof instead of through the door.   true_____   false_____

6. What did Jesus know about the man that other people could not see?
   a. The man was sad.
   b. He was hungry.
   c. The man was sorry for his sins.

7. What wonderful things did Jesus do for this man?
   a. He healed his sickness so that he could walk.
   b. He told him not to be sad because he had great friends.
   c. He forgave his sins.

Jesus: His Teaching

Bible Story: JESUS TEACHES IN NAZARETH

from Luke 4

Jesus was in Nazareth where He lived when He was a boy. Not everyone thought that Jesus was special. How could someone that lived in their town and went to school and played outside be someone sent from God?

Jesus went to the **synagogue** where people went to hear the words of God read that were written on special **scrolls**. They stood very quietly. Jesus was going to speak. He read God's Words from the scroll and then He explained exactly what the words meant. Jesus said He was the One the words were telling about. The words He read that day were from the prophet Isaiah:

"The Spirit of the Lord is upon Me, because He has **anointed** Me to preach the gospel to the poor; He has sent Me to heal the **brokenhearted**, to **proclaim** liberty to the **captives** and recovery of sight to the blind, to set at liberty those who are **oppressed**; to proclaim the acceptable year of the Lord."

The people listening to Jesus were amazed at His knowledge and understanding. He spoke with such confidence! They had never heard the other teachers speak like this. Jesus was a very special teacher. He really was the one sent from God.

WORDS TO KNOW

synagogue:	a place where people went to worship and hear the words of God read
scroll:	a roll of special paper for writing God's Word
anointed:	chosen
brokenhearted:	sad and lonely
proclaim:	to tell
captives:	slaves; those who are not free
oppressed:	those who are treated in a wrong way

Questions:
THINKING & REMEMBERING

Fill in the blanks or circle the letters of all that are right.

1. Where did Jesus return to after He had traveled to other places?
   a. Jerusalem   b. Nazareth   c. Bethlehem

2. Everyone was happy to see Jesus because they thought He was special.
   true _____   false_____

3. Why did they think He was ordinary and just like everyone else?
   a. He did all the things that all the other boys did that were his age.
   b. His parents seemed to be like other parents.
   c. Mary and Joseph told everyone that He was ordinary.

4. Where did Jesus go to read the words of God?
   a. to the temple   b. to the synagogue   c. to the library

5. Where were God's words written?
   a. in a book   b. on stone tablets   c. on special scrolls

6. What did Jesus do after He read the words?
   a. He explained what the words meant.
   b. He sat down with the other people.
   c. He left the synagogue and went home.

7. Which prophet in the Old Testament told about Jesus' coming?
   a. Jeremiah   b. John   c. Isaiah

8. To which people did the prophet say that Jesus had been sent to help?
   a. the religious leaders   e. the poor
   b. the kings   f. the brokenhearted
   c. the captives   g. the blind
   d. the oppressed   h. the rich

9. Complete the Bible Words from John 3:16.

   For God so _____ the world that He _____ His only Son, that
   _____ believes in _____ will have _____ life.

Bible Story: A NEW BIRTH
from John 3

There was a man named Nicodemus who thought that he did everything right. He had tried very hard to follow the commandments, but inside he felt sad. He knew that he could never be "good enough" all by himself. He listened to Jesus tell about God's love. One night Nicodemus wanted to talk to Jesus. He said, "You can do miracles, so God must be with you."

Jesus told Nicodemus that to have eternal life, a person must be "born again." Nicodemus did not understand. "How can a man who is grown up go back inside his mother and be born a second time?" Jesus explained that the first one was a physical birth but the second birth is spiritual.

Nicodemus listened carefully as Jesus told him that God so loved the world and sent His only Son, that whoever believes in Him will not die but will live forever. Jesus said that He was God's Son, the light that had come to shine on the earth. This was the most wonderful lesson Nicodemus had ever heard about God's love. He wanted to believe and have that special peace inside! You can know for sure that God loves you, too!

THINK ABOUT

You may think you have done everything "just right" and that your mom and dad will be pleased with what you do to help. But sometimes you can feel a little bit "not sure" that you are "good enough" all the time. Jesus loves you even when you think you are not "good enough"—that's when He is there with you saying, "Remember, I love you!" You don't have to be good all by yourself. Jesus will help you when you ask Him to!

PRAYER THOUGHT

Dear God, Thank you for loving me so much! Help me to remember that it's hard to be good all by myself and that You are always with me to help me. In Jesus Name, Amen.

Questions:
THINKING & REMEMBERING

Fill in the blanks or circle the letters of all that are right.

1. What was the name of the man who tried to be good in this lesson?
   a. Zacharias
   b. Nicodemus
   c. Zacchaeus

2. What had this man tried to do?
   a. follow God's commandments
   b. be a teacher at the temple
   c. preach at the synagogue

3. Nicodemus was a happy person because he was trying hard to be good.
   true _____   false _____

4. What did Nicodemus know?
   a. He really was a very good person and God should accept him.
   b. He could never be "good enough" by trying by himself.
   c. He didn't feel sure that God really loved him.

5. What did Jesus tell Nicodemus he must do to be right with God?
   a. He must go to the temple every week.
   b. He must try to keep following the commandments.
   c. He must be born again.

6. Nicodemus understood what Jesus meant when he told him he must be born again.   true _____   false _____

7. How did Jesus explain the second birth to Nicodemus?
   a. The second birth is a spiritual birth.
   b. The second birth is physical.
   c. The second birth shows that you are perfect and won't sin again.

8. What did Jesus tell Nicodemus that God had done?
   a. He made the commandments easy to follow.
   b. He worked on some new commandments.
   c. He sent His only Son, and by believing in Him, a person could live forever.

Bible Story: WONDERFUL WATER
from John 4

Jesus and His disciples were followed everywhere they went. People loved to hear about Jesus and the special words He was telling about God and His love for them. They wanted to hear more!

One day Jesus and His disciples were very tired. They had walked a long way. They came to a **well** where people came to get water. Jesus sat by the well and rested while the disciples went into the city to buy food.

A woman came to the well to get water. Jesus asked her to give Him a drink of water. Jesus said to the woman, "I have **living water** that will last forever. If you drink of My water, you will never be thirsty again."

Jesus knows everything about everyone. He knew that the woman needed to know about God's love. She had done many wrong things and was very unhappy. She didn't know that God loved her. She believed that Jesus was the Messiah. She ran to tell everyone she saw that she had met the Messiah. She was changed and knew that she could have everlasting life! To live forever is having living water. Jesus is the living water!

WORDS TO KNOW

well: a very deep hole dug in the ground to get water

living water: coming from God, "living water" can make joy inside a person that is different from water that you can drink that satisfies only for a little while—you always need more of that kind of water. Jesus is the "Living Water."

THINK ABOUT

The Bible says that if you keep your mind on God and follow Him, you can be sure of the way to go. Those who forget about God can be blown by the wind in many different directions—they never know which way to go and cannot decide what they should do. You can be sure that when you decide to follow Jesus that He will help you be strong—but stay close to Him, study His word, and ask Him to help you!

Questions:
THINKING & REMEMBERING

Fill in the blanks or circle the letters of all that are right.

1. What did the people want to hear Jesus tell about most?
   a. how He would be a great king
   b. God's love
   c. how he could heal people

2. Where did Jesus and His disciples stop to rest after they had walked a long way?
   a. by a well   b. by a city wall   c. near a house

3. What two things did the disciples do while Jesus stayed at the well to rest?
   a. They went into the city.
   b. They talked to people in a village.
   c. They went to buy food.

4. What kind of water did Jesus tell the woman at the well that He had?
   a. pure water   b. fresh water   c. living water

5. Jesus knew everything this woman had ever done.
   true_____   false_____

6. Who did the woman know that Jesus was?
   a. She knew that He was a nice man.
   b. She knew He was the Messiah.
   c. She knew He was different than any other man she knew.

7. What changed the woman's life and made her a new person that day?
   a. She believed in Jesus.
   b. She knew something about a different kind of water.
   c. She would have everlasting life (living water).

8. What is "living water"?   *joy   Jesus   God*
   a. Living water comes from _____.
   b. Living water will give a person _____.
   c. Who is the "Living Water"?_____

BIBLE WORDS TO REMEMBER

For God so loved the world that He gave His only Son, that whoever believes in Him will have eternal life. (from John 3:16)

Bible Story: JESUS TEACHES ABOUT LOVE
from Matthew 5

One day Jesus climbed a hillside and sat down on the grass and talked about how much God loved everyone and how God wanted people to live. He said that **obeying** God makes people happy. Jesus said that no one can obey both God and **Satan**. You must choose one or the other. He said, "If you obey God, you will do what is right. But if you listen and obey Satan, you will do what is wrong."

Jesus said to **treat** others as you want them to treat you. Sometimes we want others to be kind and do things for us, but we forget to do nice things for them. He said that you should even be kind to those who hurt you. He said that you should pray for them so they will love God, too. When you are thinking about God, you will not think bad thoughts. You will tell the truth and not lie. You should not be afraid to tell others that you love and obey God.

God can help you live right and do good if you pray and ask Him. You can talk to God and tell Him how you feel. He will always listen and help you.

WORDS TO KNOW

obeying: doing what is right and what God wants
Satan: the evil one on the earth
treat: how you behave towards others
content: to be happy with what you have

THINK ABOUT

The Bible tells us that, because God made us, He knows the best way for us to be happy. "Happy" doesn't mean that you will "feel good" all the time or be laughing at everything that happens. In the Bible, "happy" means to be **content.** You will be content when you ask God to show you from His word what He wants you to do and follow in His ways—with His help.

Questions:
THINKING & REMEMBERING

Fill in the blanks or circle the letters of all that are right.

1. Where did Jesus teach the people in this story?
   a. on the hills outside the cities and towns
   b. inside the temple
   c. by the sea

2. How did Jesus say we could be happy?
   a. by being kind to others
   b. by thinking about yourself and what you want
   c. by obeying God

3. Fill in the right words, choosing from the following:

   time   wrong   other   right

   a. If you obey God, you will do what is _____.
   b. If you listen to Satan, you will do what is _____.
   c. You cannot obey God and Satan at the same _____.
   d. You must choose one or the _____.

4. How should you treat other people?
   a. just like they treat you
   b. just like you want to be treated
   c. with kindness when you feel like it

5. What did Jesus say to do if someone hurts you?
   a. hurt them back
   b. pray for them
   c. tell them they are bad

6. What will you do if you love God?
   a. tell a lie so you won't get in trouble
   b. think about doing unkind things
   c. tell the truth

BIBLE WORDS TO REMEMBER

For God so loved the world that He gave His only Son, that whoever believes in Him will have eternal life. (from John 3:16)

Bible Story: SALT AND LIGHT

from Matthew 5

Jesus used picture stories to help us understand God's love and show us how to love others. He said that if we believe in God, we are like two very important things on earth: salt and light.

If you believe in Jesus you are like the salt of the earth. Salt gives **flavor** to the food we eat. Jesus was trying to tell us how important it is for us to live for God and do the right things. We can show others God's love by what we do and say.

You are the light of the world. If a city is up on a hill, it cannot be hidden. You do not light a candle and then cover it with a **bucket**! Don't hide the light. Let your light shine so that everyone will see that you love God and are doing His work. When they see these things, they will thank God and praise Him.

You can make a **difference** in the world. You can make it better because others will want to know about Jesus when you show your light and love from God. The world would be very dark without those who love Jesus letting His light shine. Is your light shining?

WORDS TO KNOW

flavor: taste

bucket: a can or a pail

difference: to change things and make good things happen

PRAYER THOUGHT

Dear God, Help me to share your love with others and let light come into their life. Love makes everything different, and I want everyone to know about Jesus! In Jesus Name, Amen.

Questions:
THINKING & REMEMBERING

Circle the letters of all that are right.

1. How did Jesus help people understand God's love?
   a. by writing down the words
   b. through word picture stories
   c. by reading to the people

2. What two important things are those who believe in Jesus like?
   a. bread and water
   b. flour and sugar
   c. salt and light

3. What did Jesus say believers are like?
   a. the thinkers of the earth
   b. the salt of the earth
   c. builders

4. What happens when there is no salt?
   a. Food does not have flavor.
   b. We do not need salt so it doesn't matter.
   c. Things taste just the same.

5. Why were Jesus' words about salt important?
   a. We can know that what we do and say are important.
   b. It is a good comparison for the story.
   c. It will help others see that we love God.

6. What else did Jesus say about light in the world?
   a. Those who believe are a light.
   b. If a light is on a hill, it cannot be hidden.
   c. If you put a bucket over a lighted candle, the light will go out.

7. What did Jesus say you should do with the light of God's love?
   a. Don't hide it.
   b. Keep it for yourself.
   c. Let it shine!

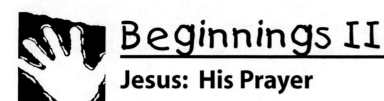

BIBLE WORDS TO REMEMBER

Ask, and it will be given to you; **seek**, and you will find;
knock, and it will be opened to you. (Matthew 7:7)

Bible Story: JESUS TEACHES ABOUT PRAYER
from Matthew 6

Jesus and His disciples were teaching and healing people all day. They were very tired at night, but Jesus did not go to sleep. First, He went off to a quiet place to be alone and pray. He knew that He needed to talk to God His Father and listen to God's voice.

The disciples couldn't understand how Jesus could stay awake and pray. But they also knew that after Jesus prayed, He had such peace. They knew that praying was very important.

One day, they asked Jesus to help them know how they should pray. Jesus told them that it is best to go to a quiet place where only God can see and hear you. You don't have to use special words for God to listen and hear your prayers. He listens to your heart. Tell Him what you are thinking. Think about God and the words you say and about what they mean.

God is your wonderful Father in heaven. He cares about you and wants you to talk to Him often. Look around you to see and feel God's love in all the wonderful things around you!

WORDS TO KNOW
(from the Bible Words to Remember—all require action!)

ask: believe and have confidence that God hears your prayer

seek: look for God to answer your prayer

knock: keep on asking so you will understand what God wants

Questions:
THINKING & REMEMBERING

Circle the letters of all that are right.

1. What does the lesson tell that Jesus and His disciples did during the day?
   a. teach
   b. heal
   c. talk to people
   d. talk to each other

2. What did Jesus want to do after such a tiring day?
   a. He wanted to go to sleep.
   b. He wanted to go to a quiet place to be alone and pray.
   c. He wanted to talk to His disciples.

3. What was Jesus doing while the disciples went to sleep?
   a. He was talking to God and listening to God's voice.
   b. He was enjoying the quiet.
   c. He went away to sleep by Himself.

4. How did the disciples know that prayer was important to Jesus?
   a. He told them they should pray and not sleep.
   b. He wanted them to stay awake while He prayed.
   c. He was peaceful after He prayed.

5. What did the disciples ask Jesus to help them learn how to do?
   a. They wanted to know how to do greater miracles.
   b. They wanted Him to teach them how to pray.
   c. They wanted to know how to stay awake longer.

6. How does God want us to pray to Him?
   a. with our hearts
   b. with our thoughts
   c. with our words
   d. all of the above, but most important is our hearts

7. How often should we pray to God?
   a. once every day
   b. a few times every week
   c. often

Bible Story: THE LORD'S PRAYER
from Matthew 6-7

Even though God knows everything you need before you ask Him, He wants you to remember that He is the One who cares most about you and He wants to listen to you. Jesus said this prayer as an **example** for us. We can use different words that are from our heart and tell God that we need Him.

Who: Our Father in heaven,   God is your Father and He is great and holy.

Honor: **Hallowed** be Your name.   May Your name be **respected.**
         Your kingdom come.   Please come soon!
         Your will be done   I **accept** what Your plan is for me.
         On earth as it is in heaven.   I accept Your plan completely.

Ask: Give us this day our daily bread.   I will be thankful for the food I need.

         And forgive us our sins,   I am sorry for the wrong things I do that hurt You.
         For we also forgive everyone   I can love and forgive with Your help.
         who does wrong and hurts us.
         And do not lead us into   Keep me from those who want me
         temptation,   to do wrong and keep me from
         But **deliver** us from the evil one. thinking bad things.

Praise: For Yours is the kingdom   I know to Whom I belong.
         and the power   I know Who is the power.
         and the glory   I know Whom I praise and worship,
         forever. Amen.   and there is no end!

WORDS TO KNOW

example: a way of showing how to do something
hallowed: honored as holy
respected: to think of in a very special way
accept: to agree with
temptation: wanting to do something that is wrong
deliver: to make free from something wrong or evil

THINK ABOUT

God is your best friend. You can talk to Him about anything you are feeling or thinking. You don't have to ever wait for a "right time" to pray. The "right time" is always—anytime or anyplace.

Questions:
THINKING & REMEMBERING

Circle the letters of all that are right.

1. How did Jesus help His followers know how to pray?
   a. He gave them lessons each morning.
   b. He gave an example of a wonderful prayer.
   c. He said God will know what is needed so not to pray.

2. What words does Jesus say that we should use when we pray?
   a. We should use exactly the words He used.
   b. We should use words from our own hearts.
   c. We should use the words from other people.

3. What should we tell God?
   a. that we need Him
   b. to give us the things we want
   c. to make us happy

4. Whom do we pray to?
   a. Jesus   b. the disciples   c. Our Father in heaven

5. What is said in the prayer about His Name?
   a. It is good.   b. It is hallowed (honored as holy).   c. It is different.

6. Whose kingdom do we want to come?
   a. Jesus' earthly kingdom   b. man's kingdom   c. God's kingdom

7. What does it say about God's will?
   a. We pray that His will be done on earth as it is in heaven.
   b. His will happens anyway.
   c. Only certain people will know His will.

8. What can we ask for every day?
   a. presents   b. bread   c. sunshine

9. Why do we need God's forgiveness?
   a. We have sinned.
   b. We want to be happy.
   c. We want to be free.

10. What does the prayer say belongs only to God?
    a. the kingdom   b. earth   c. power   d. glory

BIBLE WORDS TO REMEMBER

Ask, and it will be given to you; seek, and you will find; knock, and it will be opened to you. (Matthew 7:7)

Bible Story: THE WISE AND FOOLISH

from Matthew 7; Luke 6

One day Jesus told a story, called a parable, about two men. One of the men was wise. He wanted to build a good house so he looked until he found some ground that was on solid rock. He knew that it would be strong and safe when the winds and rain came.

The other man built his house on the sand. He was lazy and in a hurry. He had heard about houses on a solid foundation would be safe when the winds and rain came, but he didn't listen. He was very foolish.

Then the sky grew very dark. The men were inside their houses. It began to rain. It rained and rained. The wind was blowing hard. The man who built his house on the rock was safe, but the foolish man who built his house on the sand was washed away with the water. His house fell down.

Jesus told this story to teach us a lesson. He wants us to be careful and wise. We have the words that God gave in the Bible. We can know what is wise and what is foolish. We must choose.

THINK ABOUT

God gives everyone two ways to go. But there is only one right way. When you love God, you are choosing to be different from others who do not choose God's way. You do what is right instead of doing things that hurt God and other people He loves. God will show you what is wise and what is foolish when you ask Him. He loves you very much!

Questions:
THINKING & REMEMBERING

Fill in the blanks or circle the letters of all that are right.

1. What kind of a story did Jesus tell?
   a. a fairy tale   b. a parable   c. a real life story

2. Why is this kind of story different from other pretend stories?
   a. It teaches a lesson.
   b. It is a true story.
   c. It is interesting to listen to.

3. The wise man built his house on solid rock ground.
   true_____   false_____

4. Why did he choose to build there?
   a. It was beautiful.
   b. It was close to the city.
   c. It would be strong.

5. What happened when the wind and rain came down on the wise man's house?
   a. It fell down.   b. It was damaged.   c. It was safe.

6. Sand is a good place to build a house.   true_____   false_____

7. What happened to the house that was built on sand when the rain came?
   a. It was damaged.   b. It was safe.   c. It was washed away.

8. Jesus told this story (parable) to teach us a _____.
   He wants us to be careful and _____.

9. How can you know what the wise thing to do is?
   a. from your friends   b. from story books   c. from the Bible

10. Who chooses what you will do?
    a. God   b. You choose.   c. other people you know

PRAYER THOUGHT

Dear God, Thank You for sending Jesus to teach me the right way. Help me to choose to listen to Your words, and to do what is wise. In Jesus Name, Amen.

Bible Story: JESUS AND THE CAPTAIN
from Luke 7

There was a man in the city where Jesus was teaching who was a **captain** in the Roman Army. One of his servants was very sick. The captain was kind and cared about his servant and wanted to do something to help him get better, but the doctors did not know how to make him well.

When the captain heard about Jesus, he sent Him a message and asked Him to please come to his house and heal his servant. Even though the captain did not know all about God's love, he did believe that Jesus had the power to do whatever He **commanded**.

Jesus said, "I will come." As Jesus came closer, another message came from the captain. "Lord, do not come to my house. I am **unworthy** for you to come. But if you just stop where You are and say that my servant is well, it will happen as You speak."

Jesus was so surprised! He had never seen anyone with this much faith in believing what God could do. The servant was healed at that exact moment. Jesus did not need to touch the man. He did not need to continue the journey to the house. Jesus can do miracles!

WORDS TO KNOW

captain: someone who gives orders and is in charge

command: to tell others what to do

unworthy: not deserving or not good enough

THINK ABOUT

Sometimes we think that God must love people who are great and strong more than He loves those who are small and weak. Jesus tried to make us understand that each one is important to God. Whenever you start feeling sorry for yourself, STOP! Remember how important you are to God. But remember that God wants to be important to YOU. Remember to keep God first and the most important in your life!

Questions:
THINKING & REMEMBERING

Fill in the blanks or circle the letters of all that are right.

1. Who in the story was very sick?
   a. the captain   b. the captain's servant   c. one of the soldiers

2. What did the captain do when the he heard about Jesus?
   a. He went to see Him.
   b. He took his servant to Jesus.
   c. He sent Jesus a message.

3. What did he ask Jesus to do?
   a. He asked Jesus to come to his house to heal his servant.
   b. He asked Jesus to send a disciple to heal his servant.
   c. He asked Jesus to tell him what was wrong with the servant.

4. The captain believed that Jesus had the power to heal his servant.
   true_____   false_____

5. What happened as Jesus was on His way to the captain's house?
   a. There was a message that the servant was already well.
   b. There was a message that the captain believed Jesus could heal the servant by saying the words.
   c. There was a message that the captain decided to try another doctor.

6. Did the captain feel worthy to have Jesus come to his house?
   a. Yes, he was a very important person in the army.
   b. No, he thought he was undeserving to have Jesus come.

7. Jesus healed the servant without going to the captain's house.
   true_____   false_____

8. What is it called when Jesus does something no one else can do?
   a. an amazing work   b. a miracle   c. extraordinary

9. Say the Bible Words. Do you have them in your memory? If you do, no one can take those words from you. They are hidden in your heart. What do the words mean to you?_____

_____

BIBLE WORDS TO REMEMBER

Ask, and it will be given to you; seek, and you will find;
knock, and it will be opened to you. (Matthew 7:7)

Bible Story: LORD, SAVE US!
from Matthew 8; Mark 4

One day, after Jesus had been teaching by the lake, He was very tired. He and the disciples decided to go to the other side of the lake. Peter and the other disciples began rowing the boat. Jesus went to the back of the boat and lay down on a pillow. Soon He was fast asleep.

The disciples looked up in the sky and saw black clouds. The wind started blowing very hard! The disciples were so frightened. They were afraid that the big waves would make their boat tip over! They wondered why Jesus did not wake up, but Jesus stayed asleep! The disciples called to Him, "Jesus, wake up! Don't you care that we are all going to drown?"

Jesus opened His eyes. He saw the huge waves splashing up into the boat. He saw how frightened His disciples were. Jesus said, "Why are you afraid?" Jesus stood up in the boat and stretched His hands out over the angry waves. He said these words: "Peace, be still!"

At that very moment the wind stopped blowing. The waves stopped splashing. Everything was very quiet. The disciples looked at each other. They said, "Jesus is very great! Even the wind and sea obey Him!"

THINK ABOUT

There are times when a storm comes and there is such a lot of noise!
There is thunder and lightening and the whole sky seems angry. When
that happens, you sometimes feel even smaller than ever. But you do not
need to be afraid. When you love Jesus, you know He is there with you.

Questions:
THINKING & REMEMBERING

Circle the letters of all that are right.

1. What had Jesus been doing one day?
   a. teaching people by the lake
   b. fishing with His disciples
   c. praying on the hillside

2. Where did Jesus and His disciples decide to go?
   a. further down the seashore
   b. to a house close to the lake
   c. to the other side of the lake

3. What happened next on the boat?
   a. The disciples began rowing the boat.
   b. They drifted in the water to make it peaceful for Jesus.
   c. Jesus went to the back of the boat and lay down on a pillow and went to sleep.

4. Why were the disciples frightened?
   a. The wind started blowing very hard.
   b. The waves were tipping the boat and water was getting in.
   c. They thought they were going to drown.

5. When the disciples woke Jesus up what did He say to them?
   a. "Why are you afraid?"
   b. "Peace be still!"
   c. "Start rowing harder."

6. What did Jesus do then? (Put a number beside what happened in 1-2-3 order.)
   a. _____ He said, "Peace be still!"
   b. _____ He looked at the waves splashing into the boat.
   c. _____ He stretched out His hands over the angry waves.

7. When Jesus said the words, what happened?
   a. The wind stopped blowing.
   b. The waves stopped splashing.
   c. Everything was quiet.

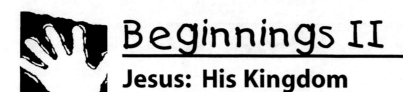

Jesus: His Kingdom

BIBLE WORDS TO REMEMBER

Let us not love in word or in tongue, but in deed and in truth.
Be doers of the word, and not hearers only.
(from 1 John 3:18 and James 1:22)

Bible Story: PLANTING SEEDS

from Mark 4

Jesus told stories called parables to help people remember His teaching. One day He told a parable about a farmer who planted seeds in his fields. The farmer wanted each seed to fall into good earth so it would grow and be a strong plant.

Some of the seed fell on the path where the ground was hard and dry. The birds flew down and ate the seed.

Other seed fell on the soil that was not very deep and was rocky. The **roots** could not go deep into the earth, and soon the plant **withered** up and died with the hot sun.

Some seed came down between weeds and thorns. These plants were soon **smothered** by the bad plants and they died.

The seed that fell on wonderful rich brown soil grew strong and healthy plants. Their roots went deep into the ground. The rain fell and watered the plants until they reached up into the sky toward the sun. These plants were good for food and **produced** even more seed for the farmer to use and plant.

Try to discover on your own what this story means. Think about the four different places the seed fell and what happened to each.

WORDS TO KNOW

roots:	the part of the plant that grows in the earth or soil
withered:	dried up
smothered:	to choke out
produced:	to make more of something

Questions:
THINKING & REMEMBERING

Fill in the blanks or circle the letters of all that are right.

1. Why did Jesus tell stories called parables?
   a. He liked to tell stories.
   b. He wanted people to remember His teaching.
   c. Parables are stories that teach a lesson.

2. The farmer planned for all the seeds to be planted in good ground.
   true_____   false_____

3. In which places did the seed fall? Write the words in the spaces.
   path   rocky   weeds and thorns   good soil
   a. hard and dry ground _____
   b. wonderful rich brown soil _____
   c. soil that is not very deep _____
   d. crowded place to be smothered _____

4. What happened to the seed that fell on the path?
   a. The wind blew it away.
   b. It just disappeared.
   c. The birds ate it.

5. What happened to the seed that fell in the rocky places?
   a. It withered and died.
   b. It grew strong.
   c. The insects ate it.

6. What happened to the seed that fell into the weeds?
   a. It grew up in a tough place.
   b. It was smothered and died.
   c. It grew crooked instead of straight and tall.

7. What happened to the seed that was planted in the good soil?
   a. The worms got into it.
   b. It grew and was strong and healthy.
   c. More plants grew from these seeds.

8. Compare people and the kinds of soil in this parable. Think about this story and be able to tell what you think it means. Jesus explains the story in our next lesson.

143

Bible Story: HOW ARE PEOPLE LIKE SEEDS?
from Mark 4

The disciples tried to understand the story of the farmer planting his seeds. They asked Jesus to explain it so they could know what they should learn from the parable.

Jesus said that the farmer is like the person who tells many people what God's Word says. The seed is like the message of God's love. The ground is like the people who hear the message.

Some people hear the message, but they forget very quickly—just like the hard ground on the path where the birds ate the seed.

There are people who are just like the seed that fell in the rocky places. They are excited at first and start to grow, but when they have any problems they give up and turn away from God's Word.

The seed that falls in the weeds and gets smothered is like the people who don't keep their eyes on Jesus and think only of themselves. Then they forget all about God.

The seeds that are planted in the good ground are like people who listen with their hearts and minds. They obey God's Word, and even when things are difficult, they remember that God loves them and will help them. They grow stronger and tell others about God's love and other people believe, too!

THINK ABOUT

Understanding the parables Jesus told is like a puzzle at first. But Jesus said that if we really listen with our ears and then think about it, we will understand with our hearts. You have to want to know! Sometimes we just want everything to be easy. We want someone to explain things quickly without trying to figure it out and think for ourselves. Jesus wants people to use the wonderful minds that God gave to discover God's message.

Questions:
THINKING & REMEMBERING

Fill in the blanks or circle the letters of all that are right.

1. How do we know that the disciples did not understand the parable?
   a. They asked each other what it meant.
   b. They asked Jesus to tell them what it meant.
   c. They asked some other teachers to explain it.

2. Who is the farmer like?
   a. the person who tells a few people about God
   b. the person who keeps the message of God just for family
   c. the person who tells many people what God's Word says

3. What is the seed like?
   a. a lot of words that have little meaning
   b. the message of God's love
   c. sayings of some great people

4. What is the ground like?
   a. people who do not listen to words
   b. people who don't want to hear messages
   c. people who hear the message

5. Into how many different kinds of places did the seed fall?
   a. one　　b. five　　c. four

6. Matching: Find the right answer below and write the number word. (There are more choices than there are matches for!)
   a. _____ What kind of people are the "path" people?
   b. _____ What kind of people are the "rocky" people?
   c. _____ What kind of people are the "weed" people?
   d. _____ What kind of people are the "good ground"?

   one) those who hear and won't accept the message of God's love
   two) those who pretend they are listening
   three) those who believe at first, but think more about themselves than God; they forget about God
   four) those who look bored when they hear God's message
   five) those who hear but give up when they have problems
   six) those who listen and obey God and are strong

BIBLE WORDS TO REMEMBER

Let us not love in word or in tongue, but in deed and in truth.
Be doers of the word, and not hearers only.
(from 1 John 3:18 and James 1:22)

Bible Story: A VERY SMALL SEED
from Matthew 13, 17

Jesus told a story about a mustard seed. It is the tiniest seed there is, but when it is planted and grows, it becomes a tree.

A farmer carefully planted a mustard seed. He made sure the ground was just right. He used a gentle spray of water and waited for God's sun to help the plant grow.

Soon a wonderful thing happened! Leaves were coming up out of the earth. They were not as tiny as the seed. They were beautiful leaves. The branches grew and became strong and tall. When it was fully grown, the birds saw the tree and came to make a nest there for their baby birds. Other birds lived under the tree and it shaded them from the hot sun.

Jesus said that the mustard seed is like His words of love. Every time someone believes His word, they will grow strong and will help others to know God's love, too. This builds God's great kingdom.

Jesus told His disciples that if they had faith as small as a mustard seed, they could move mountains from one place to another and that nothing would be impossible for them to do with God's power.

THINK ABOUT

Do you think a small seed is just as important as a large seed? Do you think a child is just as important as a grown person? God thinks so! Everything and everyone on earth has an important part in the plan of God.

Questions:
THINKING & REMEMBERING

Fill in the blanks or circle the letters of all that are right.

1. What is the name of the tiniest seed?
   a. apple seed   b. grape seed   c. mustard seed

2. The farmer wanted to plant this seed in a special place.
   true_____ false_____

3. What did he do after the seed was in the ground?
   a. He let the sun take care of it.
   b. He watered it with a gentle spray.
   c. He covered it and forgot where he planted it.

4. What kind of leaves grew from this tiny seed?
   a. beautiful   b. kind of small   c. just a few were on the branches

5. What were the branches like?
   a. thin   b. strong   c. weak

6. What happened when it was fully grown?
   a. It was a pretty bush.
   b. It was a ground bush.
   c. It was a tree that birds made their nest in and used for shade.

7. How did Jesus explain this parable?
   The mustard seed is like His _____ of _____.

8. What did Jesus say about faith and the mustard seed?
   a. It is a good thing to have faith when you can.
   b. A small faith can grow to do great things.
   c. It doesn't matter if you have faith.

9. Everything is possible to do with faith in God's power.
   true_____ false_____

PRAYER THOUGHT

Dear God, I want to share Your love with everyone. Help me remember how important little acts of kindness are in showing Your love. In Jesus Name, Amen.

BIBLE WORDS TO REMEMBER

Let us not love in word or in tongue, but in deed and in truth.
Be doers of the word, and not hearers only.
(from 1 John 3:18 and James 1:22)

Bible Story: A LITTLE GIRL LIVES AGAIN!
from Mark 5

A young girl who was loved very much by her family was sick and could not get out of bed and play or walk. The doctor did not know what to do to make her better.

Then her father remembered that Jesus could make sick people well. The father ran to find Jesus. He hurried and squeezed through all the people around Jesus. He fell down at Jesus' feet and said, "Oh, Jesus, my daughter is so sick she will die if You don't come to make her well!" Jesus said, "I will come to your house."

Because there were so many people, they could not hurry! Before they could get to the man's house, a servant met them and said, "It is too late. Your daughter has died." The father was so sad. Jesus said, "Don't be afraid. Trust me and I will help you."

They went to where the young girl lay in her bed. Jesus took her by the hand and said, "Arise!" She got up from her bed. She was well! The father and mother loved and believed in Jesus. They knew that only Jesus could do this miracle because He is the Son of God.

THINK ABOUT

Jesus is called the "Great Physician," and He is the best doctor there can ever be. That's because He is God. He has power over sickness and death. But Jesus loves doctors and nurses who want to help people get better. You can ask Jesus to be with them so that they will know just what to do.

PRAYER THOUGHT

Dear God, Thank You for taking care of me when I'm sick. Help me always to trust You. In Jesus Name, Amen.

Questions:
THINKING & REMEMBERING

Fill in the blanks or circle the letters of all that are right.

1. Why couldn't the young girl in the story get out of her bed?
   a. She was too tired.
   b. She was very sick.
   c. She didn't like to play outside.

2. The doctor knew how to help her get better.　　true_____　　false_____

3. The father believed that Jesus could help his daughter get well.
   true_____　　false_____

4. What did the father say would happen if Jesus couldn't come to his house?
   a. He would get another doctor.
   b. His daughter would die.
   c. The mother would be upset.

5. Jesus said He would come to the house of the man's daughter.
   true_____　　false_____

6. What happened before Jesus could get to the house?
   a. The young girl died.
   b. The young girl went out to play.
   c. She started getting better.

7. What did Jesus tell the father?
   "Don't be _____. Trust Me."

8. What happened when Jesus said, "Arise!"
   a. She talked to everyone.
   b. She started crying.
   c. She got up from her bed.

9. Why could Jesus make the young girl alive again?
   a. He knew the words to say.
   b. He is the Son of God.
   c. He told the doctor what to do.

BIBLE WORDS TO REMEMBER

Let us not love in word or in tongue, but in deed and in truth.
Be doers of the word, and not hearers only.
(from 1 John 3:18 and James 1:22)

Bible Story: NO ORDINARY MAN
from Mark 6; Luke 4

The people in Nazareth knew Jesus when He was growing up in an ordinary family with ordinary friends. They remembered that He had been obedient to His parents and kind to others. He had been a very good student at school. Still, He looked just like any of the other people who lived and worked in Nazareth. How could He have special power from God?

But everyone was talking about this man Jesus who was doing miracles and healing sick people. People who had been crippled were walking. People who had been blind could see clearly. There were people who had been deaf, but now they could hear.

All of the people who were healed from sickness and disease knew that Jesus had God's power. No one else could do the things He did. They believed that Jesus was the One that God had sent to earth. Jesus showed them by His love and kindness that God loved them and had not forgotten His people. Others did not believe. They were like the ones that Jesus had told about in the parable of the seeds. They heard with their ears, but not with their hearts. They rejected Jesus.

THINK ABOUT

Would you know who Jesus was if He came to your house? Jesus wants you to love all people everywhere. He said that when you do, you are really loving Him. Don't wait and look for someone special or great before you give away the love Jesus gives to you. He will always have more love to give!

Bible Words: What do they mean? To "not love in word or in tongue, but in deed and in truth" means that we should not just talk about love, we should show it by what we do.

Questions:
Thinking & Remembering

Fill in the blanks or circle the letters of all that are right.

1. Why did the people in Nazareth doubt that Jesus could have the power of God?
   a. They thought He was ordinary.
   b. They knew his family and friends.
   c. He did the things everyone else did in Nazareth.
   d. all of the above

2. What were some of the things they remembered about Jesus while He was growing up?
   a. He was obedient to His parents.
   b. He was a good student.
   c. He got in trouble sometimes.

3. What were people everywhere talking about that Jesus did?
   a. He did miracles.
   b. He was friends with fishermen.
   c. He traveled a lot of places.

4. Who were some of the people He helped?
   a. people who would not listen
   b. sick people
   c. crippled people
   d. blind people
   e. deaf people

5. The people He healed from sickness and disease knew that Jesus had God's power.   true_____   false_____

6. Why were they sure that He was from God?
   a. No one else could do the things He did.
   b. He told them about God's rules.
   c. He showed them love and kindness.

7. Who were the people like from the parable of the seeds who did not believe?
   a. like the seed that fell in between the weeds and thorns
   b. like the seed that fell on hard ground and was eaten by the birds
   c. like the seed that fell on good ground
   d. like the seed that fell in rocky ground

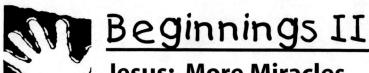

BIBLE WORDS TO REMEMBER

Jesus said: "I am the way, the truth, and the life. No one comes to the Father except through Me." (from John 14:6)

Bible Story: ONE LUNCH— 5000 HUNGRY PEOPLE
from John 6; Matthew 14

There were more than 5,000 people on the hillside listening to Jesus tell about God's love. The people listened for a long time, and they were getting hungry. The disciples said, "Let's send the people home so they can get food." Jesus said, "They do not need to go away. Give them something to eat." One of the disciples said, "We cannot buy food for all these people—there are too many!"

A little boy heard the disciples talking to Jesus. He had five small loaves of bread and two little fish in his basket. "I want to share my lunch with Jesus," he said. Jesus prayed and thanked God for the food. Then He broke the loaves and fish into pieces. He told his disciples to give everyone some food. They were so surprised! There was more and more food until everyone had enough to eat—and when everyone was full, there were twelve baskets left over!

When the people saw that Jesus had done another miracle they said, "This must be the One whom God promised to send to the world."

The little boy was so excited! He could hardly wait to get home to tell his mother about the wonderful thing Jesus did!

THINK ABOUT

God will always take care of what you need. He wants you to love Him and trust Him. He even knows when you are hungry! Remember how much He loves you and think about how 5,000 people had food to eat one day because Jesus cared that they were hungry. He did more that day than give them food to stop their stomachs from growling—He gave them a gift of love to show how much God cared for them.

Questions:
THINKING & REMEMBERING

Fill in the blanks or circle the letters of all that are right.

1. Where were the people listening to Jesus tell about God?
   a. at the synagogue
   b. on a hillside
   c. in the town of Nazareth

2. How many people came to hear about God's love?
   a. 500   b. 300   c. more than 5,000

True or False (Write T or F in the space.)

3. _____ The people brought picnic baskets with food.

4. _____ The disciples wanted to send the people home to eat.

5. _____ Jesus told the disciples to give the people something to eat.

6. _____ The disciples said they would go buy some food.

7. Who was the only one in the crowd with some food?
   a. a little boy
   b. a group from Nazareth
   c. a family that remembered to bring some food

8. How much food was brought?
   a. two loaves of bread and five small fish
   b. five small loaves of bread and two fish
   c. one sandwich with chips

9. How could Jesus feed so many people with so little food?
   a. He is the Son of God.
   b. He made the people forget they were hungry by telling stories.
   c. He had extra food that the disciples had brought.

10. How many baskets of food were left after everyone had enough to eat?
    a. seven   b. twelve   c. five

11. The people who saw this miracle believed that Jesus was the One sent from God.   true_____   false_____

Bible Story: JESUS WALKS ON WATER
from Matthew 14

Jesus wanted to be alone and talk with God His Father. The disciples went across the lake and waited in the boat for Jesus. But when it got dark, Jesus still had not come.

A great wind began to blow and carry them out further into the lake—away from Jesus! Jesus looked up and saw the storm. He started walking toward the boat.

The disciples saw the form of a man walking to them on top of the water. They thought it must be a **ghost**! They were very frightened. Then Jesus' voice called to them and said, "Do not be afraid. It is I."

Peter said, "Jesus, is it really You? Let me walk on the water to You!" Jesus said, "Come." Peter got out of the boat and began to walk toward Jesus. But then He took His eyes off Jesus and began to sink into the water. "Help me, Lord!" he cried.

Jesus put out His hand and lifted Peter up on top of the water. "Why did you **doubt**, Peter? Where is your faith?" When they came to the boat and got inside, the wind stopped. The disciples were **amazed** and worshiped Jesus. They said, "It is true! You are the Son of God."

WORDS TO KNOW

ghost: a form of a person that is no longer alive

doubt: to act unsure about something

amazed: filled with wonder and surprise

THINK ABOUT

When Jesus says you can do something, you can do it—with His help! You just need to keep your eyes on Jesus and not be afraid. Just remember Jesus will always be there beside you, helping you and loving you when you believe and trust in Him—He will give you all the confidence you need.

 # Questions:
THINKING & REMEMBERING

Circle the letters of all that are right.

1. Where was Jesus when the disciples were out on the lake?
   a. He was visiting some other friends.
   b. He was praying to God His Father.
   c. He was sitting on the seashore.

2. What happened while the disciples were waiting for Jesus?
   a. The wind started blowing and took them out further into the lake.
   b. There were some gentle waves.
   c. The disciples got impatient.

3. What did Jesus do when He saw the storm?
   a. He called to them to come for Him.
   b. He waited for the storm to be over.
   c. He walked toward the boat on top of the water.

4. What did the disciples think when they saw something coming to them?
   a. It was a ghost.
   b. It might be an unusual kind of fish on top of the water.
   c. They should row the boat away from what was coming toward them.

5. What did Jesus say to them?
   a. "Come and get me because I am getting wet."
   b. "Don't be afraid; it is I."
   c. "Don't worry, I'll come to you later."

6. What did Peter want to do?
   a. Peter wanted to get Jesus into the boat.
   b. Peter wanted to talk to the other disciples about what to do.
   c. Peter wanted to walk out to Jesus on the water.

7. Why did Peter start to sink?
   a. There was a big wave.
   b. He looked down on the water.
   c. He took His eyes from Jesus.

BIBLE WORDS TO REMEMBER

Jesus said: "I am the way, the truth, and the life. No one comes to the Father except through Me." (from John 14:6)

Bible Story: A BLIND MAN SEES
from Mark 10; Luke 18

Many people heard about the wonderful things that Jesus did. A father told the mother, she told her neighbor, the neighbor told their friends, and soon many more people wanted to go where Jesus was!

One day Jesus saw a man who was blind. His name was Bartimaeus. He could not see the beautiful blue sky or the flowers or trees. He could not see his mother or father or friends. He heard about Jesus making blind people see, and even though he could not see Jesus, he wanted Jesus to see him!

Jesus came to where Bartimaeus was sitting. Bartimaeus cried out, "Son of David, have mercy on me!" Jesus told him to come near. Then He asked him, "What do you want Me to do for you?"

Bartimeaeus said, "Lord, that I may receive my sight." Jesus loved him and wanted him to see. Jesus said, "Receive your sight; your faith has made you well." And right then Bartimeaus could see everything!

He saw how beautiful the world was—and he could see people. But most of all, he was happy to see Jesus' smiling face. He said, "Thank You, Jesus, for making me see."

PRAYER THOUGHT

Thank You, Dear God, for giving me eyes to see Your wonderful world. Help me to remember to pray for friends and people who cannot see. Let me tell them how much You love them by the many other gifts that You give them. In heaven it will be perfect and everyone will see Your face! In Jesus Name, Amen.

Questions:
THINKING & REMEMBERING

Fill in the blanks or circle the letters of all that are right.

1. How did people find out about what Jesus did?
   a. They read the newspaper.
   b. Everyone would tell someone else.
   c. They listened to the news.

2. Who did Jesus see one day?
   a. a man named Bartimaeus
   b. a crowd of people
   c. a crippled man

3. Why couldn't the man see the face of Jesus?
   a. There were too many people in front of him.
   b. He was blind.
   c. Jesus was standing behind a tree.

4. How did Bartimaeus get Jesus' attention?
   a. He cried out, "Son of David, have mercy on me!"
   b. He held out his hand to Jesus.
   c. He asked someone to tell Jesus he was there.

5. What did he ask Jesus to do?
   a. make him see
   b. help him hear
   c. help him talk

6. What could Bartimaeus do after Jesus said, "Your faith has made you well"?
   a. He could see God's beautiful world.
   b. He could see people.
   c. He could see Jesus' smiling face.

7. Write the Bible Words from John 14:6.

   _____

   _____

   _____

   _____

Bible Story: NOT ALL PEOPLE WILL BELIEVE
from the Gospels

All the **wonders** and miracles that Jesus did made many people happy. They knew that Jesus was not an ordinary man. But not everyone loved Jesus. Some people did not believe that He could be the Son of God. They didn't want the people to follow Jesus and listen to His words.

The **religious teachers** did not talk about love. They only talked about the law. They said that people must do certain things if they wanted God to listen to them pray. Jesus said these teachers were **hypocrites**. They acted like they were doing everything to please God, but they were only thinking about themselves. They thought they were better than anyone else!

So there were those who tried to hurt Jesus. They told Him to stop talking. They tried to tell everyone that He was bad because He ate dinner with people who sinned. Soon they started saying, "We must kill Jesus. He must die for saying that He is the Son of God."

Jesus was sad that these men did not understand God's love. He prayed for them and loved them even though they hated Him. That is the way Jesus is. He loves everyone!

WORDS TO KNOW

wonders: things that can amaze you because they are so wonderful

religious teachers: those who study and learn about God so they can teach others

hypocrites: people who only pretend that they are good

THINK ABOUT

Don't you wish that everyone could know how much Jesus loves them? But what is very sad is that some hear the words about God's love, and they don't care that God loves them. They think that they can be good and have the things God gives without believing in Him. That makes God sad, too. He loves people even when they don't love Him.

Questions:
THINKING & REMEMBERING

Fill in the blanks or circle the letters of all that are right.

1. Many people were happy because Jesus did _____ and
   _____.

2. Jesus was not an _____ man.

3. Not everyone loved Jesus because:
   a. They did not believe that He could be the Son of God.
   b. They didn't like His disciples.
   c. They did not want people to follow Him and listen to His words.

4. What did the religious teachers tell the people?
   a. They were not loved by God unless they followed the law.
   b. God would not listen to their prayers if they didn't do what they said.
   c. Jesus was a good teacher.

5. What did Jesus say about these teachers?
   a. They were hypocrites.
   b. They acted like they were pleasing God.
   c. They thought only of themselves.
   d. They thought they were better than other people.
   e. all of the answers above

6. What did these men who were pretending to love God say must happen to Jesus?
   a. He must stop talking.
   b. He must die.
   c. He must be taken out of the country.

7. How did Jesus respond to those who said bad things about Him?
   a. He said God wouldn't love them.
   b. He told His disciples to fight with them.
   c. He still loved them.

8. Jesus _____ for those who hated Him.

9. Jesus said: "I am the _____, the _____, and the _____."

BIBLE WORDS TO REMEMBER

Jesus said: "I am the way, the truth, and the life. No one comes to the Father except through Me." (from John 14:6)

Bible Story: PETER TELLS JESUS WHAT HE BELIEVES
from Matthew 16

Jesus did many wonderful things that made people stop and say, "Jesus does things no one else can do!" Some people asked, "How can Jesus do these things? Who is Jesus?"

One day Jesus asked His disciples, "Who do you think I am?" Peter said, "You are Christ, the Son of the living God." Peter not only saw the things Jesus did, He listened as Jesus talked about God.

When Jesus heard His disciples say that they knew who He was, He was happy. He knows that each child and each grown person can choose to believe. Some will believe that He is the Son of God. Others will choose not to believe. That will make Him very sad. But He will not force anyone to love Him.

If we believe what the Bible tells us about Jesus, we will know, just as the disciples knew, that Jesus is the Son of God.

We can know who Jesus is.
We can know why Jesus came to earth—He loves us!
We can know how Jesus came to earth.
We can know how Jesus wants us to live and have purpose in our lives.
And there is so much more!

THINK ABOUT

Some things you cannot be sure about. You cannot be sure that someone you like will be your friend next year. You cannot be sure that there will be red popsicles at the store. But you can be sure about who Jesus is and that God loves you. We never have to wonder about that—the Bible tells us and we can know for sure!

Questions:
THINKING & REMEMBERING

Fill in the blanks or circle the letters of all that are right.

1. What questions did people ask about Jesus?
   a. How can Jesus do miracles?
   b. Who is Jesus?
   c. Why is Jesus so ordinary?

2. What question did Jesus ask His disciples one day?
   a. What are people saying about Me?
   b. Do people believe that God sent Me?
   c. Who do you think I am?

3. What answer did Peter give?
   a. You are a man who can do miracles.
   b. You are Christ, the Son of the living God.
   c. You are a good teacher.

4. What two things had Peter experienced with Jesus?
   a. He saw the miracles that Jesus did.
   b. He saw that Jesus prayed to His Father if He wasn't too busy or tired.
   c. He heard Jesus tell about God.

5. Which three things listed can we know about Jesus from the Bible.
   a. Jesus wants us to be good by obeying the law.
   b. We can know how Jesus came to earth and why.
   c. We can know that Jesus loves us and that we are special to Him.
   d. We will live in heaven with Him if we do good things for others.
   e. We can know how He wants us to live and have purpose in our lives.

6. Who is Jesus?
   a. He is a wonderful person.
   b. He is a person who likes most people.
   c. He is the Son of God.

7. What makes Jesus happy?
   a. when people try to be good on their own
   b. when people choose to believe in Him
   c. when everybody tries to get along and not fight

8. Everybody will choose to believe in Jesus sometime. true_____ false_____

161

Beginnings II

Jesus: Those Who Love Him

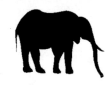

BIBLE WORDS TO REMEMBER

Jesus said: "You did not choose Me, but I chose you."
We love Him because He first loved us. (John 15:16; 1 John 4:19)

Bible Story: THE KINGDOM OF GOD
from Matthew 16

The people saw all the wonderful things Jesus did and believed that He was from God. They wanted Jesus to be a king on earth and get rid of the Roman king. But Jesus did not come to take power over the Romans. Jesus came to show God's love on earth. He was going to die for the sins of the world. He would return to heaven when His work on earth was finished.

Jesus tried to explain His message of love. Jesus said to His disciples, "I am going to suffer. Things are going to be very difficult. The religious leaders are going to turn against Me. They are trying to think of a way to kill Me. The people will listen to them and I will die, but I will be alive again after three days."

Peter was very upset. "Don't say things like that, Jesus! We want You to stay with us and be our king on earth. We don't want You to suffer and die!"

Jesus said to Peter, "I will do what God has planned for Me to do."

Jesus is the King of heaven. He wants us to live there with Him forever.

THINK ABOUT

Jesus is our king! He is not the kind of king that sits on a throne or wears a gold crown. He is the king of heaven who loves us and wants us to live with Him there. He says we are precious to Him! No earthly king can love like that. There is only one God, one king who can love perfectly.

 # Questions:
THINKING & REMEMBERING

Circle the letters of all that are right.

1. Why did some of the people want Jesus to be their king?
   a. He did wonderful things.
   b. They believed that He was from God.
   c. They wanted to get rid of the Roman king.

2. What did Jesus come to earth to do?
   a. He came to take power over the Romans.
   b. He came to show God's love on earth.
   c. He came to die for the sins of the world.

3. What did Jesus try to make His disciples understand?
   a. Things were going to be very difficult.
   b. He was going to suffer.
   c. The people were going to listen to those who hated Jesus, and He was going to die.

4. What did Jesus tell His disciples about His death?
   a. It was just pretend.
   b. He would be alive again after three days.
   c. It would not hurt.

5. Why was Peter upset?
   a. He wanted Jesus to be a king on earth.
   b. He thought he had a better plan.
   c. He didn't want Jesus to suffer.

6. What did Jesus tell Peter?
   a. He might change His mind.
   b. He would follow God's plan.
   c. Peter should think of another way.

7. What do we each need to do to be sure we will be in heaven with Him?
   a. We need to believe in Him.
   b. We need to do good things.

BIBLE WORDS TO REMEMBER

Jesus said: "You did not choose Me, but I chose you."
We love Him because He first loved us. (John 15:16; 1 John 4:19)

Bible Story: FOLLOWING JESUS

from Luke 9

Jesus did not promise that it would be easy to **follow** Him. He knew that other people would laugh and make fun of those who loved Him and wanted to be in His **kingdom**.

Jesus said to His disciples and followers, "If you choose to follow Me, there are things you will have to give up. It will sometimes be difficult to do what God wants you to do. If you want to believe in Me, don't look back. Think about what is really important and do God's work of telling others about His kingdom."

"You will have to say no to what you want and decide that loving Me is **worth** it. If you try to keep everything you have here on earth, in the end you will loose it all. You must be ready to give up everything in this world. Loving God must be the most important thing in your life."

"It might seem to you and others that you are throwing your whole life away! But if you believe in Me, you will really be keeping the only thing that really matters. You will be keeping the life that will last forever—not just life on this earth."

WORDS TO KNOW

follow: to obey, observe, and imitate

kingdom: God's place in heaven

worth: deciding the value of something

PRAYER THOUGHT

Jesus, Help me stay very close to You. Help me to choose to love You and not make the things I can have on earth more important than You. Help me to remember that what really matters is coming into Your kingdom. In Jesus Name, Amen.

Questions:
THINKING & REMEMBERING

Circle the letters of all that are right.

1. What did Jesus say about following Him?
    a. It would not always be easy.
    b. Sometimes you would like it.
    c. It would be hard all of the time.

2. What does the lesson tell that some people will do when you say you love Jesus?
    a. They will listen politely.
    b. They will laugh and make fun of you.
    c. They will tell you Jesus is not real.

3. What did Jesus say you will have to do to follow Him?
    a. follow God's rules
    b. be unkind to people who don't listen
    c. give up some things

4. When you have decided to follow Jesus, what must you ***not*** do?
    a. care about others
    b. look back
    c. think about what is important

5. What did Jesus say about trying to keep everything?
    a. It's OK to keep some things.
    b. Just keep enough things so you look rich to other people.
    c. In the end you will lose it.

6. What is the most important thing to keep?
    a. to keep Jesus the most important in your life
    b. to keep close to Jesus
    c. to keep everything you want to have

7. If we follow Jesus what will we have in the end?
    a. We will have lots of nice things that we wanted on earth.
    b. Everyone will like us again.
    c. We will have life in heaven that will last forever.

Bible Story: JESUS IN HIS BRIGHTNESS
from Matthew 17

The Bible tells that Jesus lived in heaven before He came to earth. When Jesus came to earth, He came as a man and left His brightness in heaven. He did show us some of His light so that we could believe in Him, but He is even brighter and more brilliant than any light we can look at on earth.

Jesus wanted to show His disciples His glory and heavenly brightness. One day He took three of His disciples, Peter, James and John, up on a high mountain. Jesus' face became just like the sun. It was shining! And His clothes were shining, too! They tried to look at Him, but He was so bright they had to cover their eyes. They had never seen anything so wonderfully bright before!

Then they heard a voice from the sky. "This is my beloved Son. Listen to Him." The disciples were frightened! This was the voice of God! They put their faces on the ground. Jesus touched them and said, "Don't be afraid." They looked up and they saw Jesus only.

When Jesus comes to earth again, He will let everyone see His wonderful glory. Everyone will know that He is the Son of God.

THINK ABOUT

Heaven is a wonderful place where Jesus wants us to live with Him. There is no darkness in heaven. It is a place where there is just happiness, peace and contentment. No one will ever be sad in heaven. Jesus came to show God's love and wants us to choose to believe in Him. Will you?

PRAYER THOUGHT

Dear God, I know that loving You is the most important—always! When other "things" get in the way, help me remember that I can ask You to help me. In Jesus Name, Amen.

Questions:
THINKING & REMEMBERING

Circle the letters of all that are right.

1. Where was Jesus before He came to earth?
   a. He was on a special planet.
   b. He was in a beautiful place no one knows about.
   c. He was in heaven with God the Father.

2. What did Jesus leave when he came to earth?
   a. His brightness   b. His perfection   c. His spirit

3. Why didn't Jesus bring this with Him when He came?
   a. It would show something that is a secret between God and Jesus.
   b. It would be a brighter light than our eyes could look at.
   c. He did not want people to know about it.

4. Why did Jesus show us some of His light?
   a. so people would know He didn't live in a dark place
   b. so people could be surprised in heaven
   c. so that people could believe in Him

5. What did Jesus want the disciples to see?
   a. a small amount of the light from His brightness
   b. His glory and heavenly brightness
   c. that they didn't understand about heaven

6. Which disciples did Jesus choose to show His glory to on a high mountain?
   a. Matthew   b. John   c. Peter   d. Andrew   e. James

7. What did God's voice say when Jesus showed His full brightness?
   a. "This is My beloved Son."
   b. "I am taking My Son back to heaven."
   c. "Listen to Him."

8. When will we see God's complete glory and brightness?
   a. We will see it when we sit on a mountain.
   b. We will see it when we go to a church.
   c. We will see it when Jesus comes to earth again to take us to heaven.

Bible Story: JESUS LOVES EVERYONE THE SAME
from Mark 9

Jesus wanted His disciples to listen and learn and follow the things He was teaching about God and His love. He knew that soon He would be leaving earth to go back to God the Father in heaven. When He was gone, He wanted them to keep telling others how much He loved them.

Sometimes, even though the disciples were with Jesus, they forgot to be kind and loving with each other. One day, the disciples were talking with each other and disagreeing about which one was Jesus' favorite! Jesus was sad that the disciples hurt each other by what they said.

He wanted them to understand what was the most important. He explained to them about being the greatest in the kingdom of God. A little child who had been looking at Jesus in the crowd ran toward Jesus. Jesus held the child in His arms and said, "Whoever cares about little children and loves them like I do, will be great in My kingdom. Don't talk about who is the most important and special to Me. Stop thinking about yourselves and think of others. I love everyone the same."

THINK ABOUT

Jesus' helpers were just like we are sometimes. We want to be more special than someone else—like being the teacher's favorite student. The only One who can really love us the way we need to be loved though is Jesus. He will not love Susie more than Johnny. He loves us for ourselves. He knows the good and bad about us, and it doesn't change His love for us. He wants us to think about sharing God's love with others and not worry about being the most important.

PRAYER THOUGHT

Dear God, It is so easy to just think about me—what I want and what I like and what I feel. I want to think of others and tell them that You love them too. Help me not to think about being the greatest or the most favorite. Just help me think about pleasing You. In Jesus Name, Amen.

Questions:
THINKING & REMEMBERING

Circle the letters of all that are right.

1. What three things did Jesus want the disciples to do?
   a. listen   b. learn   c. disagree   d. follow

2. What did Jesus want to get them ready for?
   a. the time when He was going to leave earth
   b. teaching in the temple
   c. being leaders over other people

3. What did Jesus want them to teach to others?
   a. that He loved people
   b. about God's love
   c. how to follow the rules of the leaders

4. Why were the disciples disagreeing?
   a. They were disagreeing about which path to take.
   b. They each wanted to be Jesus' favorite disciple.
   c. They didn't agree about Jesus' teaching.

5. Did Jesus know that they were having a problem?
   a. No, He pretended that He did not hear what they were saying.
   b. Yes, He was sad that they hurt each other with their words.
   c. No, He wasn't close to them while they were talking.

6. How did Jesus explain to them about who was important in the kingdom of God?
   a. He said only children will be important in the kingdom of God.
   b. He said those who cared about children will be great in His kingdom.
   c. He said that He would decide who was more special and important.

7. What did Jesus tell them to stop doing?
   a. He told them to stop thinking only about themselves.
   b. He told them to stop telling others what to do.
   c. He told them to stop fighting with each other.

BIBLE WORDS TO REMEMBER

Jesus said: "You did not choose Me, but I chose you."
We love Him because He first loved us. (John 15:16; 1 John 4:19)

Bible Story: THE TWO GATES
from Matthew 7

Everyone loves to think about heaven. The Bible tells that it is more wonderful than we can even imagine. But Jesus said that not everyone will choose to be in heaven. That makes Jesus very sad, because He made a way for everyone to go to heaven.

Jesus said there are two gates. One gate has a wide opening with a broad path. It is the easiest gate to go through. But this is the wrong gate. This gate will take people to the place where they will be separated from God forever.

The other gate is narrow and the path is rough and rocky. The wonderful thing about choosing this gate is that you won't have to be on this difficult path alone, because Jesus will be right there beside you. He will hold you up and help you remember that heaven is at the end of the road. God will be there waiting to bring people who choose that path into His kingdom!

Jesus promised to show us the way to His love. He will show us where His gate is, but He won't make us take this path. That is the one thing we must decide and choose.

Important things to Remember:
- *Jesus has made a way for all people to go to heaven.*
- *Everyone has two choices: to accept Jesus or to reject Him.*
- *Jesus will help you when you choose to love Him. He will always be with you.*
- *Those who love Jesus and believe in Him as their Savior will live in heaven with Him forever.*

Questions:
THINKING & REMEMBERING

Fill in the blanks or circle the letters of all that are right.

1. What does the Bible say about heaven?
   a. Everyone will go to heaven.
   b. It is more wonderful than we can imagine.
   c. We don't like to think about heaven.

2. What did Jesus do to help people understand about heaven?
   a. He made a way for people to be in heaven by dying for sin.
   b. He said that those who choose to believe will be in heaven with Him.
   c. He said we can wait and decide to choose when we are old.

3. How many gates did Jesus tell about?
   a. three   b. two   c. one   d. many

4. What did Jesus say about the gates?
   a. One is easy and wide; one is difficult and narrow.
   b. One is easy so it must be the right one.
   c. There is one that is hard so you should not go through it.

5. Which is the gate you must go through to go to heaven?
   a. the wide gate
   b. the narrow gate
   c. It doesn't matter which one.

6. Who will be with you if you choose the narrow gate to life?
   a. all your friends
   b. many people
   c. Jesus

7. Because Jesus knows you will be happy in heaven, He will force you to love Him.   true_____   false_____

8. What did Jesus promise to do?
   a. He promised to show us the way to His love.
   b. He promised to be good to us if we try hard enough.
   c. He promised not to care if we do wrong things.

9. What must you do?
   I must _____ and _____.

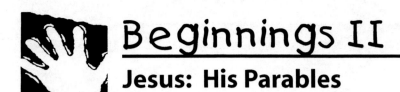

Jesus: His Parables

BIBLE WORDS TO REMEMBER

Do not worry about tomorrow. Your heavenly Father
knows what you need. (from Matthew 6:34,32)

Bible Story: GOD CARES! LILIES OF THE FIELD
from Matthew 6

Jesus and His disciples were out on a hillside. They all sat down and looked
around them. There were lilies and other flowers all over the fields. They looked
up into the sky and saw the birds with their beautiful colors flying everywhere. It
was a day that was just right!

Jesus said, "Look at the birds. God makes sure that there is enough for them to
eat. They fly to the trees or dig in the ground for worms and there is always food
there for them. Don't you think that God cares more about you than He cares for
the birds?"

"Look at the lilies out there in the field. They are so beautiful. God created them
all. The flowers don't have cloth and a needle and thread to sew their clothes, but
they are covered more beautifully in all their colors than any king who has ever
lived."

Jesus said that people should not **worry** about what they are going to eat or what
they are going to wear. God cares about people more than He cares about the
flowers and the birds. Jesus wants us to think about something more important.
We can think about God's love and giving love to others.

WORDS TO KNOW

worry: to think about and get upset about something

lesson: teaching something that is important

remind: to tell something that is to be remembered

Questions:
THINKING & REMEMBERING

Circle the letters of all that are right.

1. Where were Jesus and His disciples?
   a. by the lake   b. on a hillside   c. in a city park

2. What could the disciples see that day?
   a. other people   b. sheep eating grass   c. flowers and birds

3. What are the birds and flowers concerned about?
   a. how to get food
   b. how to be colorful
   c. nothing—God takes care of them

4. Why did Jesus say that people should not worry?
   a. God loves people more than the flowers and birds.
   b. It is not necessary to have so many things.
   c. We should not care what we look like to others.

5. What does Jesus want us to think about?
   a. God's love and loving others
   b. what kind of food we have
   c. what kind of clothes we are wearing

6. Why don't we ever have to wonder about God taking care of us?
   a. He tells in the Bible that He loves us.
   b. He sent Jesus to show us that He cares.
   c. His world is full of the good gifts He gives to take care of us.

7. What can we know for sure?
   a. If God takes care of the birds and flowers, He will take care of us.
   b. God loves us more than the other things He made.
   c. We can just hope that He will take care of us.

THINK ABOUT

Jesus wants you to know for sure that He will take care of you. He will not forget about you. Jesus gave this **lesson** to **remind** us of how God takes care of us and loves us. We don't need to wonder how we are going to get food for our lunches or worry about having just the right clothes to wear. That is not the most important!

Bible Story: ONE LOST SHEEP
from Luke 15

Jesus told this story about God's love:

There was once a shepherd who loved his sheep very much. He had one hundred sheep. He knew the name of each sheep. When he called them, he called their names.

The shepherd took care of his sheep. He let them play and eat good grass. He took them to a nice brook to drink cool water. When it became dark, the shepherd called his sheep to him. He began counting them as they went into their resting place…"one … two…three…four," and on he counted, "ninety-seven…ninety-eight…ninety-nine…" There were no more sheep—one sheep was missing! The shepherd went back to the field to look for his one lost sheep.

Then he heard the sound of his sheep far away. He hurried to the place where the sheep was. The sheep was so cold and frightened! The shepherd took the sheep in his arms and carried it safely home. He was so happy that he had found his sheep. He called his friends and neighbors and said, "Rejoice with me; for I have found my sheep that was lost."

THINK ABOUT

Jesus used this parable to tell everyone how much He loved them. This is a picture story with words that teaches a special lesson about God. Jesus wants you to make a picture in your mind.

Jesus said, "I am like a shepherd. I know your name. I will keep calling you to come to Me. I love you and will take care of you always."

PRAYER THOUGHT

Dear God, Help me to remember to listen when You call my name. I want to be ready to hear and do what You want me to do. I love You. In Jesus Name, Amen.

Questions:
THINKING & REMEMBERING

Circle the letters of all that are right.

1. What are some words for the kind of stories Jesus told?
   a. parable   b. picture story   c. fairy tale

2. Why are these stories so important?
   a. They teach a special lesson about God's love.
   b. They tell us about money.
   c. They tell us that it is OK to sometimes worry.

3. How many sheep did the shepherd own in the story Jesus told?
   a. ninety-nine   b. more than one-hundred   c. one hundred

4. What special thing did the shepherd know about each of his sheep?
   a. He knew they liked to sleep.
   b. He knew each of their names.
   c. He knew they would all run away.

5. What did the shepherd do for his sheep?
   a. He let them go wherever they wanted.
   b. He gave them food and water.
   c. He let them play in the grass.
   d. He found a place for them to rest.

6. Why did the shepherd go back into the field and mountains alone?
   a. He didn't care about the sheep while they were sleeping.
   b. He wanted to get away from the sheep for awhile.
   c. He went to find the one sheep that was missing.

7. Who are we like in this story?
   a. the shepherd   b. the sheep

8. Who is Jesus like?
   a. the sheep   b. the shepherd

9. What did Jesus say that He would do?
   a. He would let us go the wrong way.
   b. He would take care of us.
   c. He would call us by our names.

BIBLE WORDS TO REMEMBER

Do not worry about tomorrow. Your heavenly Father
knows what you need. (from Matthew 6:34,32)

Bible Story: THE MISSING MONEY
from Luke 15

This is a story Jesus told about a lost coin:

There was once a woman who worked hard to keep her home clean and keep her family happy. She did not have a lot of money, but she was careful to be wise with what she had. She had ten silver coins that she kept in a safe place to buy food for her family.

One day, she discovered that one of the coins was missing! There were only nine coins! She quickly began to search her whole house for that one coin. She took her lamp into the room and looked into each corner searching for the coin. She did not give up. She took a broom and carefully swept the floor, looking and listening for any sight or sound of the coin that might have fallen into a crack in the floor.

At last, she saw something shining! It was the coin! She went out and invited all her friends to come and celebrate with her. The lost coin was found.

Jesus said, "That is exactly how God feels when one person is found and comes into His kingdom. All the angels have a celebration when one person is lost and then is found."

THINK ABOUT

Jesus told this story to help His listeners understand that God did not just have "favorite" people. He loves everyone. If even one child or grown-up person is lost and doesn't know Jesus, He will care about them until they hear about God's love and believe in Him.

Questions:
THINKING & REMEMBERING

Fill in the blanks or circle the letters of all that are right.

1. What was Jesus' story about?
   a. money   b. sheep   c. food

2. How does this story compare with the story Jesus told about the sheep?
   a. They both are about something that was lost.
   b. Nothing is the same.
   c. There was a celebration when the lost was found.

3. What did the story say about the woman?
   a. She had a lot of money.
   b. She cared about her family.
   c. She was wise with her money.

4. How many coins did the woman have that she kept safe?
   a. seven   b. ten   c. nine

5. How much money did she discover was missing?
   a. one coin   b. nine coins   c. three coins

6. What did she do about the missing money?
   a. She cared enough to look for it.
   b. She did not give up looking until she found it.
   c. She didn't care because she had more.

7. What did she do when she found the money?
   a. She hid it in a different place.
   b. She started to get dinner for her family.
   c. She asked her friends to come and celebrate.

8. God cares when even one person is lost and doesn't know about His love.
   true_____   false_____

9. What happens when that one comes to know and believe in Jesus?
   a. Some people care.
   b. There is a celebration in heaven!
   c. No one really notices.

BIBLE WORDS TO REMEMBER

Do not worry about tomorrow. Your heavenly Father knows what you need. (from Matthew 6:34,32)

Bible Story: THE FOOLISH SON
from Luke 15

*There was a man who had two sons. One day the youngest son told his father that he wanted to have the money that he was going to get when his father died. He wanted it immediately! The father was sad that his son wanted to leave his home, but he decided to give him his **share** of money.*

The son left and went into the city where there were many things to buy. When others found out that he had money, they suggested many ways for him to spend it. Soon the money was gone. The good times were gone. The friends were gone.

*He got a job taking care of pigs. It was a terrible and dirty job. He was so hungry! He thought about his father's home. He remembered that the servants had more to eat than he did. So he thought, "I will go back to my father. I will ask him to **forgive** me and beg him to let me be his **servant**."*

Jesus knew what His listener's were thinking. They thought that the son did not deserve his father's love. The father should not allow the son to come back to his home. Will the father say "yes"?

WORDS TO KNOW

share: the part that belongs to someone

forgive: to tell someone who has done something wrong that you will excuse them for hurting you

PRAYER THOUGHT

Dear God, It is hard to tell someone when I have done the wrong thing and hurt them. Help me ask for forgiveness and to forgive those who hurt me. You always forgive me when I tell You I am sorry. I want to love others in that way, too. In Jesus Name, Amen.

 **Questions:**
THINKING & REMEMBERING

Circle the letters of all that are right.

1. How many sons did the man have in this story?
   a. three   b. two   c. one

2. What did the younger son want to do?
   a. leave home
   b. take the money he was supposed to get when his father died
   c. get the money and stay at home for awhile

3. What happened when the son was away from his home?
   a. He spent all of his money.
   b. He owned a good business.
   c. He was careful with his money and was successful.

4. What happened to those who said they were his friends?
   a. They were still his friends.
   b. They left him alone when the money was gone.
   c. They pretended they didn't know him.

5. What job did the son get?
   a. farming
   b. being a servant in the city
   c. taking care of pigs

6. What did the son decide to do?
   a. He would go back home and ask his father to forgive him.
   b. He would live with his friends.
   c. He would try to get another job.

7. What did Jesus know that the people were thinking that were listening?
   a. The son deserved the bad things that were happening to him.
   b. The father in the story should not forgive his son.
   c. The son should not be able to go back home.

8. What do you think the son's father should do?
   a. He should let him come back home if he is sorry.
   b. He should tell him to make it on his own because he made his choice.
   c. He should tell his son he loves him and will forgive him.

BIBLE WORDS TO REMEMBER

Do not worry about tomorrow. Your heavenly Father knows what you need. (from Matthew 6:34,32)

Bible Story: THE FATHER SAYS, "COME"

from Luke 15

Jesus told the rest of His story about the son who left his home:

The father did have another son whom he loved very much, but he kept thinking about the son that went away and he missed him. He stood by the road every day and watched for his son to return.

One day, the father saw his son—he was coming home! He called to him and said, "Come!" He ran to him, held out his arms, and kissed him.

The son knew that he did not deserve his father's love. He said to his father, "I have sinned. I can no longer be called your son. I do not expect you to love me." The father did not listen. He told the servants to get new clothes for his son and get ready for a big party to celebrate the son's return.

The older son who had stayed at home and had been obedient to his father could not understand how the father could still love the son who went away.

Jesus said that God celebrates when one who has gone away from Him comes back. Even though he has done wrong, God welcomes him back when he asks God's forgiveness. God does not stop loving anyone.

THINK ABOUT

How would you feel if you were the father in this story? How would you feel if you were the son who went away? How would you feel if you were the son who stayed at home? Jesus wants us to understand that God will never give up on those He loves. He waits for them to return to Him.

Questions:
THINKING & REMEMBERING

Circle the letters of all that are right.

1. How did the father in the story feel about his son who left home?
   a. He loved him and missed him.
   b. He was happy he was gone because he caused trouble.
   c. He hoped that his son was happy.

2. Did the father care about the son who had stayed home?
   a. Yes, he loved both sons.
   b. Yes, he liked having the help of the older son.
   c. No, he only thought about his younger son.

3. What did the father do because he missed the son that went away?
   a. He stayed in bed because he was so sad.
   b. He stood by the road looking for him.
   c. He tried to pretend that he didn't care.

4. What happened one day?
   a. He went to the city to find his son.
   b. The older son told his father to stop thinking about his other son.
   c. The father saw his son coming home.

5. What did the father do?
   a. He waited for him to get to the house so he could talk to him.
   b. He called out to his son and said, "Come!"
   c. He ran to him and hugged and kissed him.

6. What did the son tell his father?
   a. "I'm glad to be home. I didn't like feeding pigs!"
   b. "I don't deserve to be called your son."
   c. "I'm starved. Where's the food?"

7. What did the father do after the son said that?
   a. He told the servants to get new clothes for his son.
   b. He told his son that he could stay and work as a servant.
   c. He told the servants to get ready for a big party.

Beginnings II
Jesus: His Lessons on Love

LESSON 19 - DAY 1

BIBLE WORDS TO REMEMBER
Let each one give with purpose in his heart.
For God loves a cheerful giver. (from 2 Corinthians 9:7)

Bible Story: BEING RICH
from Mark 10

Jesus said it was easier for a camel to go through the **eye of a needle**, than for a rich man to enter the kingdom of God. Jesus said this because people who have more money than they really need do not take time to think about God. They sometimes think that they do not need God at all!

The people who wanted to be rich did not understand. Jesus knew that they could not love God *and* money. They must always think of God first and make Him the most important. It is not impossible for rich people to love God, but it is more difficult for them to choose because their life is easy.

Jesus and His disciples were sitting by the **entrance** to the temple. A rich man gave many gold coins and he wanted everyone to notice that he gave a lot of money. A woman came and gave only two small coins that were not worth very much. It was all the money she had.

Jesus said, "The rich man only gave a small part his money. The woman gave all that she has. Her gift to God is the best gift because it was given with love."

WORDS TO KNOW

eye of a needle: a small opening on a needle for the thread to go through

entrance: the place where people come into a building

THINK ABOUT

Lots of money can only make you happy for a little while. No matter how much money you have, you will want more. God gives the kind of treasure that is real and lasting. Being rich with God's love is more wonderful than all the money in the world!

182

Questions:
THINKING & REMEMBERING

Fill in the blanks or circle the letters of all that are right.

1. What question did Peter ask Jesus?
   a. "Do I need to be kind to others when they are mean?"
   b. "When do I have to forgive other people?"
   c. "If I forgive someone seven times, is that enough?"

2. How many times did Jesus say to forgive?
   a. as many times as you want to
   b. just when someone tells you they are sorry
   c. seventy times seven

3. How did Jesus answer Peter's question?
   a. He said that those who love Him should never stop forgiving.
   b. He said not to believe some people when they say they are sorry.
   c. He told a story about forgiveness.

4. What did the man owe the king?
   a. a small amount of money
   b. a lot of money
   c. an amount of money that could be paid back in a short time

5. When he could not pay the king, what did the king do?
   a. He forgave him and said he did not have to pay his debt.
   b. He made him pay the money.
   c. He would have to pay in six weeks.

6. What did the man do to another servant who owed him a little money?
   a. He said he must pay him what he owed.
   b. He said he would put him in jail if he didn't pay.
   c. He said that he would forgive because he had been forgiven.

7. What did the king do when he found out what the man he had forgiven had done to someone else?
   a. He put him in jail.
   b. He told him he was not a kind man.
   c. He changed his mind and made him pay the money he owed.

8. Because God forgives, what must we do? _____

Bible Story: A Special Visit: Mary Listens

from Luke 10

Jesus had been traveling for many days. He was teaching people wherever He went. He also healed people who were sick and did miracles to show the power of God. He knew it would be good to find a place to rest for a while.

Near Jerusalem there was a town called Bethany. Jesus' friends, Mary, Martha and Lazarus lived there so Jesus went to visit them. It was His favorite stopping place. His friends were so excited that Jesus was coming. They cleaned the house and baked good things to eat. When Jesus came, Martha found the most comfortable place for Jesus to sit. Then she hurried back to the kitchen to finish getting the dinner ready.

But Mary stayed and listened to Jesus talk about God. Martha was working hard and she was angry that Mary was not helping. "Tell Mary to help me," she told Jesus.

Jesus loved His friends. He smiled. "You both love Me and show your love in **different** ways. You are trying to make a good meal for Me and Mary is **listening** and **learning** about God. I would like you to take time to listen, too, Martha. God's words are important."

WORDS TO KNOW

different: not the same

listening: to hear what is being said

learning: understanding what you hear or read

PRAYER THOUGHT

Dear God, Help me to remember the best and most important thing—loving and serving You! I want to show love to others in the right way. In Jesus Name, Amen.

Questions:
THINKING & REMEMBERING

Fill in the blanks or circle the letters of all that are right.

1. What did Jesus talk about when He was teaching people?
   a. He talked about God and His love.
   b. He talked about how to make other people think you are good.
   c. He talked about how to tell what kind of seeds are good to grow.

2. What did Jesus do for people He met?
   a. Jesus told them where they could rest.
   b. Jesus healed the people who were sick.
   c. Jesus did miracles to show the power of God.

3. Where did Jesus go to stay with his friends?
   a. Jerusalem   b. Bethany   c. Nazareth

4. What were the names of His friends who lived there?
   a. Martha   b. Peter   c. Lazarus   d. Mary

5. How did Martha show her love for Jesus?
   a. Martha cooked a dinner.
   b. Martha sat down by Jesus.

6. How did Mary show her love for Jesus?
   a. Mary did the cooking.
   b. Mary listened to Jesus tell about God.

7. How did Jesus help Martha understand what was most important?
   a. He told Mary to help Martha with the dinner.
   b. He said they would talk about God after dinner.
   c. He said that it was more important to listen and learn about God.

8. Write the Bible Words from 2 Corinthians 9:7.

   Let each one _____ with purpose in his _____.
   For God loves a _____ giver.

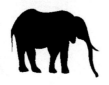

BIBLE WORDS TO REMEMBER

Let each one give with purpose in his heart.
For God loves a cheerful giver. (from 2 Corinthians 9:7)

Bible Story: A HAPPY FUNERAL
from Luke 7

Jesus and His disciples were walking up a path on their way to another town to tell people about God. They saw a crowd of people coming toward them. But it was not a happy crowd of people. A young man had died, and they were going to bury him. They were on their way to a **funeral**.

There was sad music and people were crying. The mother was **sobbing** because her only son had died. Her husband had also died, and she had no one to care for her. Jesus looked at all the sad people. He said, "Do not cry." He stood over the dead body. Everyone was very still. Jesus said, "Young man, **arise**." The man sat up and started talking! He wondered why his mother had been crying. Why were all the people looking sad? Then he saw the joy return to his mother's face. He looked at Jesus. Jesus had made him alive!

Everyone was excited about what Jesus did. The people were no longer crying and sad. They were happy! They said, "God has come to visit us!" When a person dies, it is not a problem for Jesus! He can do anything because Jesus is God.

WORDS TO KNOW

funeral: a burial for someone who has died
sobbing: to cry without stopping
arise: to get up
compassion: to show that you care about other's feelings

THINK ABOUT

The Bible tells us that there is a time to weep and a time to laugh (Ecclesiastes 3:4). Jesus had **compassion** when He saw the mother weeping. Jesus wants us to show others that we care about their sadness. Jesus can turn sadness into joy and happiness.

 # Questions:
THINKING & REMEMBERING

Circle the letters of all that are right.

1. Where were Jesus and His disciples going?
   a. They were going to a resting spot.
   b. They were going to a picnic place by the sea.
   c. They were going to another town to tell people about God.

2. What was different about the people coming toward Jesus?
   a. They were going to a place to bury someone who had died.
   b. They were going to a party.
   c. They were going to someone's house for a celebration.

3. What was happening?
   a. They were playing sad music.
   b. The people were crying.
   c. A woman was sobbing.

4. Who had died?
   a. the group's leader
   b. a little girl
   c. the son of the woman who was sobbing

5. How did Jesus show the people he cared that they were sad?
   a. He stopped and looked at them.
   b. He told them to stop crying.
   c. He kept on walking.

6. What did Jesus do?
   a. He told the man who had died to get up.
   b. He told the woman He was sorry that her son died.
   c. He told her to love God.

7. What happened?
   a. The man who was dead got up and started talking.
   b. The man said he was feeling sick.
   c. The man told all the people to stop looking at him.

8. What did the crowd of people do?
   a. They stopped crying.   b. They were happy.

BIBLE WORDS TO REMEMBER

Let each one give with purpose in his heart.
For God loves a cheerful giver. (from 2 Corinthians 9:7)

Bible Story: MANY CHANCES
from Luke 13

Jesus traveled into towns and cities. He went outside the towns to little villages. He talked to people beside the sea and in the hillsides. He spoke the words of God everywhere. Jesus wanted to tell them of God's plan.

Some people listened and went away. Others stayed and wanted to hear more. People everywhere heard the message of God's love. They were all given a chance to know and accept God's love because Jesus came to earth.

Jesus said, "Think about a man who had a fig tree on his land. Even though he watched carefully, there were no figs on the tree. The man finally told his gardener to cut it down and make room for other trees that could produce fruit. But the gardener wanted to save the tree. He said, 'Please give the tree another year. I will take good care of it and give it extra attention. If it doesn't have fruit by next year, I will cut it down. Please give the tree another chance.'"

Jesus was trying to make the people understand that He was like that gardener. He wanted to give them another chance to believe and come to God.

THINK ABOUT

Jesus came to show God's love in many ways. He didn't give up when people did not listen the first time. He kept on telling about God's love and giving love so everyone would know that God loved them.

PRAYER THOUGHT

Dear God, Help me to show Your love to others! Help me to care about people the way You do so that they will believe and accept Your love. In Jesus name, Amen.

Questions:
THINKING & REMEMBERING

Circle the letters of all that are right.

1. Where were some of the places Jesus went to talk about God?
   a. temples and churches   b. towns and cities   c. beside the sea

2. What did the people do who heard Jesus tell about God's plan?
   a. Some people yelled at Him for saying things about God.
   b. Some people listened and went away.
   c. Some people stayed and wanted to hear more.

3. What did Jesus give everyone a chance to do?
   a. to hear His latest story
   b. to know and accept God's love
   c. to find out where He was going next

4. How did God's love come to earth?
   a. through the prophets telling about it
   b. through the priests at the temple
   c. through Jesus coming to earth

5. In the story Jesus told about the fig tree, what did the owner of the tree want to do when there was no fruit on it?
   a. He wanted to cut it down to make room for trees that would have fruit.
   b. He wanted to keep taking care of it for a few more years.
   c. He wanted to stop watering it so it would die.

6. What did the gardener want to do with the fig tree?
   a. He wanted to destroy it.
   b. He wanted to give it another chance to produce fruit.
   c. He wanted to get someone else to take care of it.

7. What did the gardener do for one year?
   a. He watched it carefully.
   b. He moved the tree to a different spot.
   c. He gave the tree extra attention.

8. Whom did Jesus say He was like? _____

Jesus: More Lessons on Love

BIBLE WORDS TO REMEMBER

Jesus said, "This is My commandment, that you love one another as I have loved you." Love others as much as you love yourself.
(from John 15:12; Galatians 5:14)

Bible Story: MORE QUESTIONS, WHO IS MY NEIGHBOR?
from Luke 10

Jesus was asked a lot of questions by many different people and for many different reasons. Sometimes the questions were asked by those who wanted to find something against Him. Jesus always knew what was inside the heart of everyone who asked a question. He is wise and all-knowing—and He knew exactly how to answer the questions.

One day, a **lawyer** asked Jesus a question. He asked, "What do I need to do to have **eternal life**?" Jesus asked him a question. "What has God said to do?" The lawyer was **insulted** to be asked such a simple question. He said, "You should love the Lord your God with all your heart, with all your soul, with all your strength, and with all your mind, and your neighbor as yourself."

Jesus said, "That is exactly right. Now do that and you will live forever." The man knew that he had tried to live by the law and it was too hard to do! He tried to trick Jesus by asking another question: "Who is my neighbor?"

Jesus gave His answer in a parable. In our next lesson, see if you can understand what Jesus said about who "our" neighbor is.

WORDS TO KNOW

lawyer: one who studies the law and tells others what it means

eternal life: living forever in heaven with God

insulted: to make someone feel that they are not respected for who they are

Questions:
THINKING & REMEMBERING

Fill in the blanks or circle the letters of all that are right.

1. What were some people doing when they were with Jesus?
   a. They were asking questions.
   b. They were telling Him things they knew.
   c. They were trying to get Him to say the wrong thing.

2. How did Jesus know the reasons people asked certain questions?
   a. He is the Son of God.
   b. He can look inside and know why they asked a question.
   c. He could guess by looking at them.

3. Did Jesus ever make a mistake and give a wrong answer?
   a. Sometimes—if the person was a good actor.
   b. No, He knew exactly how to answer the questions.
   c. Yes, His disciples tried to help with the answers.

4. What was the profession of the man who asked Jesus a question?
   a. a farmer
   b. a teacher
   c. a lawyer

5. What was the man's question?
   a. "What is an easy way to heaven?"
   b. "What do I need to do to have eternal life?"
   c. "How can I get rich on earth?"

6. What question did Jesus ask him?
   a. "What has God said to do?"
   b. "Have you kept the law?"
   c. "What good things have you done?"

7. The man knew the laws of God and could tell Jesus.   true_____   false_____

8. How did the man try to trick Jesus with another question?
   a. He used God's words to challenge Jesus.
   b. He asked, "Who is my neighbor?"
   c. He asked how to know who to be kind to.

9. The man had tried to live by the _____ of God and it was too_____.

Bible Story: A GOOD NEIGHBOR
from Luke 10

This is the parable Jesus told:
One day a man was walking along a lonely road when suddenly some bad men came and beat him and took all his money. He was too hurt to walk. He waited for someone to help him.

A priest who was in a hurry to go to the temple to worship God came by. He saw the hurt man, but he did not stop. Then another man who worked at the temple came down the road. He turned his head away. He didn't want to get his hands dirty by helping—and he walked away.

Finally, there were more footsteps coming down the road. A man from another country stopped beside the hurt man. He was very kind. He washed the dirt from the man's cuts, took him to the next town to a hotel, and paid for the man to stay there until he was well.

When Jesus finished the story, He asked, "Which of the three men was a good neighbor?" There is really only one answer. It was the man who helped. This is the way God wants us to love our "neighbor." Our "neighbor" is anyone who needs help and love.

THINK ABOUT

It is easy to love ourselves. It is easy to love our family and friends and those who love us. But what about those who are not kind and are not lovable? Why did God say that we must love everyone? Did He know how hard it would be? Yes, God knew all of that. That's why God sent Jesus to earth to help us know how to love.

PRAYER THOUGHT

Dear God, I know that You love me—even when I do and say things that are unkind to others. Help me love the way You love and to care about someone today that has been unkind. They need Your love, too. In Jesus Name, Amen.

Questions:
THINKING & REMEMBERING

Fill in the blanks or circle the letters of all that are right.

1. Why did Jesus tell this parable?
   a. to tell who our "neighbor" is
   b. to show how many people will walk by a hurt man
   c. to tell people they shouldn't walk alone on a lonely road

2. What did Jesus want His listeners to learn?
   a. to be careful where they go
   b. to watch for robbers
   c. how to love like God loves

3. Who was the first to see the man who was robbed?
   a. a lawyer   b. a temple worker   c. a priest

4. Who came along the road next and why didn't he help?
   a. the temple worker who didn't want to get dirty
   b. a priest going to worship at the temple and had to hurry
   c. a man taking things to sell in the city and had to be there on time

5. How was the third man kind to the hurt person?
   a. He washed the dirt from the man's cuts.
   b. He said he was sorry, but he could not help.
   c. He took the man to a hotel to get better.

6. What question did Jesus ask the people who were listening?
   a. "Why didn't the important people help the man?"
   b. "Why didn't the man try to walk to get help?"
   c. "Which one was a good neighbor?"

7. What would Jesus want you to do if you saw a hurt person?
   a. find help for someone who is hurt
   b. pray for someone who is hurt
   c. be kind and help

8. Jesus said, "Love one another as I have _____ you."

Bible Story: BIGGER AND BETTER
from Luke 12

Many people who followed Jesus were looking for ways to have more things on earth. Jesus knew what people were thinking. He knew that they were not happy because they worried about what they didn't have instead of thinking of all the things that they did have. These people never thought about helping others or being kind because they were too busy thinking about themselves. So Jesus told them a picture story (parable) to help them think about what was important.

There was once a rich farmer who had very good **crops***. One year he had even better crops that* **produced** *more. This made him very happy. He bought a bigger house and built huge barns to store his* **grain***. He bought beautiful clothes. He did not share with others because he was so proud of how much he was getting for himself.*

That night he heard God's voice. God said, "You have been very foolish. Tonight you will die. What is going to happen to all your money and your grain now? It won't help you at all."

Jesus says that if we think only about what we have on earth, we will not be ready for treasures in heaven.

WORDS TO KNOW

crops: plants that grow as a result of planting seed in the ground

produced: what happens when a small amount grows to be a large amount

grain: that which is grown in the field and used to make flour

---

THINK ABOUT

We can spend a lot of time thinking about what we don't have. People sometimes worry about money and what they are going to buy when they get it. It is easy to put our thoughts on "things" instead of God, but "things" won't matter at all when life on earth is over. What matters is what we decide about God and loving others.

Questions:
THINKING & REMEMBERING

Fill in the blanks or circle the letters of all that are right.

1. What did Jesus know that people were thinking?
   a. how they could be kind to each other
   b. how they could love God more
   c. how they could get more things

2. What were they thinking about?
   a. God   b. themselves   c. others

3. Why did Jesus tell a picture story (parable)?
   a. to help people think about what was really important
   b. to think more about what they had on earth
   c. to help people know that they should worry about money

4. What did the man in the story do for a living?
   a. He was a banker.   b. He was a farmer.   c. He owned a bakery.

5. What happened that made him happy?
   a. He had more crops that produced more than ever.
   b. He got married and started a family.
   c. He sold his farmland.

6. What did he do with the extra money he made?
   a. He bought a bigger house.
   b. He purchased new and beautiful clothes.
   c. He built bigger and better barns to store his grain.

7. What was his attitude about the abundance he had?
   a. He wanted to share it with his neighbors.
   b. He was proud of how much he was getting for himself.
   c. He looked for ways to help the poor people.

8. What did God say would happen to him?
   a. "Tonight you will die."
   b. "You will live for a long time to enjoy what you have."
   c. "You can take some of your riches to heaven."

9. Jesus said: "If you only think about what you have on _____, you will not be ready for treasures in _____."

Bible Story: A RICH MAN GOES AWAY
from Mark 10

One day Jesus was walking on the road, and a man who was very rich came running after Him. He wanted to talk to Jesus! He had enough money to buy anything he wanted, but he wanted to be sure of one more thing. He wanted to go to heaven when he died.

So the man asked Jesus, "Please tell me what I have to do so that I will have eternal life." Jesus said, "You know all of God's commandments. Respect your parents, don't cheat, don't lie, don't murder…" "Yes, yes," said the rich man, "I have kept all the commandments all my life!"

Jesus knew the man had tried to be good. Jesus knew everything about him. And He knew that the young rich man had forgotten the most important thing. He did not really love God with all his heart and mind. He did not love others as much as he loved himself and his money. Jesus said, "If you want to be rich in God's kingdom, go and give all you have to the people who have nothing. Then come and follow Me."

The man turned and went away sadly. He could not give up what he loved most—his possessions.

THINK ABOUT

Having beautiful clothes, having a big house and the money to buy everything one wants, does not make a person happy. It's what's on the inside that counts! It is having the love of Jesus in your heart and knowing that you will be with Him forever in heaven. Not only will you feel beautiful on the inside, your face will shine on the outside showing God's love in you! What really counts the most in life? What do you need to make you happy? Whom do you need to have eternal life? How you answer these questions is important.

PRAYER THOUGHT

Dear God, I'm so glad that the things that money can buy isn't the most important thing. Help me make You the happiness in my life. In Jesus Name, Amen.

Questions:
THINKING & REMEMBERING

Fill in the blanks or circle the letters of all that are right.

1. What kind of man was running to meet with Jesus?
   a. poor   b. sick   c. rich

2. What did the man have?
   a. He had a book he wanted to show Jesus.
   b. He had something to sell to Jesus and His followers.
   c. He had money and many things that money could buy.

3. What was the one thing he wasn't sure about?
   a. He wasn't sure that he would always have enough money.
   b. He wasn't sure that he would go to heaven.
   c. He wasn't sure that his friends would like him.

4. How did Jesus answer the man's question about eternal life?
   a. He asked the man if he had kept all of God's commandments.
   b. He said to try to be good to others.
   c. He said that no one ever knows for sure that they will go to heaven.

5. Jesus already knew what the man had done and what he was thinking.
   true_____   false_____

6. What had the man **not** done?
   a. He had not loved God with all his heart and mind.
   b. He had not given money to the poor.
   c. He had not loved others more than himself and his money.

7. What did Jesus say the rich man would have to do?
   a. He would have to give all his money to the poor people.
   b. He would have to say prayers at the temple.
   c. He would have to follow Jesus.

8. What did the man choose to do?
   a. He chose to keep his money.
   b. He chose to give his money to the poor.
   c. He chose to follow Jesus.

Remember: God will give you everything you need—just believe in Him and put Him first in your life.

BIBLE WORDS TO REMEMBER

Jesus said, "This is My commandment, that you love one another as I have loved you." Love others as much as you love yourself.
(from John 15:12; Galatians 5:14)

Bible Story: TREASURE
from Matthew 13

Jesus talked a lot about what was really important. He tried to tell His disciples and the people listening that their **treasure** in heaven was more important than any treasure found on earth. He knew that they had a very hard time understanding that. Jesus told this parable:

"There was once a man who was digging out in a field. Suddenly, he hit something that was very hard. He kept digging and discovered that it was a wonderful treasure. It was worth more money than the man had ever imagined. He was so happy!

The man did not want to steal the treasure and hope that no one would ever find out. He wanted to own the treasure! He thought of a plan. He would buy the land where the treasure was. He went home and got everything that he already had and sold it. He was so excited when he had enough money finally to buy the land—and the treasure that was buried there."

Some people were beginning to understand what Jesus was telling them about God's kingdom—His kingdom is the most **precious** thing they could have. Riches weren't important—God's kingdom is the treasure!

WORDS TO KNOW

treasure: something of great value
precious: wonderfully loved and valued

THINK ABOUT

We all have things that we treasure. There are many things that are special to us—and God gives us wonderful things to enjoy. He want us to have fun and have good things. But the best treasure of all is knowing God and His love!

Questions:
THINKING & REMEMBERING

Fill in the blanks or circle the letters of all that are right.

1. Fill in the missing words from John 15:12 and Galatians 5:14.

   Jesus said, "This is My _____, that you _____ one

   another as I have _____ you." _____ others as much as you

   _____ yourself.

2. What did Jesus want people to understand?
   a. He liked to tell stories.
   b. God is the most important.
   c. that they could do what they liked

3. What did Jesus tell His listeners about treasure?
   a. Treasure in heaven is more important than treasure on earth.
   b. Having riches can make them happy.
   c. People should try to get all the money they can.

4. What did the man in the story find when he was digging?
   a. a special rock   b. a wonderful treasure   c. a different kind of plant

5. What was the treasure worth?
   a. a lot of money—more than he ever could imagine
   b. five hundred dollars
   c. enough money to buy a house

6. What plan did the man have so he could own the treasure?
   a. He would steal the treasure and hope no one would find out.
   b. He would buy the land where the treasure was buried.
   c. He would sell all that he had to get enough money to buy the land.

7. What did Jesus say was the most precious thing they could have?
   a. enough money to buy what you want
   b. God's kingdom
   c. lots of friends

Remember: God's kingdom is more precious than gold!

Beginnings II

LESSON 21 - DAY 1

Jesus: His Love

BIBLE WORDS TO REMEMBER

Pray without ceasing (stopping),
in everything, give thanks.... (1 Thessalonians 5:17-18)

Bible Story: JESUS LOVES CHILDREN!
from Mark 10

One day the children heard that Jesus was coming. They ran to ask their mothers if they could go see Jesus. The mothers wanted to see Jesus, too! They ran to the place where Jesus was talking to the people. They were so happy! What a wonderful day this was going to be!

When they came to the place where Jesus was, many people were crowded around Him. The children could not see over the people. They could hear Jesus, but they could not see Him.

Some tall men who were Jesus' helpers saw all the children trying to get close to Jesus. The children heard a voice say, "STOP! Go back. Jesus is too busy!" The children were very sad. The mothers were very sad, too.

Then they heard a very kind and gentle voice. It was Jesus! He said, "Let the children come to Me. Don't ever send the children away. I want them to come close to Me." Jesus smiled at the children and hugged them. Jesus talked with the children and said, "I love you very much!" The children knew that they were important and special. The children went home knowing that Jesus loved them.

THINK ABOUT

Would you like to think about being on earth during the time Jesus was here? Would you like to be one of the children that ran to see Jesus? Would you like to sit close to Jesus and hear Him tell you that He loves you? He would even know your name! Children are so important to Jesus! If Jesus were here on earth right now, He would give you a big hug and tell you that He loves you. By listening to Jesus' words in the Bible, you can feel hugged and loved!

Questions:
THINKING & REMEMBERING

Circle the letters of all that are right.

1. What did the children want to do when they heard that Jesus was coming?
   a. They wanted to go see Him.
   b. They wanted to play on the hillside close to where Jesus was.
   c. They wanted to hear one of the stories Jesus was telling.

2. What happened when they got to where Jesus was?
   a. They had a hard time finding Him.
   b. They couldn't tell which man was Jesus.
   c. There were too many people crowded around Jesus to get close to Him.

3. What did one of Jesus' helpers say to the children?
   a. "Come back tomorrow."
   b. "Bring a picnic when you come."
   c. "Stop! Go back."

4. Why did the Jesus' helpers want the children to go away?
   a. They said that Jesus was busy.
   b. They said that Jesus didn't like children.
   c. They said that Jesus was too important to talk to children.

5. How did the children feel when they thought they couldn't see Jesus?
   a. They were still happy because they could play in the grass.
   b. They were very sad.
   c. They were mad at the man for telling them they couldn't see Jesus.

6. What did the children hear Jesus' voice say?
   a. "Let the children come to Me."
   b. "Tell the children I will talk to them later."
   c. "Tell the children to stay with their mothers."

7. What did the children know for sure about Jesus?
   a. He wasn't too important to care about children.
   b. He was the boss of His helpers.
   c. He loved children.

Bible Story: THE GOOD SHEPHERD
from John 10

Jesus wanted everyone to know how important it was to choose life instead of death. God sent Jesus to show God's love to everyone. He died for all the wrong things (sin) that people did and are still doing today. The way to life is through Jesus. There is no other way!

Jesus said, "If a person tries to get into the **sheepfold** by some other way, he is a **thief** and a **robber**. Everyone must enter by the door. I am the door. A shepherd calls his own sheep and leads them. The sheep know his voice and follow him. They will not follow strangers. I am the good shepherd and I will give My life for the sheep. I know My sheep and they know Me. My sheep hear My voice and they follow Me. I give them eternal life, and they shall never **perish**." Then Jesus said, "I and My Father are one."

When Jesus said those words about being God, the people tried to kill Him. But it was not the time yet for Jesus to die. He went away where others would listen again to His words about God. He was sad for the people who hated Him.

WORDS TO KNOW

sheepfold:	a place where the sheep are safe
thief and robber:	those who are trying to steal something that does not belong to them
perish:	to die forever instead of live in heaven

THINK ABOUT

Jesus wants to be your shepherd. He loves you and He knows your name! He will call for you and you will know that it is His voice if you love and believe in Him. Remember that there is only ONE WAY. If you have not asked Jesus to live in your heart, you are trying to be good all by yourself. It won't work. Jesus is the only way to God.

PRAYER THOUGHT

Dear God, You sent Jesus to give me eternal life. I can never come to You by any other way. Help me to stay close to You through Jesus. In Jesus Name, Amen.

 **Questions:**
THINKING & REMEMBERING

Circle the letters of all that are right.

1. What did Jesus want everyone to know?
   a. He wanted them to know how important it is to choose life.
   b. They should be quiet and listen to Him talk about God.
   c. They should work hard to be good.

2. What is the way to life?
   a. going to church every Sunday
   b. singing songs about Jesus
   c. believing in Jesus

3. What things do people do to find other ways to God?
   a. being good, loving your family and obeying your parents
   b. pretending to love everyone and doing good things for others
   c. going to church, reading the Bible, praying, getting baptized
   (These are right things to do, but believing in Jesus and asking Him to forgive you is FIRST.)

4. What did Jesus call the people who tried to come to God without believing in Him?
   a. sincere people   b. thieves and robbers   c. ordinary people

5. What did Jesus say His sheep would do when they hear His voice?
   a. follow Him   b. have eternal life   c. come when they feel like it

6. What did Jesus say about His Father?
   a. "We are joined in our spirits only."
   b. "We are friends."
   c. "I and My Father are one."

7. Why were the people so angry?
   a. They thought He was just an ordinary man.
   b. They said He was not God!
   c. They wanted Him to talk about something else.

BIBLE WORDS TO REMEMBER

Pray without ceasing (stopping),
in everything, give thanks.... (1 Thessalonians 5:17-18)

Bible Story: ONE MAN SAYS, "THANK YOU"
from Luke 17

Jesus and His disciples were on their way to the city of Jerusalem. There were ten men standing on the side of the road who had a very terrible disease. No one wanted to get near them. When people saw them coming, they ran away and shouted at the men to get back away from them!

The men heard that Jesus was coming, and they knew that He made sick people well. They were sure He could make their disease go away. They called to Him, "Jesus, please help us!" Jesus was not afraid of being close them. He said, "Go and show yourselves to the priest. He will tell you that you are well."

As they were walking away, the disease that had covered their bodies was gone! They looked just like everyone else walking along the road! No one was running away from them any more.

One of the men stopped. He ran quickly back to Jesus. He knelt down and worshiped Jesus. "Thank You, Jesus, for making me well again!" Jesus said, "I healed ten men. Where are the other nine?" Jesus was glad that the one man remembered to thank Him. He said, "Your faith has made you well."

THINK ABOUT

Always remember to say Thank You to God for all the things He gives you and all the wonderful things He does for you! Jesus gives us many gifts of love every day.

PRAYER THOUGHT

Dear God, There are so many things I want to thank You for. I really don't deserve all the gifts You give me, and I want to learn to be thankful every day. Thank You for sending Jesus. Thank You for Your love. Thank you for my family. Thank You most of all for caring about me and showing Your love in so many ways! In Jesus Name, Amen.

Questions:
THINKING & REMEMBERING

Fill in the blanks or circle the letters of all that are right.

1. Where were Jesus and His disciples going?
   a. to Bethlehem   b. to Nazareth   c. to Jerusalem

2. Who were standing along the side of the road?
   a. crowds of people
   b. some of the followers who were waiting for Jesus
   c. ten men with a terrible disease

3. What were other people afraid of?
   a. that they would get the disease
   b. that they would miss seeing Jesus
   c. that their children would get sick

4. Why did the men want to come to Jesus?
   a. They heard that He made sick people well.
   b. They knew He could make the disease go away.
   c. They thought He would know what to do.

5. Jesus was afraid to be close to the sick men.   true_____   false_____

6. What did Jesus tell them to do?
   a. He told them to put lotion on their sores.
   b. He told them to show themselves to the priest.
   c. He told them to go back and stay away from people.

7. What happened when they obeyed Jesus' command?
   a. They were immediately well.
   b. It looked like they had fewer sores on their body.
   c. They didn't get well until they got to the temple.

8. What did one of the ten men do?
   He ran to Jesus and _____ down and _____ Him.

9. What did He say to Jesus?_____

10. How many men forgot to say, "Thank You"?_____

11. Fill in the missing Bible Words:
    In _____ , give _____ .

207

Bible Story: THE TWO SONS
from Matthew 21

Jesus was coming closer Jerusalem. The religious leaders followed Him and tried to argue about His message. They could not understand how Jesus could say He was from God and then eat dinner with people who were "sinners"!

Jesus knew what they were saying about Him. He knew that they were angry and trying to find a reason to kill Him. But He loved them. He would keep teaching until God told Him that His work on earth was finished.

Jesus told this story: *A father had two sons. One morning he said, "I want both of you to work today in my vineyard." One son said, "No! I don't want to work today!" But after a short time, he was sorry he had said that, and he went right to work. The other son said, "I will go and work," but he did not go.*

Jesus asked His listeners, "Which son obeyed his father?" The religious leaders said, "Of course it was the son who worked." "Yes," Jesus said. "Think about what you are doing. You believe you are saying all the right things. You are saying *yes* to God, but you are not *doing* what God says."

THINK ABOUT

Remember . . . to remember. That means "don't forget!" Sometimes we choose not to remember important things that we know we are supposed to do. Then we say, "I forgot." God wants you to listen to your parents and teachers because they know what is best and they will help you make the right choices to grow and be strong in many ways. God's words are very important to know so that you will remember the promises He has given and be ready for Jesus when He comes again!

PRAYER THOUGHT

Dear God, I know that I do not always obey You. There are times that I just want to say "no" when my mom or dad tells me to do something. I know that you want me to obey my parents. Help me do the right thing and ask Your forgiveness when I do wrong. In Jesus Name, Amen.

Questions:
THINKING & REMEMBERING

Circle the letters of all that are right.

1. Into which city was Jesus coming?
   a. Jerusalem   b. Samaria   c. Bethany

2. Why were the religious leaders following Jesus?
   a. They were arguing with Him about His message.
   b. They were telling Him about the temple.
   c. They wanted to know more about God.

3. What did they think that Jesus should not do?
   a. say He was from God   b. talk about God   c. eat dinner with sinners

4. What did Jesus know that the leaders were saying about Him?
   a. that He was the Son of God
   b. that He would be a priest in the temple
   c. that He should be killed for saying that He was God

5. How did Jesus feel about the people who were angry?
   a. He loved them.
   b. He hoped they would stop talking.
   c. He didn't care about them because He was too busy.

6. What story did Jesus tell to help them think about what they were doing?
   a. a story about a rich man
   b. a story about a father who asked his two sons to work
   c. a story about a shepherd

7. What did the two sons do differently?
   a. One said he would work and didn't. One said he would not work and did.
   b. They each worked on different parts of the vineyard.
   c. They worked on different days.

8. Why did Jesus tell the religious leaders that they did the same?
   a. They said they were working for God, but they weren't.
   b. They believed they were saying *yes* to God, but then did not *do* it.
   c. They made everyone think they knew what God said.

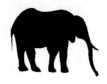

BIBLE WORDS TO REMEMBER

Pray without ceasing (stopping),
in everything, give thanks.... (1 Thessalonians 5:17-18)

Bible Story: VIEW FROM A TREE
from Luke 19

Jesus and His friends were going through the town of Jericho where a man named Zacchaeus lived. Zacchaeus had a lot of money, but he wasn't happy. Zacchaeus didn't have any friends. He was a tax collector and a lot of times took extra money for himself.

Many people were crowded in the streets of Jericho to see Jesus. Zacchaeus wanted to see Jesus, too. Finally, He came close to Jesus, but he was a very short man and too many people were in front of him. Then Zacchaeus had a great idea. He climbed up a tree and waited. Now he could see everything. Jesus was coming toward the tree where he was!

Jesus stopped and looked right up at Zacchaeus. He said, "Zacchaeus, come down—I'm going to your house today." Zacchaeus was so surprised! Jesus even knew his name! He hurried down the tree, and they went to his house. Zacchaeus told Jesus about the money he had taken from other people. He felt sorry. He said, "I am going to give back all the money I took and more. Thank You, Jesus, for showing me how God wants me to live. Thank You for caring about me."

THINK ABOUT

We can never be "good enough" all by ourselves. We can never do all the "right things" on our own. We cannot love others just by saying the words. We need the love of Jesus inside us to help us.

PRAYER THOUGHT

Dear God, Thank You for caring about me and knowing my name. Help me to learn the things I should and to obey Your Word. In Jesus Name, Amen.

Questions:
THINKING & REMEMBERING

Fill in the blanks or circle the letters of all that are right.

1. What town were Jesus and His friends going through?
   a. Jerusalem   b. Nazareth   c. Jericho

2. Even though Zacchaeus had enough money, what didn't he have?
   a. a big enough house   b. a place to put his money   c. friends

3. What job did Zacchaeus have?
   a. He worked in a bank.   b. He was a tax collector.   c. He owned a store.

4. Give the reason people did not like him.
   a. He was short.
   b. He thought he was better than everyone else.
   c. He kept money for himself that wasn't his.

5. Why couldn't Zacchaeus see Jesus?
   a. There were crowds of people in the way.
   b. He was too far away.
   c. He was too short to see over all the people.

6. What idea did Zacchaeus have so that he could see Jesus?
   a. He would run ahead of all the people.
   b. He would politely ask people to let him through to get closer.
   c. He would climb up a tree and wait for Jesus to come by.

Write T or F (True or False) beside each letter.

7. What did Jesus do when He came to the tree where Zacchaeus was?
   a. _____ He was walking too fast to notice Zacchaeus.
   b. _____ He looked up in the tree.
   c. _____ He called to Zacchaeus by his name
   d. _____ He said He was coming to his house that very day!
   e. _____ He told Zacchaeus to come down from the tree.

8. What did Zacchaeus tell Jesus?
   a. _____ He would give back more money than he had taken.
   b. _____ He was sorry for doing wrong.
   c. _____ He wanted to obey God.
   d. _____ He thanked Jesus for loving him and caring about him.
   e. _____ He liked being a tax collector.

BIBLE WORDS TO REMEMBER

Let us not grow weary while doing good …
As we have opportunity, let us do good to all.… (Galatians 6:9-10)

Bible Story: THE WORKERS
from Matthew 20

Jesus told this parable to show that everyone who comes to God is important:

*There was once a man who had a great **vineyard**. When the grapes were ready to pick, he did not have enough workers to do the job. So he went early in the morning to the **marketplace** to find more workers. He told some men, "If you can work for the day, I will pay you a **silver coin**." They were happy to work and agreed that the pay was good. A little while later, the man could see that he needed even more workers. He went to find them. When he told them that he would pay them fairly, they agreed and went to work.*

*At lunchtime, he needed more workers. Then in the afternoon, he **hired** even more men. Each time the men were glad to have work and were willing to go to the vineyard and work as long as they could for whatever the man paid them.*

At the end of the day, when there was only an hour left to finish the work, the man asked a few more workers if they could help. They worked until it was finished.

WORDS TO KNOW

vineyard:	a large garden where grapes are grown
marketplace:	the place where people sell their crops
silver coin:	an amount of money
hired:	to ask someone to work for money

THINK ABOUT

Jesus told the story about the workers to help people understand that everyone who comes to God is important. Everyone who believes in Jesus and wants to be part of His kingdom is welcome to come.

Questions:
THINKING & REMEMBERING

Fill in the blanks or circle the letters of all that are right.

1. What was Jesus teaching in this parable?
   a. Everyone who comes to God is important.
   b. You must work a long time to be noticed by God.
   c. The people who work a short time will not be very great.

2. What was the parable about?
   a. a man who had a vineyard
   b. a man who hired workers
   c. a man who liked grapes

3. Where did the man go first to find help to pick grapes in his vineyard?
   a. He went to another town close to his vineyard.
   b. He went to the city office.
   c. He went to the marketplace.

4. What was the pay that he offered?
   a. one silver coin
   b. as much as they thought they were worth when they finished
   c. ten silver coins

5. Were the men happy with what the man was going to pay?
   a. They were happy to work and agreed that the pay was good.
   b. They thought if they were good workers they might get more.
   c. They wanted to discuss the pay before they accepted.

6. When he discovered he needed more workers later, how many times did he go to find them?
   a. two times   b. one more time   c. four times

7. All of the men agreed to work for whatever pay the man would give.
   true_____   false_____

8. Before Jesus told this story, the people were concerned about who would be the greatest. This parable helps the people understand that
   a. everyone is important to God.
   b. God loves everyone.
   c. everyone who wants to be part of God's kingdom is welcome to come.

Bible Story: PAYMENT TIME

from Matthew 20

Jesus continued His parable:

The man who owned the vineyard and had hired each group of men at different times of the day told his servant to pay all the men. The pay for each was one silver coin. All the workers lined up to get their pay. The men who had started working last were called to get their pay before the others. The men who had worked since morning were very grumpy! They said, "This is not fair—why are they getting the same pay? We deserve more pay than the others because we worked longer—and we were here first! Why are we the last to get paid?"

The man said very kindly. "I have kept my promise. You agreed on the pay. When I asked you to work for one silver coin, you were happy. If I choose to give the others the same, that is for me to decide, not you."

Jesus said, "Everyone who comes to God and believes in Me will be in heaven. It won't matter who first believes or who is last. In God's kingdom, the last may be first, and the first may be last."

THINK ABOUT

Do you worry a lot about what is fair? Sometimes people spend so much time and energy on fairness, they use up the time they could be spending on positive things. When we remember that our real reward is heaven, who gets the most and best right here and now won't matter, and we will be able to do more of what God wants us to do. Life here on earth was never promised to be fair. Jesus is the perfect one. He knows exactly what is in each person's heart and He will be the perfect judge of what is fair. Check yourself in the next few days and see how many times you say, "It isn't fair!" Decide how you can change your attitude. Saying those words is just about YOU. Try to think about others and what God wants you to do and be.

PRAYER THOUGHT

Dear God, Thank You for Your gift of Jesus and all of Your promises. Help me remember that things will not always be fair, and help me think of You and others before myself. In Jesus Name, Amen.

Questions:
THINKING & REMEMBERING

Fill in the blanks or circle the letters of all that are right.

1. Write T or F (true or false) beside each letter.
   a. _____ The first group of workers was promised one silver coin.
   b. _____ The first group agreed to the pay that was offered.
   c. _____ The workers that were hired later in the morning, at noon, afternoon, and late in the day received more than one silver coin.

2. What was paid to each worker in each group? _____.

3. Which group was upset?
   a. the last group, because they didn't get to work as long
   b. the first group, because they had worked the longest for the same pay as all the others
   c. the three groups hired in between the first and the last because they really didn't want to work

4. What did the man who paid the workers tell the first group?
   a. "Be glad you had a job today."
   b. "You didn't work very hard all day."
   c. "I kept my promise and gave you what I said I would pay."

5. What is this parable about and what did it mean?
   a. It is about who would be in God's kingdom.
   b. It will not matter who believed first or last.
   c. All believers will be in heaven.

6. When will those who believe in Jesus receive their reward?
   a. They will receive it when they help people on earth.
   b. They will receive it when they ask God if they can have it.
   c. The great reward will be received in heaven.

7. What matters most?
   a. believing in Jesus
   b. trying to make everyone happy
   c. demanding that everything in this life be fair

BIBLE WORDS TO REMEMBER

Let us not grow weary while doing good ...
As we have opportunity, let us do good to all.... (Galatians 6: 9-10)

Bible Story: ONE FOOLISH SERVANT
from Matthew 25

Jesus told this story about **trust** and **loyalty**:

A man who had a great amount of money was leaving on a long journey. He called three servants to him and told them he was trusting them to be in charge of his riches while he was gone. The first servant was given 5,000 gold coins by his master. The second was given 2,000 and the third, 1,000.

The first two servants found ways to increase the amount of money given to them. The third servant dug a hole in the ground when no one was looking and buried it.

*When the master came back, he asked each of them what they had done with the money. The first two servants had twice the amount of money their master had left with them. He was very pleased and rewarded them. He said that they were loyal servants who could be trusted with more. The third servant was **trembling**. "Here are the one thousand coins you left. I did not want to **risk** losing it, so I buried it." The master was very disappointed. "I will give your money to the others. You should never stop using everything you have for good."*

WORDS TO KNOW

trust: to believe in someone and be able to depend on them
loyalty: to stay true to someone and do what is right
trembling: shaking with fear
risk: take a chance

THINK ABOUT

God has given each of us special gifts to help His kingdom grow bigger. Whatever God gives us—whether it is a lot or just a little—we should use it wisely.

 **Questions:**
THINKING & REMEMBERING

Fill in the blanks or circle the letters of all that are right.

1. What was the parable about that Jesus told His followers?
   a. being sincere   b. loyalty   c. being careful   d. trust

2. Where was the master in the story going?
   a. He was going to live in a different city.
   b. He was going on a long journey.
   c. He was going to visit family in another country.

3. How many servants did he call and speak to?
   a. four   b. one   c. three

4. What did he want these servants to do?
   a. be in charge of his wealth
   b. be wise with the money he gave them while he was gone
   c. spend the money on themselves

5. How much did he give the first servant?_____

6. How much did he give the second servant?_____

7. How much was the third servant given?_____

8. What did the first two servants do?
   a. They increased (made more) the amount of money given to them.
   b. They buried it.
   c. They bought new houses.

9. What did the third servant do?
   a. He lost it.   b. He spent it.   c. He buried it.

10. What was Jesus teaching in this parable?
    a. We should be careful and hide our money.
    b. We should use everything God gives us in a wise way.
    c. Whatever God gives us—a little or a lot—we should use it for Him.

11. Fill in the Bible words from Galatians 6:10.
    As we have _____, let us do _____ to all.

Bible Story: BEING READY
from Matthew 25

Jesus told this parable and asked His listeners to discover the meaning:

It was the wedding day! The bride and her friends needed to be prepared when the bridegroom came. There were ten girls waiting for the bridegroom to call them for the wedding.

*It was already getting dark, and the bridegroom had not come. They got their lamps ready. Five of the girls had oil to keep their lamps lit. But the other five were **careless** and foolish. They thought, "Oh well, we will get more oil on the way if we need it."*

*When the bridegroom called for them to come, the five foolish girls went into a **panic**! They had no oil for their lamps! Their lamps had gone out! The shops were closed. It was too late to get ready. They were not prepared for his coming.*

The five wise girls followed the bridegroom to the wedding. The wedding celebration began. The door to the house was closed. When the five foolish girls arrived very late, the bridegroom said, "Go away. I do not know you. If you were my friends, you would have been ready to come when I called."

WORDS TO KNOW

careless: not thinking about what is important

panic: a terrible fear of knowing what will happen

THINK ABOUT

Jesus, our king will come back to earth someday. We will not know the exact time, but we must be ready and prepared when He comes. When He comes, it will be too late to change your mind and follow Him. You will be left behind if you have not believed in Him. He is calling everyone to come to Him. He loves you and wants everyone to be in heaven with Him.

PRAYER THOUGHT

Dear God, I want to be ready when Jesus comes! Help me to know each day what to do and what to say. I want to be able to pray "Come quickly, Lord Jesus!" In Jesus Name, Amen.

Questions:
THINKING & REMEMBERING

Fill in the blanks or circle the letters of all that are right.

1. What kind of celebration was Jesus telling about in His story?
   a. a birthday   b. a wedding   c. a Christmas celebration

2. Whom did the bride and her friends have to wait for?
   a. the parents of the bride   b. the bridegroom   c. some other friends

3. Did they know exactly when he would come for them?
   a. Yes, it would be before the sun went down.
   b. No, it would be sometime during the wedding week.
   c. No, they just had to be ready when he came.

4. How many girls were waiting for the bridegroom?
   a. seven   b. twelve   c. ten

5. How many kept their lamps burning so they would be ready when he called? _____

6. How many got tired of waiting and were not prepared when he came?
   _____

7. What happened after the celebration began?
   a. The door to the house was closed.
   b. Everyone was waiting for the five late girls.
   c. The gate was open but the door was shut.

8. What did the bridegroom say to those who came late?
   a. "I'm sorry that you missed some of the celebration."
   b. "Go away. I do not know you."
   c. "If you were my friends, you would have been ready when I called."

9. Whom are we waiting for now who is our king? _____

10. Will you be ready for Him when He comes?_____

Remember: Jesus promised that He would come back to earth and take us to heaven if we believe in Him. Jesus always keeps His promises. We do not know the exact time that Jesus will come back for us. We need to always be ready.

BIBLE WORDS TO REMEMBER

Let us not grow weary while doing good …
As we have opportunity, let us do good to all.…(Galatians 6: 9-10)

Bible Story: DIVIDING THE SHEEP AND GOATS
from Matthew 25

Jesus said that a shepherd keeps his flocks of animals in separate pastures. He **divides** them and puts the sheep in one field and the goats in another. It will be like this when the kingdom of God is ready and prepared for those who love Him. God wants everyone to come. He has **invited** them all to be in His kingdom.

Jesus, our King, will come with all the angels for those who love Him and are ready. He will sit on a great white throne and He will judge everyone fairly. Everyone who has ever lived will be there to stand before Him. He will divide all the people into two groups. There are only two choices. One is to **accept** Jesus, and the other is to **reject** Him. There is not a choice to be "almost" ready.

Then Jesus said, "I will tell the people who believe to stand on the right side. They will go into the kingdom of heaven where My Father is. There is a wonderful place prepared for them there." Those who rejected God's love, He will tell to stand on the left side. They chose to live in darkness far away from Jesus forever.

WORDS TO KNOW

divide: to make into two parts or places
invite: to ask people to come
accept: to trust and believe
reject: to refuse to believe or accept

THINK ABOUT

Can we get ready for Jesus by sitting in our house looking out the window waiting for Him to come? Jesus says that we should first believe in Him and ask Him to forgive our sins. We can show others by how we live that we believe. Then we should tell others about His love for them. Jesus wants everyone to go to heaven, and only those who have trusted Him will be ready when He comes. He loves you very much!

 # Questions:
THINKING & REMEMBERING

Fill in the blanks or circle the letters of all that are right.

1. Where does a shepherd keep his flocks of animals?
   a. He keeps them all together in the same place.
   b. He keeps them in separate pastures.
   c. He lets them go wherever they want to go.

2. How does he divide the animals?
   a. by their kind—sheep and goats
   b. by how old they are
   c. by their color

3. What did Jesus say the division would be like?
   a. people in the world living in different countries
   b. the kingdom of God
   c. the earth and space

Write T or F (true or false) beside the number.

4. _____ Jesus has invited everyone to come into the kingdom.
5. _____ All people will accept the invitation and believe in Jesus.
6. _____ There will be some who thought about accepting Jesus, but waited too long to make a decision.

7. Where will the people go who believe in Jesus?
   a. They will go to a very nice place on earth.
   b. They will go to heaven—a wonderful and perfect place where there will be no sickness, sadness or pain.
   c. They will go to a place where they can do more good works until they are good enough to go to heaven.

8. What will happen to the people who did not choose to love Jesus?
   a. They will be in darkness forever.
   b. Jesus will say, "I never loved you."
   c. They will not be in heaven because they rejected Jesus.

Remember: God never wants anyone to live in that darkness away from Him, but He will not force anyone to love and believe in Him. He lets each person choose where they will spend eternity.

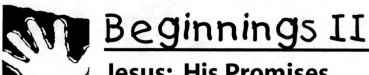

Beginnings II

Jesus: His Promises

BIBLE WORDS TO REMEMBER

Watch, stand fast in the faith, be brave, be strong.
Let all that you do be done with love. (1 Corinthians 16:13-14)

Bible Story: A BROTHER LIVES AGAIN
from John 11

Jesus and His disciples were on their way to Jerusalem. Jesus' friends, Mary and Martha, sent a message for Jesus to come quickly because their brother Lazarus was very sick. By the time He got the message, Jesus already knew that Lazarus was dead. He also knew that He had power over death.

Lazarus was buried in a tomb. The sisters cried and wished that Jesus could be there. When Martha saw Jesus coming she said, "If only You had been here, my brother would still be alive. But I do know that right now, if You ask God for anything, He will do it."

Jesus cried when he saw how sad His friends were. He knew how much they loved Lazarus. He knew that God would be with Him to bring Lazarus back to life. When they got to the place where Lazarus was buried, Jesus prayed, "Thank You for hearing Me, Father. Please let everyone know that You have sent Me to give life."

Then He said in a loud voice, "Lazarus, come out!" Lazarus slowly came out of the grave! His sisters were so happy! The people who saw this miracle said, "This must be the Son of God!"

PRAYER THOUGHT

Dear God, Thank You for sending Jesus to show power over death. Thank You for caring when I am sad. Help me remember always that You will be with me. In Jesus Name, Amen.

Questions:
Thinking & Remembering

Fill in the blanks or circle the letters of all that are right.

1. Why did Mary and Martha send a message to Jesus to come quickly?
   a. They had dinner ready.
   b. Their brother Lazarus was very sick.
   c. They wanted Jesus to come and help them.

2. Jesus got there in time to help before Lazarus died.   true_____   false_____

3. What did Mary and Martha do?
   a. They waited for Jesus to tell them what to do.
   b. They told all their friends that Lazarus wasn't really dead.
   c. They buried Lazarus in a tomb.

4. What did Martha say to Jesus when He came?
   a. "If only You had been here, my brother would still be alive."
   b. "Why were you so long in coming?"
   c. "Lazarus is dead. We have buried him."

5. What did Martha know that Jesus could do?
   a. Whatever He asked God to do would happen.
   b. He could bring Lazarus back to life.
   c. He could comfort all their family and friends.

6. When Jesus saw how sad his friends were, what did He do?
   a. He hugged them.   b. He cried.   c. He told them not to worry.

7. What was Jesus' prayer to the Father?
   "Thank You for hearing Me, Father. Please let everyone _____
   that You have _____ Me to give _____."

8. What did Jesus do when they got to the tomb?
   a. He asked everyone some questions.
   b. He thought about what He was going to do.
   c. He told Lazarus to come out.

9. What did everyone who saw this miracle know about Jesus?
   a. He was very powerful.
   b. He was the Son of God.
   c. He loved Lazarus.

Bible Story: A PRECIOUS GIFT
from John 12

Jesus was having dinner with His friends. He was happy to be with friends who loved Him. But He was sad because He would not be with them much longer. He knew that He was going to Jerusalem and would **suffer** and die a very **painful** death for the sins of the world. He knew people would turn against Him. Many would not believe that He came to bring God's love.

Martha served a wonderful meal. She loved cooking for Jesus! Mary wanted to show her love to Jesus, too. She had a **precious** gift she was saving. Mary poured **perfume** over Jesus' feet and wiped them with her hair.

The whole room smelled sweet with this wonderful perfume. Then an angry voice said, "What a waste! That perfume was worth a lot of money. It should have been sold and the money given to the poor." Judas said these words. He was the disciple who would turn away from Jesus in Jerusalem.

Jesus said to Judas, "Don't say that to Mary. She has given this for My **burial**. The poor will always be with you, but I will be leaving you soon." Mary gave the very best that she had to show her love.

WORDS TO KNOW

suffer: to experience a great deal of pain

painful: to feel severe hurt

precious: worth a lot

perfume: a liquid that smells very sweet and wonderful

burial: to put a dead person in a grave

THINK ABOUT

What is our very best gift to Jesus? When Mary wanted to give her very best perfume to Jesus, Jesus saw more than the perfume—He saw that Mary's heart was full of love. That is what He sees and knows when we give a gift to Him or others. He sees what is in our heart.

Questions:
THINKING & REMEMBERING

Fill in the blanks or circle the letters of all that are right.

1. What was happy about this dinner Jesus was having with His friends?
   a. He was with friends who loved Him.
   b. He liked Martha's cooking.
   c. He wanted to see if Mary would give Him a gift.

2. What made Jesus sad?
   a. He would not be with them much longer.
   b. He was thinking about what was going to happen in Jerusalem.
   c. Some people would not believe that He came to bring God's love to them.

3. What was going to happen to Jesus very soon in Jerusalem?
   a. People were going to turn against Him.
   b. He was going to suffer and die a very painful death.
   c. He would be made a king.

4. Why was Jesus going to die?
   a. to make people finally believe that He was God's Son
   b. for the sins of the world
   c. so that He could go back to heaven

Write Mary or Martha for the right sentence.

5. Who showed her love for Jesus by pouring perfume on His feet?_____

6. Who showed her love for Jesus by making a wonderful meal?_____

7. What did Judas say about Mary's gift?
   a. "That was a waste!"
   b. "That was a wonderful gift."
   c. "That perfume should have been sold and the money given to the poor."

8. What did Jesus know that Judas was going to do in Jerusalem?
   a. be His best friend   b. turn against Him   c. take care of the money

PRAYER THOUGHT

Dear God, Thank You for sending Jesus, Your very best gift to earth to show how much You love me. Help me to give all of my gifts with love. In Jesus Name, Amen.

BIBLE WORDS TO REMEMBER

Watch, stand fast in the faith, be brave, be strong.
Let all that you do be done with love. (1 Corinthians 16:13-14)

Bible Story: A KING COMES INTO JERUSALEM
from Luke 19

Just before Jesus and His disciples came into Jerusalem, He told two of his disciples to go and bring Him a donkey to ride into the city. He said they would find the donkey tied to a post just outside a village. If anyone asked them why they were taking the donkey, they should say, "The Lord needs it."

When they brought the donkey, Jesus carefully got on its back. The children in Jerusalem were very happy. This was an exciting day! "Here comes Jesus riding on a donkey," they shouted. The children sang and waved palm branches from the trees to show Jesus how much they loved Him.

Many people were following Jesus and singing, "**Hosanna**! Hosanna!" They wanted Jesus to be their king on earth. They did not understand that Jesus is a heavenly king.

Some people were not singing. They did not want the people to love Jesus. They were angry because Jesus said He was the Son of God. They told Jesus to make the children stop singing. Jesus did not tell the children to stop singing. He said, "I love the children, and I like to hear them sing. It shows that they love Me, too."

WORDS TO KNOW

Hosanna: to show worship; in Hebrew, it meant "Save Us!"

THINK ABOUT

God's plan is perfect. Jesus was part of God's plan to bring love to the world. He loved us more than we can ever understand. He came to die for us so that we could live forever. Jesus did not ask God to change His mind even though He would have to suffer and die. He wanted to make a way for everyone who believed to go to heaven.

Questions:
Thinking & Remembering

Fill in the blanks or circle the letters of all that are right.

1. What instructions did Jesus give His disciples?
   a. They should sneak into a village.
   b. They would see a donkey tied to a post outside the village.
   c. If someone saw them, He told them what to say.

2. What did Jesus tell them to explain to someone who asked about the donkey?
   a. "We are just going to borrow the donkey for a few days."
   b. "Don't worry, we won't hurt the donkey."
   c. "The Lord needs the donkey."

3. How did Jesus arrive in Jerusalem?
   a. He was walking with His disciples.
   b. He was riding on a donkey.
   c. He went on a path not many people knew about.

4. Cross out the wrong word in the sentence and write the correct word.
   The children in Jerusalem were sad when they saw Jesus coming.

   _____

5. What did the children and people do to welcome Jesus?
   a. They sang, "Hosanna!"
   b. They threw flowers at Him.
   c. They waved palm branches from the trees.

6. Why did some people hate Jesus?
   a. They didn't believe that Jesus was the Son of God.
   b. They didn't want the people to love Jesus.
   c. They thought He made the crowds too noisy.

7. What did the men tell Jesus to make the children stop doing?
   a. dancing
   b. waving branches
   c. singing

8. How does Jesus feel about children?
   He _____ the children and He likes to hear them _____.
   He said, "It shows that they _____ Me, too."

Bible Story: THE END OF THE AGE
from Matthew 24

Jesus and the disciples were in Jerusalem. The disciples wanted to ask Jesus some questions. They were **confused** about what was going to happen. They wanted to learn more before He left to go back to heaven.

The question they asked Jesus was about the **end of the world**. What would happen? What would it be like? Would Jesus tell them when He was coming back to bring the **new kingdom**? Jesus said, "You cannot know everything about that time. Only God knows the time that the world will end. He wants everyone to hear about Him so they can choose to love Him and be in His kingdom."

Jesus wants us to be ready for His return right now! He doesn't want us to wait and think we will have time to get ready when we get older or when we decide to make up our minds.

Jesus said that sad and terrible things will happen before He returns. The terrible things will happen because people are **turning away** from God. He will warn them to come to Him before it is too late and there are no more **chances** to believe.

WORDS TO KNOW

confused:	to not understand
end of the world:	the time when God has given everyone a chance to believe and will send Jesus to take those who love Him to heaven
new kingdom:	a new heaven and a new earth just as wonderful as it was in the beginning!
turning away:	to reject what has been heard about God
chances:	all the possibilities and opportunities given

THINK ABOUT

Jesus talked about those who will try to tell us not to believe in God. He said there will be someone at the end times who will say he is God. If you stay close to Jesus, you will know the difference! Talk to God every day and listen to His words to you in the Bible. You will know who the real Jesus is, and no one will be able to trick you. Right now Jesus is in heaven getting a place ready for you. Don't keep this wonderful news a secret! Tell others what is true and let them know that you love Jesus and that He loves them too!

Questions:
Thinking & Remembering

Fill in the blanks or circle the letters of all that are right.

1. Where were Jesus and His disciples?
    a. by the sea of Galilee   b. in Jerusalem   c. with friends in Bethany

2. What were the disciples confused about?
    a. what was going to happen when Jesus went back to heaven
    b. who their friends were going to be after Jesus left
    c. what they were going to do the next day

3. What did the disciples ask Jesus about the end of the world?
    a. what would happen and what would it be like
    b. when He was coming back to bring the new kingdom
    c. if they could go to heaven with Him right now

4. What did Jesus tell them that they could not know?
    a. the exact time   b. that He would get a place ready

5. What did Jesus tell them was most important?
    a. to tell everyone that Jesus loved them
    b. to give everyone a chance to believe and be ready for Him
    c. to tell people they had a long time to decide

6. Should we ever think we can wait and decide later to follow Jesus?
    a. No, we should choose to follow Him right now.
    b. Yes, we can wait until we are older.
    c. Yes, it won't really matter in the end.

7. Why will terrible and sad things happen before He comes back?
    a. People will reject God's love more and more.
    b. People who have heard will turn away from God.
    c. People will decide not to be nice.

8. What will God try to do?
    a. He won't care anymore.
    b. He will warn the people to come to Him before it is too late.
    c. He will let people do whatever they want and forget about them.

9. Bible Words: _____, stand fast in the faith, be brave, be strong. (1 Corinthians 16:13)

BIBLE WORDS TO REMEMBER

Watch, stand fast in the faith, be brave, be strong.
Let all that you do be done with love. (1 Corinthians 16:13-14)

Bible Story: BEING READY FOR JESUS
from Matthew 24

Jesus told His disciples that they should be happy when they were thinking about His coming back. When we see bad things happening, it is easy to feel frightened—unless we remember how much He loves us. Whatever happens, He will come to be there with us! God is in control of the whole universe! We can be thankful that God loves us and wants us in His kingdom.

When we know Jesus, we will be able to know the things that will happen and be excited because it is getting closer to the time when He will return. Jesus always keeps His promises! He is getting a beautiful place ready for us in heaven. Then He will come back for those who believe in Him. In heaven, nothing bad will ever happen again. It will be a place of complete joy and happiness!

Jesus said that while we are watching and waiting, we must show others by how we live that we love God and tell them about His love. Problems are never too big for God and there will never be a reason that He will not love anyone who believes and asks Jesus to be in their heart.

Write the Bible Words from 1 Corinthians 16:13-14 on the lines below.

_____

_____

_____

Questions:
THINKING & REMEMBERING

Read Matthew 24. Jesus tells some of the things that will happen before He comes back. Put True or False (T/F) beside what you can know is already happening.

1. _____ Many others will say that they are the Messiah.

2. _____ There will be many wars and talk about more wars.

3. _____ There will be places in the world where there is not enough water to grow food and many people will die.

4. _____ There will be more people dying from terrible diseases.

5. _____ There will be more earthquakes in unusual places.

6. _____ People will hate each other. They will even stop pretending to be good. They will just give up.

7. _____ People will stop loving each other in families and do evil things to each other.

8. _____ The Bible will be told and read to many people. Some will believe—some will not.

9. _____ People will be killed for believing in Jesus.

10. So when we see these things happening, should we be afraid? _____

Remember: God loves you and whatever happens, He will be with you. When we love Jesus, we know that He is in control and that everything will turn out right!

Come Quickly, Lord Jesus!

Discuss these things with a parent or teacher.

PRAYER THOUGHT

Dear God, Help me to remember what You have told in Your Word about the end of the world. Help me to not be afraid but look up to heaven and know that JESUS is coming soon! In Jesus Name, Amen.

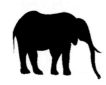

BIBLE WORDS TO REMEMBER

Be of good comfort, be of one mind, live in peace; and the God of love and peace will be with you. (2 Corinthians 13:11)

Bible Story: OUR KING AND AN ENEMY
from Matthew 26

When Jesus rode into Jerusalem on a donkey, everyone had been excited. They wanted Jesus to be a king on earth. The disciples also wanted Jesus to be a king. They didn't want the Romans to rule them any longer.

Jesus tried to tell His disciples and followers that He was not an earthly king. He was a heavenly king. He was going to die, live again, and go back to heaven.

Judas, one of the disciples, would not accept a king that was not going to rule on earth. He wanted a king to make him wealthy and powerful in an earthly kingdom. When he saw that Jesus was not going to do that, he gave himself to evil.

Judas knew that the Jewish priests wanted to kill Jesus. He went to the priests who said they would give thirty silver coins for helping them find and arrest his "master." Judas agreed and left to try to pretend that he still was Jesus' disciple. He thought, "I will at least make some money for all the time I have wasted following Jesus." Jesus knew all about Judas and what he had done. Jesus loved Judas, and He was very sad for him.

THINK ABOUT

The whole plan of God is about His love for people. It is about people loving Him. It is about people loving each other. God knew that it took more than rules and commandments for love to be in our hearts. Jesus is our heavenly king. That is wonderful because we know that earth is not perfect. People are not perfect. Only God is perfect, and He is making us a perfect place to be forever!

Questions:
THINKING & REMEMBERING

Circle the letters of all that are right.

1. Why were the people so excited when Jesus came into Jerusalem?
   a. They wanted Him to be king.
   b. They thought He was kind.
   c. They wanted to get rid of the Romans who ruled them.

2. Who else wanted Jesus to be an earthly king?
   a. the disciples   b. the priests   c. the Romans

3. What did Jesus tell His disciples and followers?
   a. He would stay on earth and become a king.
   b. It was not time for Him to take over the Romans.
   c. He was a heavenly king, not an earthly king.

4. What was Jesus' purpose in coming to earth?
   a. He came to die.
   b. He would live again.
   c. He came to visit before He went back to heaven.

5. Which disciple was angry about Jesus not being a king on earth?
   a. Peter   b. John   c. Judas

6. What did this disciple do?
   a. He went to the priests who wanted to kill Jesus.
   b. He agreed to help them find Jesus and capture Him.
   c. He decided to believe in Jesus even though He was not the kind of king he wanted.

7. How much money did the priests offer to give him for bringing Jesus to them? a. 50 pieces of silver   b. 20 pieces of silver   c. 30 pieces of silver

PRAYER THOUGHT

Dear God, Help me to be brave when someone asks me if I believe in Jesus. I want to say, "YES!" and be able to tell them WHY I love Jesus so much! In Jesus Name, Amen.

BIBLE WORDS TO REMEMBER

Be of good comfort, be of one mind, live in peace; and the God of love and peace will be with you. (2 Corinthians 13:11)

Bible Story: THE SUPPER
from Matthew 26; Mark 14; Luke 22

It was the **celebration** of the Passover for the Jewish people in Jerusalem. This was a time of remembering God's promise to take His people from Egypt where they were slaves to a new land where they could be free.

Jesus and His disciples were planning to have a special supper together. Jesus knew that this would be the last time He would be with all of His disciples before He died.

Jesus gave instructions to Peter and John: "Go into the city, and a man will meet you carrying a **pitcher** of water. Follow him. Wherever he goes in, say to the owner of the house, 'Jesus said you would take us to the guest room where He will have the Passover meal with His disciples.'" Jesus said it would be a large **upper room**. It would already be **furnished**. He said to make everything ready.

In the evening, Jesus came with the other disciples. The twelve disciples ate the **Passover supper** together. Then Jesus wanted to tell His disciples some important things before He died on the cross and went back to heaven. They still did not understand why Jesus was going to die for the sins of the world.

WORDS TO KNOW

celebration:	a time to remember something very special
pitcher:	a container like a jar that holds water
upper room:	a room that is above another
furnished:	all the things needed
Passover supper:	the meal to remember God's promise to the Israelites

Questions:
THINKING & REMEMBERING

Fill in the blanks or circle the letters of all that are right.

1. What were the Jewish people doing in Jerusalem?
    a. They were there to see Jesus.
    b. It was the celebration of the Passover.
    c. It was a nice time of the year to go to Jerusalem.

2. What was the meaning of this celebration?
    a. to celebrate the birth of Jesus
    b. to honor the Romans
    c. to remember that God made them free from being slaves in Egypt

3. What were Jesus and His disciples planning?
    a. to have the Passover supper together
    b. to find out what the priests were going to do with Jesus
    c. to make people unhappy with the Roman government

4. This was the last time that Jesus would be together with all of His disciples before He died.   true_____   false_____

5. What instructions did Jesus give to Peter and John?
    Put the following in the order in which they happened:
    a. _____ Follow a man with a pitcher of water.
    b. _____ Go into the city.
    c. _____ Get everything ready.
    d. _____ Ask the man where the room is for Jesus to have the Passover meal with His disciples.
    e. _____ Wherever the man with the pitcher goes, go and talk to the owner of the house.
    f. _____ The man will show you a large upper room, furnished and prepared.

6. How many disciples were at the supper? _____

PRAYER THOUGHT

Dear God, You always show how much You care about me. Help me to be kind and love others like You love me. In Jesus Name, Amen.

Bible Story: JESUS SHOWS LOVE
from John 13

In the time that Jesus lived on earth, people who came into the house at dinner always took their **sandals** off at the door. A **servant** would wash their feet because they were so dusty from walking on dirt roads.

When Jesus and His disciples went to the room for their Passover meal, there was no one to wash their feet and none of the disciples thought it was their job to do it. Jesus wanted to teach His disciples a special lesson about being a servant and loving each other.

Jesus took a towel and a bowl of water and began to wash their feet. Jesus knelt at Peter's feet and Peter was **ashamed** of himself. "No, Jesus! You are not the servant. You are our Master. You shall never wash my feet!"

Jesus said, "You do not understand, Peter. But some day you will know that the person who loves is the person who helps. I am showing my love by doing what a servant does."

When Jesus **finished** washing the feet of all His disciples, He told His friends, "I have washed your feet to teach you to do kind things for each other and for other people." It was an important lesson.

WORDS TO KNOW

sandals: a shoe that has open spaces with straps

servant: someone who helps and works for others

ashamed: to feel sorry about something you have done

finished: to get something done

PRAYER THOUGHT

Dear God, I have so many lessons to learn. I just want to say, "That is not my job," when it is something I don't like to do—or don't want to do! I am forgetting what is most important—loving You and loving others. When I remember that, it really doesn't matter what the job to do is, it's getting it done. Help me remember! In Jesus Name, Amen.

Questions:
THINKING & REMEMBERING

Fill in the blanks or circle the letters of all that are right.

1. Why did people in the time of Jesus take off their sandals?
   a. It was polite.
   b. It kept the floors clean.
   c. Their feet were dusty from walking on dirt roads.

2. Why were Jesus and His disciples having a special dinner?
   a. They were going to celebrate the Passover.
   b. They just liked to be together.
   c. They were hungry.

3. There was a servant at the door to wash their feet when they went into the room.   true_____ false_____

4. Which one of the disciples wanted to wash the feet of the others?
   a. Peter   b. Matthew   c. James   d. none of them

5. What lesson did Jesus teach His disciples?
   a. He taught them how to be a servant to others.
   b. He taught them how to do some of the work.
   c. He taught them how to love each other.

6. Who washed all of the disciples' feet? _____.

7. Which disciple said to Jesus, "You shall never wash my feet"? _____

8. Who did Peter say that Jesus was? _____

9. What did Jesus want Peter to understand?
   a. Washing feet was not an unpleasant job.
   b. If you love others, you will help them.
   c. You should serve others when it is something easy to do.

10. What did Jesus want His disciples to remember?
    a. They should always love each other.
    b. He showed them how to do kind things for each other.
    c. They didn't need to wash feet because they would just get dirty again.

11. Bible Words to Remember: …be of one _____, live in _____.

237

Bible Story: JUDAS GOES AWAY
from Matthew 26; Luke 22

Jesus and His disciples finished their Passover meal. Jesus knew that it would soon be time for Him to leave the special friends that He loved. When Jesus looked at Judas, He was very sad. He said, "One of you will **betray** Me and will give Me to the **enemy**."

All the disciples looked at each other. They were **shocked**! All of them loved Jesus! They followed and believed in Him. Which one of them could do such a thing? They each asked, "Is it I, Lord?"

Jesus said, "I will give a piece of bread that I dip into the cup to the one who will betray Me." He gave it to Judas and said, "Judas, Go quickly and do what you planned." Judas left. He made His **final** choice.

Jesus knew that the others would be afraid too. Jesus said to the disciples, "You will also all leave when the enemies come to take Me." Peter said, "Maybe the others will, but I will never leave You!" Jesus said, "Peter, before the rooster crows in the morning, you will say you do not know Me three times. I will understand and I will always love you."

WORDS TO KNOW

betray: be disloyal to

enemy: someone who is against someone enough to hurt them

shocked: very surprised and upset

final: something that cannot be changed

THINK ABOUT

A friend is someone you can talk to and share special times with. Friends can tell each other how they really feel and still like each other. Friends can make mistakes and forgive each other. You can know that Jesus is always your best friend. He is the only friend that will never stop loving you! Jesus loved each one of His disciples. They were so different from each other. He thought of the times they had been together. They had laughed and cried together. They had become friends. Jesus thought, "I have loved these who are in the world, and I will love them to the end."

Questions:
THINKING & REMEMBERING

Fill in the blanks or circle the letters of all that are right.

1. How long would Jesus keep loving His friends?
   a. He would always love them.
   b. He would love them until He went back to heaven.
   c. He would love them if they didn't make any mistakes.

2. Why was Jesus sad when He looked at Judas?
   a. Judas had not loved Jesus the way the others had.
   b. Judas turned against Jesus.
   c. Judas was going to betray Jesus.

3. Why were the disciples shocked?
   a. They all loved Jesus.
   b. They followed Him and believed His message of love.
   c. They believed that He was the Son of God.

4. What question did each of the disciples ask Jesus?
   a. "Do you mean that the religious leaders will betray you?"
   b. "Do we have any enemies we don't know about?"
   c. "Is it I, Lord?"

5. How did Jesus show which disciple was going to betray Him?
   a. He dipped bread in the cup and gave it to Judas.
   b. He told everyone that it was Judas.
   c. He took Judas to the door and told him to go out.

6. What did Jesus tell the other disciples after Judas left?
   a. "There is someone else who will leave Me."
   b. "All of you will leave when the enemy comes to take Me."
   c. "Some of you will run away."

7. When Peter said he would never leave Jesus, what did Jesus say?
   a. "Before the rooster crows, you will say you do not know Me three times."
   b. "I know that you love Me, Peter."
   c. "I think you will always do the right thing."

8. Would Jesus stop loving Peter? _____
   Jesus said, "I will understand and I will always _____ you."

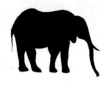

BIBLE WORDS TO REMEMBER

Be of good comfort, be of one mind, live in peace; and the God of love and peace will be with you. (2 Corinthians 13:11)

Bible Story: THE NEW COVENANT
from Mark 14; John 13-16; Luke 22:20

The meal that Jesus had with His disciples is called the "**Last Supper**" because it was the last time that they were all together. Jesus told His disciples that He was going to die, but He would be alive again.

When Jesus shared the bread with each of His disciples He said, "This is My body that will be broken for you. Take and eat. Whenever you do this, remember Me." Then He took the cup and said, "This cup is the **new covenant** in My blood, which is given for you." It is a sign between believers and God. God will accept all people who believe in Me from all **nations**."

Then Jesus said, "Very soon, it will seem to you that everything has gone wrong. It will be hard for you to understand. But keep trusting and believing. I will be leaving you, but I will be alive again, and we will meet together before I go back to My Father."

The disciples did remember—and they celebrated this supper again after Jesus went back to heaven. All the people who believed after this time still remember Him by sharing this meal together, until He comes to earth again.

WORDS TO KNOW

Last Supper: the meal that Jesus had with His disciples before He died. This meal is also called The Lord's Supper or Communion.

new covenant: a promise between God and those who believe in Jesus

nations: all the countries in the world

Questions:
THINKING & REMEMBERING

Circle the letters of all that are right.

1. Why was the meal Jesus had with His disciples called The Last Supper?
   a. because Judas was not going to eat with them again
   b. because it was the last time the disciples would be together
   c. because it was the last time Jesus and the disciples would eat together before He died

2. What did Jesus tell His disciples that He was going to do?
   a. He was going to talk to the people who didn't like Him.
   b. He was going to die for the sins of the world.
   c. He was going to stay with them a few more months.

3. Would Jesus stay in the grave?
   a. He would stay only for about a week.
   b. He would stay until God could see that people were trying to be good again.
   c. No, He is alive today!

4. What did Jesus give that was a sign of something important?
   a. He gave a new covenant (promise) that would change the world forever.
   b. He gave the old promise with a new condition added.
   c. He gave a different kind of promise about ways to get to heaven.

5. To whom was this promise for then, now and in the future?
   a. It is to those who will obey the ten commandments.
   b. It is to all those who believe in Jesus as their Savior.
   c. It is to the people who do good works on earth.

6. What did Jesus tell His disciples to do whenever they ate bread and drank together?
   a. to remember that He healed people on earth
   b. to remember that He loved most of the people
   c. to remember that His death on the cross for sin was for everyone

7. How did Jesus say that the disciples would feel when the enemy took Him to the cross?
   a. They would be angry enough to kill Roman soldiers.
   b. "It will seem to you that everything has gone wrong."
   c. They would blame the religious leaders.

Beginnings II

LESSON 25 - DAY 1

Jesus: The Savior

BIBLE WORDS TO REMEMBER

Love one another as I have loved you.
If you love Me, keep My commandments. (from John 13:34; 14:15)

Bible Story: A NEW COMMANDMENT

from John 13

Jesus talked a lot about love. He came to earth to show God's great love for people. All that Jesus did on earth was an **example** of that love. Then He gave His life to **express** the greatest love **possible**. He died so that we can live.

Before people can love each other, they must first love Him. Jesus wanted His followers to show everyone that when they love Him, they will love each other in a special way. He gave a new commandment to all of those who would believe in Him then—and now. It is about an **exceptional** love that believers should have for each other. He said:

"Love one another as I have loved you.
Then others will know that you are My disciples,
if you have love for one another."

Jesus knew that His friends were going to have sadness and gladness happen in their lives. He wanted them to stick together and make each other strong. But most of all, if a believer says they love Jesus but are mean and unkind to others, they are not following Jesus' commandment. Other people will know that believers love Jesus and are His by how they treat each other.

WORDS TO KNOW

example:	to show someone by doing it first
express:	to do or say
possible:	something that can happen because of what has been done already
exceptional:	unusual; not ordinary

242

Questions:
Thinking & Remembering

Fill in the blanks or circle the letters of all that are right.

1. What did Jesus talk about during His time on earth?
   a. He talked about how people should follow the law.
   b. He talked about love.
   c. He talked about about being good.

2. What did Jesus do that He talked about?
   a. He showed God's love to everyone.
   b. He was an example of love in everything He did.
   c. He expressed love in the greatest way possible.

3. What was the greatest expression of love?
   a. dying on a cross for the sins of the world
   b. paying the price so we would not die in sin
   c. making it possible for us to live in heaven forever

4. What must happen before people can love others?
   a. We must read a book on how to be kind.
   b. We must listen to others tell us how to love.
   c. We must love God first.

5. What was the new commandment that Jesus gave His disciples?
   a. "First love the people who hate you."
   b. "Love one another as I have loved you."
   c. "Do kind things for each other."

6. What is so exceptional about this kind of love?
   a. It is a love that comes from God, not what we can do ourselves.
   b. God's love does not count mistakes. That is what our love should be like.
   c. It is a love that doesn't stop every time we get upset with someone.

7. How do we know the kind of love Jesus wanted His disciples to have?
   a. It was written about in the Old Testament.
   b. The disciples showed this love.
   c. Jesus showed us by what He did on earth.

8. Jesus promised that everything on earth would be perfect for us.
   true_____ false_____

Remember: Jesus wants us to stick together and love each other until He comes back.

243

Bible Story: I Am the Way

from John 13-14

Jesus told His disciples many things before He died. He knew that it would be a difficult time for them. It would seem like they were in a fog and nothing would make sense. But then everything would be clear and they would understand when He went to heaven.

Jesus told His disciples not to be afraid or **troubled**. He said, "You believe in God, now also believe in Me. You can trust Me."

Jesus said, "In My Father's house are many **mansions**; if it were not so, I would have told you. I'm going to prepare a place for you. Then I will come back to get you and take you there. I want you to be where I am. You now know the way to go to be with Me. I am the way, the truth, and the life. No one can come to God except through Me."

When the disciples asked Jesus if they could see God, He said, "You have seen Me. I am in God the Father, and God the Father is in Me. The words I speak are the words God told Me to tell you. He helps Me do all the things you have seen Me do."

Words to Know

troubled: upset and worried

mansions: a beautiful home—more wonderful than we can imagine

Think About

Many people want to decide for themselves "the way" to get to heaven. They may think that "the way" is to go to church every Sunday or be baptized. Some people think that if they try to do many good things that God will accept them. These are good things God wants you to do, but they won't count unless you do what God says to do *first*. The only way to God is by believing in Jesus and asking Him into your life.

Prayer Thought

Dear God, I know that the only way you can accept me is if I believe in Your own precious Son, Jesus. Help me not to try other ways but just to trust You. In Jesus Name, Amen.

Questions:
THINKING & REMEMBERING

Fill in the blanks or circle the letters of all that are right.

1. Why didn't the disciples understand everything Jesus was telling them before He died?
   a. It was too difficult.
   b. They should have asked more questions.
   c. They should have written down things so they could remember.

2. Jesus knew that they would understand the words He said after a time.
   true_____   false_____

3. What did Jesus say about being troubled and afraid?
   a. He said that they should be afraid because of what was going to happen.
   b. He said not to try to understand the things that were happening.
   c. He said not to be afraid or troubled.

4. Why did He want them to be confident?
   a. because they believed in God and they could believe in Him
   b. because it would turn out good in the end
   c. because they could trust Jesus

5. What did Jesus say was in His Father's house?
   a. many angels   b. many mansions   c. many good things

6. What did He say He was going to do when He went away?
   a. He was going to rest for a while.
   b. He was going to talk to God about His time on earth.
   c. He was going to prepare a place for the people who love Him.

7. What did Jesus promise to do someday?
   a. He promised to come back to earth.
   b. He promised to make the earth perfect.
   c. He promised to take us to be with Him in heaven.

8. Who is the way, the truth, and the life? _____
   Fill in the Bible Words from the book of John: "Love one another as I have
   _____ you. If you _____ Me, keep My commandments."

BIBLE WORDS TO REMEMBER

Love one another as I have loved you.
If you love Me, keep My commandments. (from John 13:34; 14:15)

Bible Story: PROMISE OF THE SPIRIT
from John 16

Jesus gave a new promise to those who believed in Him. He said that when He went back to heaven, He would not leave believers in the world alone without a helper. "I will send the **Holy Spirit** to live inside of you. He will be your friend and will guide and help you. The Holy Spirit can not be seen with your eyes, but you will know in your heart and mind that I have sent Him." The Holy Spirit will be the believer's **invisible** helper.

"The Holy Spirit will be close to you and make you strong and will be a **comfort** to you when you are sad and afraid. He will be with you to help you remember all the things I have told you that you do not **understand**. He will make you brave and give you the **power** to tell others that I love them."

The Holy Spirit will be your teacher. Since He is God the Spirit, He knows all the things that are important to love God even more. Since He lives inside you, He knows exactly what you need and will **guide** you to find the right answers for everything.

WORDS TO KNOW

Holy Spirit:	the part of God who is a helper for those who believe in Jesus
invisible:	not being seen
comfort:	to give peace
understand:	to believe and accept
power:	strength and courage
guide:	to show the way to go

Questions:
Thinking & Remembering

Fill in the blanks or circle the letters of all that are right.

1. What words did Jesus give to His disciples and believers in this lesson?
   a. a new promise   b. a new covenant   c. a new commandment

2. When would they know that this was true?
   a. immediately
   b. when Jesus went back to heaven
   c. when Jesus thought they were in trouble

3. What was the promise?
   a. He would send prophets to help them.
   b. Religious leaders would be there to guide them.
   c. He would not leave believers alone in the world without a helper.

4. Who was the helper Jesus sent? _____

5. Where would He live when a person asked Jesus to be their Savior?
   a. He would be available every time you asked for help.
   b. He would live in heaven until you got into trouble.
   c. He would live inside you all the time.

6. What things does the Holy Spirit do?
   (Circle the letters of all that He does—cross out what He is not.)
   a. He is our friend.   b. He is our guide.
   c. He is our comforter.   d. He is our teacher.
   e. He is our helper.   f. He is our Savior.

7. Fill in the blanks from these words in the lesson:

   invisible   need   power   strong   remember

   a. The Holy Spirit will be close to you and make you _____.
   b. The Holy Spirit knows exactly what you _____.
   c. The Holy Spirit will make you brave and give you the _____
      to tell others that Jesus loves them.
   d. The Holy Spirit will be your _____ helper.
   e. The Holy Spirit will help us _____important things
      that God tells us in the Bible.

247

BIBLE WORDS TO REMEMBER

Love one another as I have loved you.
If you love Me, keep My commandments. (from John 13:34; 14:15)

Bible Story: JESUS PRAYS FOR HIS FOLLOWERS
from John 17

Jesus wanted to prepare His disciples for the difficult days when He would do what God sent Him to do—die for the sins of the world. Jesus told His disciples about the peace that they could have in their hearts—no matter what happened. He talked about those who would believe and those who would say, "Jesus cannot be God!" He talked to them about the sadness they would feel and that He would send a comforter.

Then Jesus prayed. His prayer was for His disciples. He prayed that the Father would be **glorified**. He prayed that God would give eternal life to all of the special helpers God had given Him on earth. He prayed that people everywhere would know God and believe in Him whom God sent.

Jesus said that He had given these special followers the words that God gave Him and that they had accepted and believed. Jesus prayed that God would keep those who listened to God's Words faithful to Him. He asked God that His followers would have joy. He knew that those who loved Him must stay in the world, but Jesus asked God to keep them from the **evil one**.

WORDS TO KNOW

glorified: honored and adored

evil one: Satan—the one who tries to make us sin

THINK ABOUT

God shows His love in many ways. Then God will wait until you take the first step. Believe that Jesus is God's Son and know that you can trust Him. That is the first step. Tell Him you are sorry for the wrong things you think and do. That is the next step. Ask God to forgive you. Ask Him to be with you always. He will take you step by step and show you the way He wants you to live. Pray to Him every day and thank Him for sending Jesus to die on the cross for your sins. Jesus will be praying for you and asking God to help you. He will send the Holy Spirit to be your helper. God loves us a lot!

Questions:
THINKING & REMEMBERING

Fill in the blank or circle the letters of all that are right.

1. What did Jesus say would happen to His followers after He left?
   a. They would all be very happy.
   b. There would be difficult times.
   c. They wouldn't be friends anymore.

2. What did Jesus say they could have in their hearts during this time?
   a. joy   b. peace   c. hate   d. bitterness

3. Which two kinds of people did Jesus mention?
   a. those who believe and those who do not believe
   b. those who love and those who hate
   c. those who are happy and those who are unhappy

4. When Jesus died He knew His disciples would feel _____.
   sad   happy   angry

5. Whom did Jesus promise to send to comfort them?
   a. He promised to send someone else to take His place.
   b. He promised to send holy men who knew the scriptures.
   c. He promised to send the Holy Spirit.

6. In this lesson, whom did Jesus pray for?
   a. He prayed for the leaders who hated Him.
   b. He prayed for His disciples and those who would follow Him.
   c. He prayed for the people who were bad.

7. What did Jesus ask God to keep the disciples from?
   a. friends who try to make them do wrong things
   b. people who don't love God
   c. from the evil one

8. What will Jesus do for us always?
   a. Jesus will pray that God will keep us from sin.
   b. Jesus will pray that God will love us.
   c. Jesus will pray that God will help us love one another.

BIBLE WORDS TO REMEMBER

Love one another as I have loved you.
If you love Me, keep My commandments. (from John 13:34; 14:15)

Bible Story: PRAYER IN THE GARDEN
from Matthew 26

Jesus and His disciples went to a garden called Gethsemane. When they entered the garden, Jesus said to them, "Stay here while I go and pray. Watch and pray."

Jesus was all alone. It was a quiet and dark night. Jesus knelt down by a large stone and began to pray to His Father in heaven. Jesus was very sad. He was sad because people did not love God. He was sad because men would soon come to take Him and nail Him to a cross so that He would die. Jesus was going to die because people sinned against God.

Jesus said, "I will die so that people who believe in Me can live forever." Jesus did not have to die. He could ask God to send angels to stop the men from putting Him on a cross. But Jesus knew that we would be punished for sin and He loves us so much, He said He would be punished instead.

The disciples were tired. They fell asleep while Jesus was praying. Jesus was sorry that His disciples did not pray with Him. But God was with Jesus to make Him strong so that He could do God's will.

THINK ABOUT

Before Jesus came to die, people had to sacrifice an animal as payment for their sins. God wanted people to know that because Jesus was willing to die, they would no longer have to offer a blood sacrifice for sin. The New Covenant (Promise) means that God was going to accept people because Jesus was taking the punishment for our sin. People who believe that Jesus did this for them, can live forever in heaven with Him. God promised from the very beginning, when sin happened in the Garden of Eden, that He would send Jesus to save people from their sins.

PRAYER THOUGHT

Dear God, You let Your own Son come to earth and die so that I could be alive with You in heaven. Thank You for keeping all Your promises! In Jesus Name, Amen.

Questions:
THINKING & REMEMBERING

Circle the letters of all that are right.

1. What was the name of the garden in which Jesus prayed?
    a. the Garden of Eden
    b. the Garden of Gethsemane
    c. the Mount of Olives Garden

2. What did Jesus ask His disciples to do?
    a. He asked them to take a rest while He prayed.
    b. He asked them to watch for enemies.
    c. He asked them to watch and pray.

3. Why was Jesus so sad?
    a. He was sad because people did not love God.
    b. He was sad because He didn't think people were worth dying for.
    c. He was sad because His disciples were tired.

4. What was the most important thing that Jesus knew was going to happen?
    a. He was going to see His disciples sleeping.
    b. He was going to die for the sins of everyone in the world.
    c. People would kill Him.

5. Why did Jesus decide to be punished and die for our sins?
    a. He loves us.
    b. He wants us to be grateful.
    c. He wants us to be able to live in heaven with Him forever.

6. What would Jesus have the power to do?
    a. stop the men who would put Him on the cross
    b. keep the soldiers from tying His hands
    c. ask God to send angels to keep Him from the ones who would kill Him

7. What did the disciples do while Jesus was praying?
    a. They went to sleep.   b. They were ready to fight.   c. They prayed.

8. Who was with Jesus to comfort Him and make Him strong enough to accept God's plan?
    a. angels   b. Peter   c. God

251

Beginnings II

Jesus: Seeing and Believing

BIBLE WORDS TO REMEMBER

And walk in love, as Christ also has loved us
and given Himself for us. (Ephesians 5:2)

Bible Story: A SAD DAY
from Luke 22-23

There were some people who did not love Jesus. They did not believe that Jesus was the Son of God. They paid Judas money to show them where Jesus was. Then they sent some soldiers into the garden where Jesus was praying with His disciples and took Him to the ruler in Jerusalem. They were mean to Jesus. They beat Him and laughed at Him. Jesus' friends were very sad and afraid. They all went away.

Then the men who hated Jesus started saying, "Kill Him!" The crowd got louder and louder. It was such an ugly, angry sound! The men gave Jesus a wooden cross and made Him carry it to a hill. Jesus died on the cross. But before He died, He asked God to forgive the men who hated him.

Jesus' friends could not believe what had happened. They were so sad. They thought they would never be happy again. They carefully took Jesus from the cross and took Him to a special place where they wrapped Him in soft white cloth and buried Him in a tomb. They forgot that Jesus had told them that He would be alive again after three days. A happy day was coming!

THINK ABOUT

Because God loves you so much, you can share His love with your family first, then your friends and others. God has enough love to reach to everyone in the whole world—and He sent Jesus to help us see that love and give it away to all people everywhere.

PRAYER THOUGHT

Dear God, From the beginning You had a perfect plan to bring us back to You. Thank You, Jesus, for dying for my sin so I can live in heaven with You. In Jesus Name, Amen

 # Questions:
THINKING & REMEMBERING

Fill in the blanks or circle the letters of all that are right.

1. What reason did some people have for not loving Jesus?
    a. Jesus said that He was the Son of God.
    b. He told leaders they had not followed God's commandment of love.
    c. He didn't have money and a place to live.

2. What was Jesus like on earth?
    a. He was just like an ordinary man.
    b. He was perfect.
    c. He was God in a human form.

3. Which disciple betrayed Jesus?
    a. John   b. Judas   c. James

4. Where did this disciple take the men to find Jesus?
    a. He took them to the house where they had the Passover supper.
    b. He took them to the temple.
    c. He took them to the Garden of Gethsemane.

5. How was Jesus treated?
    a. They asked Him some questions and let Him go.
    b. They beat Him and laughed at Him.
    c. They treated Him like a king.

6. What did Jesus' disciples do?
    a. They went away and pretended they didn't know Him.
    b. They stayed with Jesus to help Him.
    c. They went to get help from some other friends.

7. How did the disciples feel?
    a. sad   b. afraid   c. angry

8. Why did Jesus die on the cross?
    a. He died for our sins.
    b. He loved us.
    c. He wanted us to live in heaven with Him.

9. What did Jesus' friends forget that Jesus had told them?
    He would be _____ again after _____ days.

BIBLE WORDS TO REMEMBER

And walk in love, as Christ also has loved us
and given Himself for us. (Ephesians 5:2)

Bible Story: JESUS IS ALIVE!
from Mark 16; John 20

Early on Sunday morning, after that awful day when Jesus died, three sad women walked into the garden where they were going to be surprised. They brought perfume to put on Jesus' body.

When they reached the garden, the sun was peeking up over the trees and the flowers. The women thought, "How will we ever get that heavy stone rolled away from the door of the tomb?" When they came to the tomb, suddenly they stopped and looked. The stone had been moved away!

They ran inside where Jesus had been laid, but He was not there! Then the women saw an angel sitting outside the tomb. They were afraid because the angel was so bright. The angel said, "Don't be afraid. You are looking for Jesus who died. He is not here! He is alive! Go and tell His friends."

The women were so happy! This was wonderful news. Jesus was alive! They ran quickly to tell the others. Two of the disciples came and looked inside the tomb and it was empty. It was true. Then they remembered that Jesus had tried to tell Him that He would not stay in the grave—He would live again.

THINK ABOUT

There are many things that we cannot keep. Your mom buys clothes that are just right, and then you get taller. You make your bed, and the next day it needs to be made again! Your dad mows the lawn, but the next week the grass is tall again. All the time we get things and do things. There is one thing that will matter forever, though. That one thing is believing that Jesus died on the cross because He loves you. That cannot change or be taken away. Keep what is important, the most important—loving Jesus.

Questions:
THINKING & REMEMBERING

Fill in the blanks or circle the letters of all that are right.

1. What day was sad for Jesus' friends?
   a. The day Jesus died was sad for Jesus' friends.
   b. The day of the Passover supper was sad for Jesus' friends.
   c. The day they came into Jerusalem was sad for Jesus' friends.

2. Where were the women going on the Sunday after Jesus died?
   a. They were going to see their friends and talk about Jesus.
   b. They were going to the tomb to put perfume on Jesus' body.
   c. They were going to the temple to worship.

3. What did they see there?
   a. They saw a man working in the garden.
   b. They saw some guards by the tomb.
   c. They saw the stone rolled away from the tomb.

4. What did they discover when they looked inside the tomb?
   a. The body of Jesus was not there.
   b. There were angels inside the tomb.
   c. The guards were there discussing where the body was.

5. Whom did the women see outside the tomb?
   a. The women saw some of Jesus' friends who were crying.
   b. The women saw the gardener taking care of the flowers.
   c. The women saw an angel.

6. What did the angel tell the women?
   a. "Do not be afraid."   b. "Jesus is alive!"   c. "Go and tell His friends."

7. How many disciples believed the women and came to see if what they told them was true?   a. two   b. twelve   c. four

8. Jesus had told the disciples that He would live again.   true_____   false_____

9. What is most important to you? _____
   Which part of your life that matters will you give the most time to?

   _____

Bible Story: ANOTHER SURPRISE FOR JESUS' FRIENDS
from Luke 24

That was such an exciting day that first Easter Sunday! So many strange things happened. Jesus' tomb was empty. Jesus had risen from the dead, even with soldiers outside to guard it! But some of Jesus' disciples still didn't believe that Jesus was alive. They were confused.

As two of Jesus' disciples were walking down the road, talking about the things that had happened that day, another man joined them. This man was really Jesus, but they did not **recognize** Him. The men told Him all about their wonderful friend Jesus who died on the cross.

When the men came to their house, they asked the stranger to stay and eat dinner with them. Then, when Jesus began to pray, the men suddenly **realized** that this man was not a stranger—the man they had talked with was Jesus! He was alive! They hurried to tell Jesus' other friends that they had really seen Jesus. "Jesus is alive again!" they shouted. "He walked with us and ate with us!"

The disciples were not confused any more! Now they understood that Jesus died because He loved them so much. He had arisen from the dead because He is the Son of God.

WORDS TO KNOW

recognize: to know who someone is
realize: to understand

THINK ABOUT

When God's Son Jesus came to earth, He showed love to everyone. Part of that love was to die on a cross. He was buried, but then three days after that Jesus came alive again! He did that because He loves you. Jesus paid the price for everything bad you think or do. Because of Jesus, you can live in heaven forever. This is God's best gift of love!

PRAYER THOUGHT

Dear God, I know that Your plan is always perfect. I needed a Savior to die because of my sins, and You planned for the way to come to You through Jesus dying on the cross. When I think how Jesus suffered because of sin, I wish there had been an easier way—but I know how holy and pure You are, and I am so thankful that Jesus was willing to do this because He loves me. In Jesus Name, Amen.

Questions:
THINKING & REMEMBERING

Fill in the blanks or circle the letters of all that are right.

1. What happened on the first Easter Sunday?
   a. Jesus arose from the grave.   b. The angels sang.   c. Jesus' tomb was empty.

2. Why was this happening so strange and unusual?
   a. The stone in front of the grave was very heavy.
   b. No one saw Jesus leave.
   c. There were guards at the grave.

3. Why were Jesus' disciples confused?
   a. They wondered where He could be.
   b. They didn't remember what He told them.
   c. They hadn't seen Jesus with their own eyes.

4. Did they know who the man was that came to walk with them?
   a. No, but they thought He knew a lot about what they were talking about.
   b. No, they did not recognize him.
   c. Yes, they understood it was Jesus.

5. When did the men finally realize that they were talking with Jesus?
   a. They knew it was Jesus when He told them who He was.
   b. They knew it was Jesus when He prayed to God.
   c. They knew it was Jesus when He talked about how He had died.

6. What did they do because they were sure Jesus was alive?
   a. They stayed and talked with Him.
   b. They asked Him to keep them safe.
   c. They ran to tell all Jesus' other disciples.

7. What changed for the disciples that day?
   a. They were not confused any more.
   b. They were sure that Jesus was alive.
   c. They knew that what He had told them came true.

8. Write the Bible words from Ephesians 5:2.

   _____

   _____

Bible Story: MORE FRIENDS SEE JESUS
from Luke 24; John 20

Some of the disciples were still afraid. They thought that the men who had put Jesus on the cross would try to find all of Jesus' friends and kill them. They went inside a house, shut the doors, and locked them.

Suddenly, Jesus came and stood right in the room so they could all see Him! At first, they were terrified and frightened—they thought that they had just seen a spirit because He didn't come through the door.

Then He showed them His hands where the nails had been put when He was nailed to the cross. He showed them His side where the soldiers had **pierced** Him with their **spear**. Jesus wanted them to know for sure that they knew He was the Son of God.

Jesus looked at each one and saw that they believed. He was not angry that they had all run away in the garden because they were afraid. He said, "Peace to you!" He told them that He was sending them into all the world to tell others what they saw and believed. Now they would be a light in the world. The Holy Spirit would give them power to do God's work.

WORDS TO KNOW

pierced: to be stabbed with a sharp weapon (Jesus was stabbed with a spear.)

spear: a long stick that is sharp on the end to hurt or kill

THINK ABOUT

When we know about God's love, we will not want to just keep it to ourselves. We cannot pretend that God's love didn't happen! Love spills out all over when we know that God thinks we are precious. We do not want to keep God's love a secret from anyone. When we have the light of Jesus, others will be able to see God's love by what we do and say. If you are covering your light, it will soon go out—like a candle whose flame is smothered when something is put over it.

Questions:
THINKING & REMEMBERING

Fill in the blanks or circle the letters of all that are right.

1. Why were some of the disciples still afraid, even after they saw that Jesus was alive?
   a. They were not sure about anything after knowing that Jesus died.
   b. They thought that the men who killed Jesus would kill them, too.
   c. They were afraid of the Roman guards.

2. What did they do so they would feel safe?
   a. They went to another town.
   b. They hid in the hills outside of Jerusalem.
   c. They went inside a house and shut the doors and locked them and talked quietly.

3. What happened when the disciples were in the room?
   a. Jesus came and stood right in the room so they could all see Him.
   b. Someone started knocking on the door and frightened them.
   c. There were some noises that scared them.

4. Why did the disciples think they were seeing a spirit instead of Jesus?
   a. Jesus didn't come in the room through the door.
   b. It was like a floating body.
   c. It didn't seem like a real person.

5. What did Jesus show them to convince them that it was really Him?
   a. He showed them His hands where they put the nails.
   b. He showed them His side where the spear had pierced Him.
   c. He said to just trust His word.

6. What did Jesus want them to know for sure?
   a. He loved them.
   b. He was the Son of God.
   c. He had kept His word.

7. What words did He say to the disciples?
   a. "Peace to you!"
   b. He said that He was sending them into the world to tell others.
   c. He said that they would be a light in the world after He was gone.

8. Who will give power to those who believe to do the work of God?

_____

BIBLE WORDS TO REMEMBER
And walk in love, as Christ also has loved us
and given Himself for us. (Ephesians 5:2)

Bible Story: A SPECIAL ASSIGNMENT
from John 20; Matthew 28

There was one disciple that was missing when all of the others saw Jesus. It was Thomas. He said, "I will not believe until I touch the place where they hurt Jesus and feel the scars." I want to see Jesus, too.

A few days later Jesus came into a room where they all were together. He said "Peace to you!" Then He told Thomas to touch His hands and side. Thomas finally believed. Jesus told him, "There are many who will believe without seeing. They are very **blessed**."

Many people today believe in Jesus from the words in the Bible. Do you believe that Jesus is the Son of God? If you do, you can live with Him in heaven forever!

Jesus gives you important work to do until He comes back to take you to heaven. It is a very special **assignment** to those who love Him. Jesus said that we should be a light in the world. We must tell others about God's love and that Jesus came to earth as Savior and Lord. Tell others about the promises of God so they will believe. Jesus said, "You can be sure that I will always be with you, even to the end of the world."

WORDS TO KNOW

blessed:	set apart because they are a special kind of believer
assignment:	an important job or task; a responsibility
resurrected:	a new body that was heavenly and had no barriers (something that stops an object from passing through)

Questions:
THINKING & REMEMBERING

Circle the letters of all that are right.

1. Which disciple had not been with the others and had not seen Jesus?
   a. Matthew   b. Thomas   c. Andrew

2. When did he say that he would believe?
   a. when he could touch the place where they hurt Jesus and feel the scars
   b. when he could talk to Him
   c. when someone told him for sure

3. How was it possible for Jesus to just appear in a room?
   a. He had a **resurrected** body that has no barriers.
   b. He walked in very quietly.
   c. It was just the disciple's imagination that He was there.

4. What words did He say to His disciples when He appeared?
   a. "Do you have a dinner ready?"
   b. "Don't be afraid!"
   c. "Peace to you!"

5. What did Jesus ask the disciple who doubted to do?
   a. He asked him to touch His hands and His side.
   b. He asked him to stop asking questions and believe that He was alive.
   c. He asked him to accept what the other disciples had said.

6. What did Jesus say about those who believed without seeing?
   a. He loved them more.
   b. They would be the greatest in God's kingdom.
   c. They were blessed.

7. What is one way that we can know and believe in Jesus today?
   a. by the words in the Bible
   b. by what someone else thinks is right
   c. by reading history books at school

8. When you believe in Jesus, what is your assignment?
   a. to stay in a safe place like a house or a church
   b. to read the words in the Bible and keep them to yourself
   c. to tell others about the love of Jesus

Beginnings II

God: His Promises

BIBLE WORDS TO REMEMBER

Jesus said, "I am with you always, even to the end of the age."
(from Matthew 28:20)

Bible Story: BREAKFAST WITH JESUS
from John 21

The disciples kept thinking about all the things Jesus told them. They were happy, sad, and confused all at the same time. They were happy because Jesus was alive. They were sad because He was leaving them. They were confused because they didn't know exactly how they were going to do what Jesus told them they could do. So they waited. They wondered if they would see Jesus again.

Peter said to the other disciples, "Well, I'm going to go fishing"—that was one thing Peter knew how to do. "We are going with you, too," the others said. They fished all night long, but they didn't even catch one fish!

When morning came, they saw a man standing on the shore. The man asked, "Have you caught any fish?" "No," they answered. They did not know that the man they were talking to was Jesus. Jesus said, "Put your nets in the water on the right side of the boat." The disciples did as Jesus said. The nets were so full of fish they could not even lift them into the boat! Then Peter knew who it was that was on the shore—it was Jesus! They had breakfast together. Jesus had not left. He was with them again!

THINK ABOUT

Jesus came to love. Jesus said that there are two important rules. The number one rule is to love God with all your heart. The number two rule is to love others as much as you love yourself. When you love God, He helps you love others because God is love.

PRAYER THOUGHT

Dear God, I know that when You help me to do the right thing, I can do anything You ask! Make me strong and learn to love You more. In Jesus Name, Amen.

Questions:
THINKING & REMEMBERING

1. Review Question: From Lessons 23-26, put the following events in the order that they happened:

   a. _____ The soldiers come to take Jesus.

   b. _____ Thomas sees and believes Jesus.

   c. _____ Jesus comes into Jerusalem.

   d. _____ Jesus and His disciples have the Last Supper together.

   e. _____ Jesus died on the cross.

   f. _____ Jesus prayed in the garden.

   g. _____ Jesus walked with the two disciples.

   h. _____ Jesus is not in the tomb and is alive!

Choose one correct answer.

2. What made the disciples happy?
   a. Jesus was alive.
   b. They were glad the people were not following them around anymore.

3. Why were the disciples sad?
   a. They didn't have anywhere to go.   b. Jesus was going to go away.

4. What were they confused about?
   a. They were confused about how to do what Jesus told them they could do.
   b. They were confused about who should be their leader.

5. What did Peter and the others decide to do?
   a. They waited for Jesus in the upper room where they had their supper.
   b. They decided to go fishing.

6. How many fish had they caught during the night?
   a. none   b. many   c. a few

7. They knew the man who called to them from the shore and told them to put their nets on the other side of the boat.   true_____   false_____

8. What made them know who it was who called to them?
   a. He was someone they knew when they were fishermen.
   b. They caught so many fish. It was a miracle only Jesus could do.

Bible Story: PETER REMEMBERS
from John 21

Jesus had met with His disciples three times since He arose from the grave. They wanted to be with Him more! After they had finished eating breakfast, Jesus asked Peter an important question—three times!

> Jesus asked, "Do you love Me more than anything?"
> Peter said, "Yes, Lord; You know that I love You."
> Jesus said, "**Feed My lambs**."
> Jesus asked again, "Do you love Me?"
> Peter answered again, "Yes, Lord; You know that I love You."
> Jesus said, "**Tend My sheep**."
> Then Jesus asked once more, "Peter, do you love Me?"
> Peter was sad that Jesus kept asking. He was sure that Jesus could see inside his heart and know how much he loved Him.
> He said, "Lord, You know everything; You know that I love you."
> Jesus said, "**Feed My sheep** and follow Me."

Then Peter remembered the time that he said that he did not know Jesus. He said it three times after they left the garden before Jesus died. Peter didn't think he was the right one to "feed Jesus' lambs." Jesus was asking him to be a leader and take care of all those who would believe in Him. Peter looked at John and asked Jesus, "Why didn't you choose John?" Jesus said, "Don't be concerned about that—I want you to follow Me."

WORDS TO KNOW

"Feed My lambs": Jesus was not talking about food or animals. He was telling Peter to give the young—those who first hear about God (lambs are baby sheep) God's words.

"Tend My sheep": After people have heard God's words, they need to be watched carefully so they can grow (learn more) of God's way.

"Feed My Sheep": Some people believe at first, but forget God's words. Jesus wants them to be fed (hear God's words again) so they will be strong followers.

PRAYER THOUGHT

Dear God, Help me be strong and remember that You will always be with me. In Jesus Name, Amen.

Questions:
THINKING & REMEMBERING

Fill in the blanks or circle the letters of all that are right.

1. How many times did Jesus meet with His disciples after He arose from the grave?   a. not sure   b. seven   c. three

2. How many times did Jesus ask Peter the same question?
   a. three   b. once   c. two

3. What was the question Jesus asked Peter?
   a. "Are you sorry you said you didn't know Me?"
   b. "Are you sure you believe that I am God's Son?"
   c. "Do you love Me?"

4. What was Peter's answer each time?
   a. "I will follow You always."
   b. "Yes, Lord; You know that I love You."
   c. "I know I ran away once, but I won't do it again."

5. Put Jesus' instructions in the order that He gave them to Peter:
   a. _____ "Tend My sheep."
   b. _____ "Feed My sheep and follow Me."
   c. _____ "Feed My lambs."

6. What did Peter remember that he had done three times before?
   a. He told others that he did not know Jesus.
   b. He said he would pray with Jesus in the garden.
   c. He told the other disciples he would stay with Jesus.

7. What did Jesus want Peter to be to followers and believers?
   a. the light of the world
   b. a leader
   c. one of the disciples with no special responsibility

8. What did Peter think about what Jesus asked Him to be?
   a. He thought John should be the leader.
   b. He did not think he was the right one for the job.
   c. He was too afraid to do what Jesus asked him to do.

Remember: God never makes a mistake when He chooses you!

BIBLE WORDS TO REMEMBER

Jesus said, "I am with you always, even to the end of the age."
(from Matthew 28:20)

Bible Story: JESUS RETURNS TO HEAVEN
from Matthew 28; Acts 1

Before Jesus went back to heaven, He talked to His disciples about what they should do. He said, "Go everywhere into the whole world, and tell everyone how much God loves them. Tell them that I came to earth so that they can choose to live in heaven forever if they believe in Me." His promise was special and wonderful: "I am with you always, even to the end of the **age**."

Then Jesus began to go up into the clouds until the disciples could not see Him anymore. They knew He was back in heaven with God the Father. But the disciples weren't sad. Jesus had said He would be with them always. Even though His body went to heaven, He would send His Spirit to be with all who believed in Him.

The disciples were still looking up in the sky when two angels appeared and said, "Why are you looking up in the sky? Jesus will come back again the same way you saw Him go." The disciples knew that they must do what Jesus had asked them to do—tell everyone about Him. They were excited. They did want to tell everyone how wonderful Jesus was so that others could believe in Him too.

WORDS TO KNOW

age: the time here on earth before Jesus returns

Remember these things:
- Jesus is in heaven, but He said He will come back. He always keeps His promises.
- Jesus wants us to tell others about how much He loves them.
- Jesus promises that, even though we cannot see Him, He is always with us.
- Jesus will come back and take those who love Him to heaven to live forever.

Questions:
THINKING & REMEMBERING

Circle the letters of all that are right.

1. What did Jesus tell His disciples to do?
   a. "Go everywhere and tell everyone how much God loves them."
   b. "Stay in safe places, away from people."
   c. "Get together and be good friends."

2. What reason did Jesus give for what He asked them to do?
   a. so people would know that they should have listened
   b. so that many people could believe in Him
   c. He wanted everyone to live in heaven with Him.

3. What wonderful promise did Jesus give so the disciples would know that they did not have to do this important work by themselves.
   a. "I will always be with you."
   b. "God will send angels if you need them."
   c. "I will be watching from heaven."

4. How long would the promise He gave be true?
   a. It would be true until they learned how to do the work alone.
   b. It would be true until the end of the age.
   c. It would be true until the Holy Spirit came.

5. What happened next?
   a. They had a last lunch together.
   b. Jesus went up in the clouds into heaven with God the Father.
   c. Jesus just disappeared but they did not see Him go.

6. Whom had Jesus promised to send to be with them?
   a. an angel   b. the Holy Spirit   c. some more disciples to help them

7. Why weren't Jesus' friends sad when He went to heaven?
   a. They knew His Spirit would be with them, as He promised.
   b. They were excited about the important work He wanted them to do.
   c. He made a promise to be with them always.

8. What did the angels tell the disciples?
   a. They said to stop looking in the sky.
   b. They said that Jesus would come back again the same way they saw Him go.

BIBLE WORDS TO REMEMBER
Jesus said, "I am with you always, even to the end of the age."
(from Matthew 28:20)

Bible Story: A WONDERFUL HELPER—THE HOLY SPIRIT
from Acts 2

Jesus promised His disciples—and all of those who believe in Him that He would send a Helper for them so that they could do what He asked them to do. The Helper is called the Holy Spirit.

The disciples stayed together in one place. They were waiting for the promise of the Holy Spirit to come to them. They prayed and sang hymns to God. They knew that Jesus would keep His promise.

Then the day came! There was a very loud noise! It was like a powerful, rushing wind. It filled the whole house where they were sitting. They were amazed as they saw small flames of fire come above each of them. The Spirit had come to live inside each of them! They were not afraid to do what Jesus said—go tell others.

The Holy Spirit gave them the power to tell all the people who were outside all about Jesus and His love for them. People from many different nations could hear God's message of love in their own language. The Holy Spirit helped the people understand that God loved them and changed their hearts. What a wonderful helper Jesus sent!

THINK ABOUT
Something Important to Understand and Remember:
> The Holy Spirit is part of God.
> God is three persons, but only one God.
>   God is the Father; God is the Son, Jesus; God is the Holy Spirit.
> These three parts of God each have a special purpose.
>   Each is part of God in a different way to bring His love to the world.
> God is our Father who made us in His image (likeness).
> God the Son came to earth as a man to die for us and be our Savior to
> us to God.
> God the Holy Spirit gives us a new heart that can love God.

Questions:
THINKING & REMEMBERING

Fill in the blanks or circle the letters of all that are right.

1. What is TRUE about the Holy Spirit? Check the right ones.
    a. _____   Jesus sent a helper who is the Holy Spirit.
    b. _____   The Holy Spirit would be with the disciples for a short time.
    c. _____   The Holy Spirit was sent to all believers to help them tell others about Jesus.
    d. _____   The Holy Spirit helps people understand God's word and His love.
    e. _____   The Holy Spirit would only help believers.
    f. _____   The Holy Spirit gives power to those who love Jesus.
    g. _____   The Holy Spirit is a comforter.

2. Write beside each one the name for the three parts of God:
    Jesus   God   Helper

    a. The Father _____
    b. The Son _____
    c. The Holy Spirit_____

3. What ONE purpose do the three parts of God have?
    a. to bring love to the world so that people can be with God forever
    b. to make everyone happy, whether they believe or not
    c. to make earth a perfect place to live

4. How are the three parts of God different?
    a. They live in different places.
    b. They are ALL God in different ways to bring His love to the world.
    c. All of the parts are not needed all of the time.

5. How did the Holy Spirit come to the disciples?
    a. He quietly entered the room.
    b. He came like a powerful, rushing wind.
    c. He came to each of them at different times.

6. What did the Holy Spirit give the disciples power to do?
    a. to tell all the people about Jesus and His love for them
    b. to speak to people from different nations in their own language
    c. to go outside the room without being afraid anymore

Bible Story: JESUS' FRIENDS WORK TOGETHER
from Acts 4

After the Holy Spirit gave the disciples power to speak in different languages, three thousand people believed in Jesus! Every day there were more who knew that Jesus came to die for their sins. They wanted to accept God's message of love. All of the new believers became friends and helped each other. If someone needed food or clothes, everyone helped.

They wanted to be baptized and worship God. They didn't have a church building, so they all went to one of their friend's houses. They prayed and sang songs about God. They talked about what Jesus had told them to do when He was with them. They asked God to help them be brave and strong.

Soon everyone was working together. The more they helped each other, the happier and more loving they became. They were like one big family! They were all in God's family just as we are part of God's family if we love Him.

The disciples were also given the power to heal people from their sickness and disease. They were able to do miracles in Jesus' name. They did everything to show others how much God loved and cared for them. They were doing what Jesus told them to do.

THINK ABOUT

Jesus wants each of us to follow Him because we believe and love Him. He has special things for you to do too, just as He had for the believers in the Bible. He will help you know what is important when you listen to His words. And when God's people work together, more people can learn about Jesus and they can be part of God's family.

PRAYER THOUGHT

Dear God, Thank You for sending the Holy Spirit to come and live in my heart. I want to have a new heart that can love You more. Help me tell everyone about Jesus, and help them believe and understand Your love. In Jesus Name, Amen.

Questions:
THINKING & REMEMBERING

Circle the letters of all that are right.

1. By whose power were the disciples able to speak in different languages?
   a. Jesus told them that He would help them speak in different languages.
   b. The Holy Spirit gave them the power.
   c. They had power in themselves they did not know about before.

2. How many people became believers in Jesus by hearing about Him in their own language?
   a. 300   b. 3,000   c. too many to count

3. What did all of these people do after they believed?
   a. They were baptized.
   b. They told everyone how great they were.
   c. They went to church.

4. Where did they go to worship together?
   a. the synagogue   b. church buildings   c. friends' houses

5. How did they worship God?
   a. They prayed.   b. They ate.   c. They sang.

6. What did they ask God to help them do?
   a. get new leaders in the church
   b. get new leaders in the government
   c. be brave and strong believers

7. What did the disciples have the power to do?
   a. to heal people from sickness and other disease and do other miracles
   b. to know whom they should tell about Jesus
   c. to tell all the new believers what they should do

8. What did the believers do for each other?
   a. They helped whoever was in need.
   b. They pointed out the wrong things other believers did.
   c. They loved each other like family.

Beginnings II

Jesus: He Makes Us Strong

BIBLE WORDS TO REMEMBER

Be strong in the Lord and in the power of His might. The things which are impossible with men are possible with God.
(from Ephesians 6:10 and Luke 18:27)

Bible Story: THE BRAVE BELIEVERS

from Acts 6-7

There was a man named Stephen who loved and believed in Jesus. God gave him power to do miracles. Stephen helped people understand God's words.

Those who hated Jesus heard Stephen telling others about how God loved them and sent Jesus. They did not want any more people to believe and become Christians. They said, "Do not listen to Stephen. He is telling you wrong things about God. Jesus is not God's Son!"

Stephen was not afraid. The Holy Spirit made him very brave. He kept telling people about Jesus. They were so happy to know that Jesus died for all the wrong things they had done. They asked God to forgive them and wanted to be baptized to show others that they believed in Jesus.

Soon, the angry men took Stephen, hurt him, and killed him. Before he died, he said, "I see Jesus!" He asked the Lord to forgive the men who hurt him. He knew that they were listening to Satan and did not know God's love in their hearts. He did not hate them. He wanted them to know and believe in Jesus. God's love helped him love others and have peace in his heart.

Write the Bible Words to Remember from Ephesians 6:10 and Luke18:27.

_____

_____

_____

_____

Remember: God's love can help us love others, even when they want to hurt us. Someday they may remember the words you tell them about Jesus and love Him.

Questions:
THINKING & REMEMBERING

Circle the letters of all that are right.

1. What was the name of the man who was not afraid to talk about Jesus?
   a. Paul   b. Luke   c. Stephen

2. What did the men who hated Jesus do to stop Stephen from telling about Jesus?
   a. They told people that Stephen did not love God.
   b. They said that Stephen was telling people wrong things about God.
   c. They said to listen to what Stephen said.

3. What did the men say about Jesus?
   a. Jesus was sent by God.
   b. Jesus was not God's Son.
   c. Jesus was a good man.

4. What did Stephen do?
   a. He kept telling people about Jesus.
   b. He was afraid of the men who hated him.
   c. He told them they were bad men.

5. Who helped Stephen be brave?
   a. the other disciples   b. people who loved Jesus   c. the Holy Spirit

6. What did the people do who heard Stephen tell about Jesus?
   a. They asked God to forgive them.
   b. They believed in Jesus.
   c. They were baptized.

7. What did the angry men do to Stephen?
   a. They hurt him and killed him.
   b. They told him to go to another city.
   c. They put him in prison.

8. What did Stephen ask God to do before he died?
   a. He asked God to kill the bad men.
   b. He asked God to forgive the ones who hurt him.
   c. He asked God to stop loving those who killed him.

Bible Story: A CHANGED LIFE
from Acts 9

Saul hated people who believed in Jesus. He helped those who killed Stephen for telling others about Jesus. Saul did not believe that Jesus was God's Son. He did not believe that Jesus was the One that God promised to send as a light and the Savior of the world. Saul thought that it was not true that Jesus was alive again after being killed on a cross. He was angry that people believed in Jesus.

Jesus loved Saul and was sad that he was hurting Christians. God had plans for Saul to tell others about Jesus! One day, Saul was traveling to another city to put Christians in jail for believing in Jesus.

Suddenly, a light from heaven blinded Saul! The Lord's voice said to Saul, "Saul, why are you hurting Me?" Saul was frightened! "Who are You, Lord?" The voice answered, "I am Jesus, whom you are hurting." Saul said, "Lord, what do You want me to do?"

The Lord told Saul that He wanted him to be for Him, not against Him. Saul knew that Jesus was the Son of God. Jesus gave him a new name—Paul. Paul went to many places to tell people about Jesus.

THINK ABOUT

We should always ask God to help us use the right words to tell about Jesus. Ask Him to help you tell about Jesus at the right time and in the right way. That does not mean that you should be afraid or wait to tell! When you treat your friends in a kind way and love them, they will want to know about Jesus and His love. Then you can tell them that it is because you know that God thinks you are precious—and that they are precious to God, too!

PRAYER THOUGHT

Dear God, There are many people who do not know about Your love and how You sent Jesus as a Savior to the world. Help me to know the right words to tell them about You. In Jesus Name, Amen.

Questions:
THINKING & REMEMBERING

Fill in the blanks or circle the letters of all that are right.

1. How did Saul feel about people who believed in Jesus?
   a. He thought they were OK.
   b. He didn't want to be friends with them.
   c. He hated them.

2. What did Saul say about Jesus?
   a. He was not the Son of God.
   b. Jesus was dead.
   c. Jesus was a kind man.

3. What made Jesus sad?
   a. Saul didn't like Him.
   b. Saul was hurting Christians.
   c. Saul didn't understand the Bible.

4. What plans did God have for Saul?
   a. He wanted Saul to stay away from Christians.
   b. God didn't have any plan for Saul.
   c. He wanted Saul to tell others about Jesus.

5. What happened to Saul on the way to another city to put Christians in jail?
   a. Saul decided it was too far to the next city.
   b. His soldiers left him.
   c. He was blinded by a great light from heaven.

6. What did the Lord say to Saul?
   a. He wanted Saul to stop hurting Him.
   b. He wanted Saul to be for Him and not against Him.
   c. He wanted Saul to tell the world about Him.

7. How did this experience change Saul that day?
   a. He believed that Jesus was the Son of God.
   b. He decided to go back home and not hurt Christians.
   c. His name was changed to Paul.
   d. Instead of hurting Christians, he wanted to go everywhere and tell people about Jesus.

8. Bible Words: Be _____ in the _____... (from Ephesians 6:10)

BIBLE WORDS TO REMEMBER

Be strong in the Lord and in the power of His might. The things which are impossible with men are possible with God.
(from Ephesians 6:10 and Luke 18:27)

Bible Story: A KIND WOMAN

from Acts 9

The Bible tells about a woman named Dorcus who loved Jesus very much. She thought about ways to tell others about Jesus and His love. She could not go into the city to preach like Stephen did. She could not go to other lands to tell many people like Paul did. But God had a plan for her, too!

She began helping people in the best way that she knew how. She made beautiful clothes for others to wear. While she was sewing, she told them about Jesus! Soon Dorcus had many friends. She was so kind. She listened to them and cared about them in a special way that showed she loved Jesus.

One day, Dorcus became very sick. She could not get well and she died. All her friends were so sad. They remembered all the nice things she had done for them and all the beautiful clothes she had made for them.

Peter, a disciple of Jesus, came to Dorcus' house. He knelt by the bed and prayed to God. He told Dorcus to get up out of bed. Her eyes opened and she was alive! The friends were so happy! They ran to tell everyone, "Dorcus is alive! God made her alive again!"

THINK ABOUT

Jesus said many words of love. When you are kind to others, it is like giving a gift of God's love. By loving and doing things for others, that love grows and grows. God can make love very big from even a small act of love.

Remember: God has a plan for everyone who believes in Jesus!

Questions:
Thinking & Remembering

Fill in the blanks or circle the letters of all that are right.

1. What was the name of the woman who loved Jesus?
   a. Mary   b. Dorcus   c. Martha

2. What did she want to do?
   a. She wanted to tell others about Jesus and His love.
   b. She wanted to do miracles.
   c. She wanted to travel with the disciples.

3. Which people are important to God?
   a. missionaries who travel to tell others about Jesus
   b. preachers who tell others what God says in the Bible
   c. those who tell others about Jesus in their work
   d. all people who tell others about Jesus

4. What did the following people do? (Write the name in the space.)
   Dorcus   *Paul*   *Stephen*

   a. _____ went to other lands as a missionary.
   b. _____ made clothes for other people.
   c. _____ preached in the city.

5. What did Dorcus do that was important?
   a. She cared about people in a special way.
   b. She told the people she was helping about Jesus.
   c. She fed poor people.

6. What sad thing happened?
   a. Her sewing machine broke.
   b. She became very sick and died.
   c. Her friend moved away.

7. What happened when Jesus' helper came to the home of Dorcus?
   a. He prayed to God.
   b. He gave her some medicine.
   c. He told Dorcus to get up out of bed.

8. Who had the power to make Dorcus alive again?
   a. God   b. Peter   c. Paul

Bible Story: PETER'S FRIENDS PRAY
from Acts 12

Peter was one of Jesus' most brave disciples now. He wanted to tell everyone about how much Jesus loved them. The king hated Christians and sent spies and soldiers to find those who loved Jesus. They heard Peter talking about Jesus and put him in prison.

Peter's friends knew that God had the power to do anything—even help Peter get out of prison. So they prayed. "Dear Jesus, we know that you can help Peter. Take care of him and protect him. Please let him get out of prison so he can tell more people about You." They did not stop praying. They prayed through the night.

At the prison, an exciting thing happened! It was very quiet when suddenly the chains fell off from Peter's hands. An angel came to Peter and said, "Put your sandals and your coat on and come with me." Peter went with the angel. When they came to the gate, it was locked. But God made the gate come open for them!

Peter knew that the Lord sent the angel to make him free. He went to his friend's house where they had been praying. They were so happy to see Peter! God had answered their prayers!

THINK ABOUT

Sometimes we pray for things that really seem impossible. But then we remember that the Bible tells us "nothing is impossible with God." Peter's friends prayed for something that would be impossible for anyone to do but God. When God answered their prayers, they could hardly believe it! Think of someone you need to pray for who needs God's help. When we pray for things that we know are God's will from His Word, we should not give up! And don't be surprised when God answers your prayer!

PRAYER THOUGHT

Dear God, Thank You for hearing all my prayers. Thank You for sending angels to watch over me. Even though I cannot see them, I know that they will be near me to take care of me, because I belong to You. In Jesus Name, Amen.

Questions:
THINKING & REMEMBERING

Fill in the blanks or circle the letters of all that are right.

1. Who was one of Jesus' brave disciples? _____

2. What did he want to do?
   a. go fishing   b. tell everyone about Jesus   c. be friends with the king

3. What did the king tell his soldiers to do to Christians?
   a. He said to tell them to stop talking about Jesus.
   b. He said to make them move to a different city.
   c. He said to put them in prison for telling about Jesus.

4. When Peter was put in prison, what did Peter's friends know and believe?
   a. God had the power to help Peter get out.
   b. Peter was not afraid.
   c. They didn't need to be scared of the king.

5. How long did Peter's friends pray?
   a. for a few minutes   b. for two hours   c. through the night

6. What happened at the prison?
   a. The chains fell off Peter's hands.
   b. The guard disappeared.
   c. An angel came and told Peter to follow him.

7. How did they get through the gate that was locked?
   a. God opened it.   b. The angel had a key.   c. A soldier opened it.

8. What did Peter's friends do when they saw Peter?
   a. They were surprised and happy.
   b. They started singing loudly.
   c. They knew that God had answered their prayers.

9. Bible Words: "The things which are _____ with men are
   _____ with _____." (from Luke 18:27)

BIBLE WORDS TO REMEMBER

Be strong in the Lord and in the power of His might. The things which are impossible with men are possible with God.
(from Ephesians 6:10 and Luke 18:27)

Bible Story: PAUL TELLS EVERYONE ABOUT JESUS
from Acts 16

Paul was a **missionary** who loved Jesus. He did not care what other people thought. He just kept telling everyone about Jesus and how much God loved them. After he told the people in one city, he would go to another city or town.

The leaders did not want people to follow Jesus. They put Paul and his friend Silas in prison and told Paul not to talk about Jesus anymore. But Paul could not stop! He knew God would take care of him. Even though he was having troubles and was in prison, he was happy because he was obeying God.

The **jailer** put chains on their feet and hands so Paul and Silas could not move. But they were not afraid. They started singing in the jail! They sang about Jesus so the other men in the jail could hear them.

Suddenly there was a lot of noise and crashing—the chains were broken and the doors of the jail opened. Paul and Silas were free! God's angels had come to open the jail gates! The jailer was frightened. Nothing like this had ever happened before! Paul said to him, "Don't be afraid—our God is very great." The jailer said, "I want to believe in Jesus, too. He is very powerful!"

WORDS TO KNOW

missionary: someone who tells others a special message

jailer: one who keeps prisoners locked up in jail

Remember: Thank God for all the special things that happen to you and for you. God makes these things possible. When you praise God, you make everyone around you feel happy and loved because you are remembering how much God loves you.

Questions:
THINKING & REMEMBERING

True or False:

1. _____ Paul was afraid to talk about Jesus because the leaders put Christians in prison.

2. _____ Paul was happy because he was obeying God.

3. _____ Paul and Silas started crying when they were tied up with chains in prison.

4. _____ Paul and Silas started singing about Jesus in prison.

5. _____ Paul stopped telling about Jesus when they put him in prison.

6. _____ The jailer called for more guards when he saw that Paul and Silas were free.

7. _____ God's angels came and opened the jail gates.

8. _____ The jailer was frightened and ran away.

9. _____ The chains fell off Paul and Silas' hands and feet.

10. _____ The jailer believed in Jesus.

11. Write the Bible Words to Remember from Ephesians 6:10 and Luke 18:27.

_____

_____

_____

_____

_____

PRAYER THOUGHT

Dear God, Help me always to give You the very best that I have and to make You the most important every day. In Jesus Name, Amen.

BIBLE WORDS TO REMEMBER

Love is patient and kind. Faith, hope and love; the greatest of these is love. (from 1 Corinthians 13:4,13)

Bible Story: GOD HELPS US LOVE— A LETTER FROM PAUL

from 1 Corinthians 13

Jesus gave the two most important rules:
   1. Love God first.   2. Love others as much as you love yourselves.

Paul wrote that when Christians love, they are patient with others. Love is not being jealous of others, what they have or what they are able to do. Love does not hurt other people's feelings by saying mean and unkind things. When others say they are sorry, we love by forgiving them.

Love thinks of others first and wants good things to happen for them. Love helps people who are sad and lonely and those who do not have as much as you have. Love will never be happy when bad things happen to others. Love will not be glad with evil.

Love thinks of good things, not bad. God's love gift is the best gift we can give! Love is full of joy when true things are said. Love will protect others. Love always trusts. Love always hopes. Love never gives up. Love does not fail. Three things that are important are faith, hope and love. And the greatest of all three is love. Let God help you love the way He loves, and you will always know that loving God's way is best.

THINK ABOUT

The Bible tells that love is much more than a feeling. Feelings change all the time. Love is an action. It is something you do. Jesus loves everyone the same. He does not have a list of things you must do before God can love you. When you say nice things but are unkind, you miss the most important thing—LOVE!

Questions:
THINKING & REMEMBERING

Fill in the blanks or circle the letters of all that are right.

1. What are the two most important rules Jesus gave about love?
   a. Love yourself first, then love God.
   b. Love others first, then love God.
   c. Love God first, then love others as much as you love yourself.

2. What do we do when we love?
   a. We are patient.   b. We forgive others.   c. We are kind.

3. What do we *not* do when we say we love others?
   a. We are not jealous.
   b. We do not say mean things.
   c. We do not talk to others in an unkind way.

4. When we love, what do we want for others?
   a. We want bad things to happen for them.
   b. We want a few good things to happen for them.
   c. We want all good things to happen for them.

5. What are three important things?
   a. kindness, fairness and happiness
   b. faith, hope and love
   c. joy, toys and friends

6. What is the greatest of all three? _____

7. Where can we find out what true love is?
   a. in the dictionary   b. in the Bible   c. in lots of books

8. What is love?
   a. It is just a feeling.   b. It is an action sometimes.   c. It is something you do.

9. Why can't love just be a feeling?
   a. We don't understand feelings.
   b. Feelings change all the time.
   c. We feel different if things are going the way we want.

Challenge! Memorize 1 Corinthians 13:4-8 from your Bible.

Bible Story: ANOTHER LETTER FROM PAUL
from Galatians

Some Christians who had been excited about Jesus forgot what Paul had taught them about loving each other. They started to be unkind to others. They were **jealous** and said mean things. They were **selfish** with what they had and did not want to share. These things made God very sad.

When Paul heard about the Christians' **behavior**, he sent them a letter reminding them how to love each other. They would never be happy acting in this way. Others who did not even know about Jesus' love would see Christians fighting with each other and think, "We don't see God's love in these people. They act just like everyone else, even though they say they love God!"

Paul wrote in his letter that Christians must let God's Holy Spirit help them live in a different way—in a way that showed love. He gave them some words that they should learn. These are the important words: *love, joy, peace, patience, kindness, goodness, faithfulness, gentleness,* and *self-control.*

Think about each word and know whether it is something we do to others or something we have inside us so that we can love others the way God wants us to love.

WORDS TO KNOW

jealous: wanting what someone else has

selfish: keeping things to yourself; not sharing

behavior: what you do; the way you act

THINK ABOUT

We cannot live for God without the help of the Holy Spirit. The Spirit helps us want to live in God's way. It is not just saying words like love, joy, peace and all the other wonderful words of the way to live. It is showing His love by the way you act—your behavior. When you let the Holy Spirit help you, then others will want to know the Jesus you love. Which words will you choose to work on this week to show God's love?

Questions:
THINKING & REMEMBERING

Fill in the blanks or circle the letters of all that are right.

1. What was the name of the man who went many places to tell about Jesus?
   a. Matthew   b. Peter   c. Paul

2. What happened to some Christians?
   a. They forgot what they had been taught about loving each other.
   b. They remembered what Paul had taught them.
   c. They wanted another missionary to tell them what to do.

3. What are some of the things they did that made God sad?
   a. They were mean and unkind to each other.
   b. They talked to people who were not Christians.
   c. They were jealous and selfish and didn't share.

4. What did Paul do when he heard how they were behaving?
   a. He wrote them a letter.
   b. He went back to visit them.
   c. He sent someone to tell them what to do.

5. Of what did Paul remind them?
   a. Paul reminded them how to love each other.
   b. They should start telling others about Jesus.
   c. They should separate so they wouldn't fight.
   d. Others would not want to love Jesus when Christians were acting in the wrong way.

6. Who would help them love in the way God wanted them to love?
   a. other Christians   b. their leaders   c. the Holy Spirit living inside them

7. Which of the following will be shown in your character if you allow the Holy Spirit to have control in your life? You should be able to check nine characteristics.

   _____ joy   _____ anger   _____ peace
   _____ love   _____ kindness   _____ gentleness
   _____ selfishness   _____ faithfulness   _____ jealousy
   _____ self-control   _____ goodness   _____ patience

BIBLE WORDS TO REMEMBER

Love is patient and kind. Faith, hope and love; the greatest
of these is love. (from 1 Corinthians 13:4,13)

Bible Story: LOVE IS OBEDIENCE
from Ephesians

There are important words in the Bible just for children! The words are, "Children, obey your parents." God wants children to listen to their parents. When children listen, they will learn quickly about God's love and His commandments. A wonderful thing about remembering to obey is that families can love each other in God's way. Best of all, God gives a special promise to children who obey their parents. The promise is that they will enjoy life longer and be successful in life.

From the very beginning, God had a wonderful plan for your family. He chose a mother and father especially for you! In the Bible, God tells your parents that they are in charge of you, just as God is in charge of your parents. God tells parents to give you love (that's not hard for parents!) and **guidance** (God tells in His word what is right). God also tells parents to **discipline** you (that is harder, because parents like to be nice all the time). But if parents do not discipline like God tells them, they are not obeying God, and you will not grow up to be like God wants you to be.

WORDS TO KNOW

guidance: to show, to tell, to help know what to do

discipline: to train with control; to correct and result in obedience

punish: to make a consequence (the result) for doing wrong and disobeying

THINK ABOUT

God has chosen your parents to prepare you for the very special plan He has for you. When you say "no" to your parents, you are disobeying God and your parents. It may seem like your mom and dad are not showing love when they must **punish** you for not doing what you are told to do; but if your parents teach you what is right and wrong, you will grow up and be able to choose God's way.

 # Questions:
THINKING & REMEMBERING

Fill in the blanks or circle the letters of all that are right.

1. Which words are in the Bible just for children?
   a. "Children should just be happy."
   b. "Children, obey your parents."
   c. "Children, do whatever you want."

2. What do children learn when they listen?
   a. They learn about God's love.
   b. They learn about how they can get their own way.
   c. They learn about God's commandments.

3. True or False—Children who obey their parents:
   a. _____ have love in their home.
   b. _____ have happy parents, but the children are angry.
   c. _____ make their home a happy and peaceful place to be.

4. What promise does God give children who obey their parents?
   a. They will never have any problems.
   b. They will enjoy longer life.
   c. They will have more friends.
   d. They will be successful.

5. Who planned for families to be together in the beginning? _____

6. What responsibility did God give to parents?
   a. to give their children lots of toys and things
   b. to be in charge of their children
   c. to make sure their children are always happy

7. What three things does God tell parents to do with their children?
   a. love   b. play   c. guide   d. ignore   e. discipline

8. What does God want parents to teach their children?
   a. what is right and wrong from the words in the Bible
   b. how to be happy
   c. how to be able to do whatever you want to do

Remember: God will help you do what is right, even when your parents are not watching. The Holy Spirit will guide you and show you what God wants.

Bible Story: THINK ON THESE THINGS
from Philippians

When Paul was in prison, he did not **complain**. He thought about God and knew that God's plan for him would work out. He was thankful that he could write letters to Christians and know that they were praying for him, too. Paul thanked God every time he thought of them, and he prayed that God would be with them. He knew that God would finish the work that was already started in their life of loving Jesus.

Paul said, "Keep your eye on the **goal**." The goal should be to forget the things they had done wrong that God had forgiven them for and look forward to what was ahead—God's very best for their lives! God will give the **prize** in the end to those who follow and obey Him. It was important for all Christians to work together in love, follow the same rule, and do what God said in His word. They should not separate and go in different directions. If they did, they would forget what was important—being with Jesus in heaven!

Paul said not to be worried about anything, but pray and be thankful that you can ask God for whatever you need. He said to think about what is true, **noble**, **just**, pure, lovely and that is of a good report.

WORDS TO KNOW

complain: to whine and be grumpy

goal: what your purpose to do is

prize: reward

noble: goodness that others can see

just: fair

THINK ABOUT

How much "thinking time" do you have? You can remember that the great people in the Bible and people who do great things today are those who take time to think about important things and consider what God wants them to do. The people who make good decisions are those who pray in their quiet times and ask God what He wants them to do. Take some time today to pray and think.

Questions:
THINKING & REMEMBERING

Fill in the blanks or circle the letters of all that are right.

1. From where did Paul write this letter to Christians?
    a. from his home in Jerusalem   b. from prison

2. What was Paul's attitude like in prison?
    a. He thought God had forgotten him.
    b. He rejoiced and knew God's plan would work out.
    c. He complained about being in prison.

3. What was Paul doing while he was in prison?
    a. He was praying for the Christians.
    b. He was writing letters about how God wanted Christians to live.
    c. He was wasting time.

4. What was Paul very sure of?
    a. The Christians would forget about him.
    b. God would finish the work He started in them.
    c. He would get out of prison.

5. What is the important goal for Christians?
    a. It is to keep looking forward to the best and important thing—Jesus.
    b. It is to keep remembering the wrong things we have done.
    c. It is to try by ourselves to do good and love others.

6. How can Christians get to this goal?
    a. We can reach this goal by being perfect all the time.
    b. We can reach this goal by working together in love.
    c. We can reach this goal by staying out of trouble.

7. What did Paul say Christians could talk to God about and ask Him for?
    a. They can ask for new things to play with.
    b. They can ask for whatever they need.
    c. They can ask to have a happy life.

8. What things did Paul say that Christians should think of?
    a. what is true   d. what others think is right
    b. what is noble   e. things of a good report
    c. what feels good   f. lovely things

BIBLE WORDS TO REMEMBER

Love is patient and kind. Faith, hope and love; the greatest of these is love. (from 1 Corinthians 13:4,13)

Bible Story: LIVING FOR JESUS
from Colossians

In a letter Paul wrote, he said to Christians, "Don't give up!" He wanted them to keep learning more about Jesus and tell others. There were people who thought that they were smarter and stronger than God. He told believers that they should not want what the world has—because all of those things will perish. They do not have eternal value.

There is only value in the things of God. They should think of heavenly things—not earthly things. Jesus makes us new. We are created in God's image and when we ask Jesus to live in us, we can have the power from Him to be kind and patient. Because Jesus forgives us, we must also forgive each other. Most of all, love each other and let the peace of God rule in your hearts.

It is important to know that God has given us gifts to use for Him. Use each gift God has given you and He will give you even more! Hiding your gift and putting it where no one can see it will be of no value to you or to God. God wants to give you even more—not just "things," but also your talents, which are gifts from God.

THINK ABOUT

Think of what can you do well right now. Work on that first. Sometimes we jump from one thing to another, never sticking with something. God will be with you when you trust Him to show you. Think of what you can do that will last forever—not just what other people think is important or popular on earth. We won't be on earth forever—we will be with Jesus in heaven some day if we believe in Him!

Questions:
THINKING & REMEMBERING

Circle the letters of all that are right.

1. What important words did Paul write to believers from prison?
   a. Start making money.　　b. Get me out of prison!　　c. Don't give up!

2. What did Paul want the Christians to keep doing?
   a. He wanted them to learn more about God.
   b. He wanted them to pretend that they were believers.
   c. He wanted them to tell others about Jesus.

3. What did some people who were not believers think?
   a. They were smarter and greater than God.
   b. Christians were strange people.
   c. Jesus was just an ordinary man who was dead because they killed Him.

4. What did Paul want to tell God's people not to do?
   a. Don't care about things and people on earth.
   b. Don't want things that will not last and will perish.
   c. Don't think about things that do not have eternal value.

5. What is the most important thing for Christians to think about?
   a. what other people have
   b. how smart we are compared to other people
   c. living for Jesus and being in heaven

6. What does God give us the power to do through the Holy Spirit?
   a. God gives us the power to be able to change people who do wrong things.
   b. God gives us the power to be kind and patient.
   c. God gives us the power to forgive others because Jesus forgives us.

7. What did Paul say about peace?
   a. He said to let the peace of God rule in our hearts.
   b. He said to make other people be peaceful.
   c. He said to stop making noise.

8. What does God give each of us that we should use for Him?
   a. gifts—abilities and talents
   b. money to get what we want

BIBLE WORDS TO REMEMBER

The grass withers, and its flower falls away, but the word of the Lord endures forever. (from 1 Peter 1:24,25)

Bible Story: A GOOD EXAMPLE

from Thessalonians & Timothy

Timothy's mother and grandmother loved God and they wanted Timothy to know and love God, too. They read to him from God's book and told him that God wanted him to love others and to be kind. They taught him that the important thing was to love and obey God. Timothy listened carefully to the words in the Bible and obeyed God and his parents.

When Timothy got older, he went with Paul to many places to tell other people that God loved them. Paul told others about God in a way that they would listen. Paul wrote some letters to Timothy when he was in another country to help him become a good worker for God. Paul knew that Timothy had a special gift for telling others about Jesus.

Timothy read the words that Paul wrote and knew that he wanted to be like Paul. He wanted to be strong. Paul said that even though it would not always be easy to follow Jesus, God will always be faithful to us.

Timothy knew that even though he was young and had a lot to learn, he wanted to say the words that Paul said, "I have fought the good fight, I have finished the race, I have kept the faith. I will not give up!"

THINK ABOUT

The Bible is God's letter to you! He wants you to know that what is written in His book is important for everyone who believes. God's truth is like a rock, and nothing can make it go away. The Lord knows all those who love Him. God will help you do the right thing and be strong. Then you can say the words, "I have fought the good _____. I have finished the _____. I have kept the _____. I will not _____ _____!"

Questions:
THINKING & REMEMBERING

Circle the letters of all that are right.

1. Which people in this lesson taught Timothy to love God?
   a. His grandfather   b. His mother   c. His grandmother   d. Paul

2. What were some of the things Timothy learned?
   a. He learned how to love others and be kind.
   b. He learned how to love and obey God.
   c. He learned how to obey his parents.

3. Whom did Timothy travel with to learn more about God?
   a. Paul   b. his friends   c. other disciples

4. What else did Paul do to help Timothy know how to tell others about God?
   a. He invited him to his house to tell him how to tell others about Jesus.
   b. He wrote letters to instruct and encourage him.
   c. He took him to meetings with other disciples.

5. What did Paul tell Timothy about following Jesus?
   a. It would sometimes be difficult.
   b. It would always be easy.
   c. People would always listen when he talked about Jesus.

6. Even though Timothy was young, what did he want to do?
   a. He wanted to travel with Paul to learn as much as he could.
   b. He wanted to be a good worker for Jesus.
   c. He wanted to travel to see other parts of the world.

7. Why did Timothy want to be like Paul?
   a. Paul loved God and kept his eyes on the goal.
   b. Paul was strong .
   c. Paul told others about Jesus in a way that they would listen.

8. What did Timothy want to be able to say?
   a. "I have fought the good fight."
   b. "I have finished the race."
   c. "I have kept the faith."
   d. "I think I did the right thing."

Bible Story: NEW LIFE
from Titus and Philemon

Paul wrote to the Christians who were leaders. He wanted to help them know what God **expected** them to do. He knew that there would be many questions about how to live for Jesus in the best way. He knew that they would have to make important decisions so that Christ's church would grow strong in the right way.

Many of the new Christians were excited about knowing Jesus as their Savior. Sometimes, though, they thought they were free from all of God's rules that will make people happy. Jesus didn't come to **erase** God's rules. They are still very important. Jesus did come to make it possible for us to follow God's rules. With His power, we can love others as we should.

Paul said that Christians should stop arguing and being unkind. Knowing God's love makes that possible. Those who have accepted Jesus' love should be a **pattern** of good works. We should live our lives so that others will not have anything bad to say about us. Always be ready to do good things for others. Don't say bad things about others. Be peaceable, gentle and don't show off about anything. Remember to show love in all the ways that you can so others will want to know Jesus, too!

WORDS TO KNOW

expected: required behavior
erase: wipe out or cancel
pattern: to model or guide

THINK ABOUT

If we love Jesus, we know that He has forgiven the wrong things we have done—and even thought about doing. Sin separates us from God. We could only come to God because Jesus paid for our sin on the cross. We must forgive others who do wrong things to us, too. When someone starts believing in Jesus and begins a new life, we should not keep reminding them of the wrong they did. That is not forgiving! God does not keep reminding us of our sins. The Bible says He remembers them no more. Jesus was so wonderful to be willing to die for our sins to bring us back to God!

Questions:
THINKING & REMEMBERING

Circle the letters of all that are right.

1. Whom was Paul teaching in the letters he wrote?
   a. Christians who were leaders
   b. those who didn't love Jesus
   c. new Christians (those who just started believing in Jesus)

2. What did Paul know that they would need to learn?
   a. how to live for Jesus in the best way
   b. how to make decisions to help Christ's church grow strong
   c. how to tell people where they should live

3. How did the new Christians feel about knowing Jesus?
   a. They wanted to wait and see if following Jesus was worth it.
   b. They wanted Jesus to solve all their problems.
   c. They were excited!

4. What did they sometimes think?
   a. They thought that rules were for other people.
   b. They thought that they didn't need to follow God's rules anymore.
   c. They thought that it was hard to follow God's plan.

5. What did Jesus come to do?
   a. He came to make everything in life easy.
   b. He came to make it possible to follow God's rules.
   c. He came to give us power to love others as we should.

6. What did Paul say that Christians should stop doing?
   a. Christians should stop arguing with each other.
   b. They should stop having too many dinners together.

7. What did Paul say Christians should do if they love Jesus?
   a. They should be a pattern of good works.
   b. They should live their lives so that others will not have anything bad to say about Christians.
   c. They should always be ready to do good things for others.
   d. They should be peaceable, gentle, and not show off what they have and can do.

295

BIBLE WORDS TO REMEMBER

The grass withers, and its flower falls away, but the word of the Lord endures forever. (from 1 Peter 1:24,25)

Bible Story: FAITH THAT WORKS

from Hebrews and James

Faith is what we **hope** for even when we cannot see it with our eyes or hold it in our hands. Faith is **trusting** God—not just when things are going great—but all of the time. We should have our highest hope when things are difficult or seem **impossible**. The Bible tells about many people who lived with **courage** and hope. That is faith. It is knowing that God has everything in **control**!

Those who really believe in God, follow Him. It shows in what they say and do. Some people try to **pretend** they love God, but they **continue** to follow Satan and do the things that hurt other people and make God sad.

God gives a promise of rest for those who love and believe in Jesus. It is the place where we can be **secure** knowing that our faith and trust is in Him—not other things. Those who have not put their trust in Jesus will not know or understand the comfort and security of God's rest. When we have entered God's place of rest, He promises that we will share all that belongs to Christ if we are faithful to the end. God will always help us stay in His wonderful place of rest if we pray and ask Him.

WORDS TO KNOW

faith:	trust and confidence
hope:	knowing that you can trust what is promised
trust:	to believe without any doubt
impossible:	something that seems hopeless to us
courage:	bravery
control:	to have power over
pretend:	to act like something is real
continue:	to keep on
secure:	protected and safe

Questions:
THINKING & REMEMBERING

1. True or False:

   a. _____ Faith believes without seeing.

   b. _____ We can pretend to love Jesus and live in heaven.

   c. _____ We can know and be confident that God has everything in control.

   d. _____ Loving God must show in what we say and do.

   e. _____ We can choose to stop trusting God and have His rest.

   f. _____ God promises that we can be in His place of rest if we believe in Jesus and love Him.

   g. _____ We can have our highest hope when things seem impossible.

   h. _____ Some things are impossible for God to do.

2. When should we trust God?

   a. We should trust God when things are good.

   b. We should trust God when things are difficult.

   c. We should trust God when we feel like it.

3. What do people do who believe in God?

   a. follow Him   b. trust and obey Him   c. continue to follow Satan

4. Write the word that matches the meaning.

     faith   continue   pretend   trust   hope
     courage   control   secure   impossible

   a. _____ to act like something is real

   b. _____ trust and confidence

   c. _____ bravery

   d. _____ to keep on

   e. _____ something that seems hopeless to us

   f. _____ knowing that you can trust what is promised

   g. _____ to believe without any doubt

   h. _____ to have power over

   i. _____ protected and safe

Bible Story: LIVING LOVE
from 1 Peter and 1 John

When Jesus asked Peter to be one of His disciples, He could see inside Peter and knew what Peter could become. Peter didn't start out to be a gentle person. He was a rough fisherman. But after He met Jesus and let Jesus change him on the inside, he knew how to love.

Peter wrote a letter to Christians everywhere and said that what we look like on the outside is not as important as what we look like on the inside. When we let Jesus' love live in our hearts, others will see "a gentle and quiet spirit, which is very precious in the sight of God." John was also a disciple of Jesus. The longer He loved Jesus, the more he learned about love! He said that when love is perfect, there is no fear. "Love one another, for love is of God. Everyone who loves is born of God and knows God. He who does not love does not know God, for God is love."

Loving God and believing in His Son Jesus will result in a wonderful and bright forever! All of God's promises will come true! Everything on earth comes to an end, but this earth is not the end for people who believe in Jesus as their Savior.

WORDS TO KNOW

refrain: to stop doing

evil: doing wrong continually

deceit: to not be honest and not tell the truth

seek: to search for

pursue: to follow after

THINK ABOUT

Jesus wants you to live forever with Him in heaven. You can have that life—but you must choose. Heaven is just a place for those who have asked Jesus to forgive them from their sins and live in their heart. Remember these words from the Bible in 1 Peter 3:10-11:

> "He who would love life and see good days, let him **refrain** his tongue from **evil**, and his lips from speaking **deceit**. Let him turn away from evil and do good; let him **seek** peace and **pursue** it."

Questions:
THINKING & REMEMBERING

Fill in the blanks or circle the letters of all that are right.

1. Write and memorize the Bible Words from 1 Peter 1:24,25.

   _____

   _____

   _____

   _____

2. What did Jesus see in Peter that He also sees in us?
   a. Jesus sees that we can be perfect.
   b. Jesus sees what we can become on the inside.
   c. Jesus sees all the bad stuff.

3. What was Peter like before He let Jesus change him?
   a. He was gentle most of the time.
   b. He tried to be in control by himself.
   c. He was a rough fisherman who talked a lot.

4. What words tell us what is precious to God?
   a. to have a gentle and quiet spirit
   b. saying whatever comes to our mind before we think about it
   c. thinking it is honest to hurt other people's feelings with our words

5. What did John write that he had learned about love?
   a. We don't have to love anyone as long as we love God.
   b. There is no fear in perfect love.
   c. Love one another, for love is of God.

6. What does the Bible say about peace in the book of 1 Peter?
   a. We should look for it and follow it.
   b. There will never be peace.
   c. God does not promise peace.

7. If we say we love God, but do not love others, we are lying.
   true_____   false_____

BIBLE WORDS TO REMEMBER

The grass withers, and its flower falls away, but the word of the Lord endures forever. (from 1 Peter 1:24,25)

Bible Story: COME QUICKLY, LORD JESUS!
from Jude and Revelation

Everything was perfect in the beginning. But sin spoiled the beautiful world God made. The bad things that happen now, happen because of sin. The Bible tells us not to listen when people pretend to love God and say things that are wrong. When you know God's words for yourself, you will know the difference. Jesus sent the Holy Spirit to keep you from falling away from God.

When Jesus showed His disciple John what heaven would be like in a vision, it was so bright and beautiful that John had to cover his eyes. God told John to write about what he saw. Heaven looked like it was made of gold and beautiful jewels. God told John that there would never be night there because it would always be light with the brightness of God's glory. God will be there for us to worship all the time. Everything will praise God, and there won't be any more sadness or sickness.

Jesus promises that when He comes back, everything will be beautiful and wonderful again! Right now Jesus is in heaven making a place for those who love Him. It will be more wonderful than we can imagine. Everyone who loves and believes in Jesus will live there forever with Him.

THINK ABOUT

It will be a wonderful day when Jesus comes again to take us to His beautiful new home in heaven! Never forget Jesus' words and remember always to obey His teaching so that you will be ready when He comes back! We hope Jesus will come soon!

PRAYER THOUGHT

Dear God, Help me always listen to You and know Your words so that I can stay close to You. Make me strong so that I will be ready for Jesus when He comes. Thank You, Jesus for making a place for me to live with You forever. Please come soon! In Jesus Name, Amen.

Questions:
Thinking & Remembering

Circle the letters of all that are right.

1. What phrase describes what the world was like in the beginning?
   a. a nice place   b. a perfect place   c. a pleasant place

2. What word tells what spoiled the beautiful world God made?
   a. sin   b. people   c. animals   d. plants

3. Why do bad things happen here on earth?
   a. People don't know how to be happy.
   b. People are not kind and don't love each other.
   c. Bad things happen because of sin (all wrongdoing).

4. What promise did Jesus make when He comes back to earth?
   a. He will talk to people who do wrong things.
   b. He will make the earth a better place to live.
   c. He will make everything beautiful and wonderful again.

5. Where is Jesus right now?
   a. He is in heaven talking to God.
   b. He is in heaven making a place for us to live with Him.
   c. He is making a plan.

6. What did John tell that heaven looked like in his vision?
   a. Heaven is more beautiful than we can imagine.
   b. Heaven will be an ordinary place that we will like.
   c. Heaven looked like it was made of gold and beautiful jewels.

7. What else did John write about heaven?
   a. It would never be night there because it would always be light with the brightness of God's glory.
   b. God will be there for us to worship all the time.
   c. Everything will praise God.
   d. There will not be any sadness or sickness there.

8. Fill in from the Bible Words to Remember.

   The_____ of the _____ endures _____.